The Necessary Transition
The Journey towards the Sustainable Enterprise Economy

THE **NECESSARY TRANSITION**

The Journey towards the Sustainable Enterprise Economy

Edited by Malcolm McIntosh

Greenleaf
PUBLISHING

© 2013 Greenleaf Publishing Limited

Published by Greenleaf Publishing Limited
Aizlewood's Mill
Nursery Street
Sheffield S3 8GG
UK
www.greenleaf-publishing.com

Cover by LaliAbril.com
Art by Kay Lawrence. 'Kyoto Protocol#2' (2011), 6,912 photographic pieces,
staples, 1.8m × 2.4m approx.
Photographer: Rhys Jones

Printed in the UK on environmentally friendly, acid-free paper
from managed forests by CPI Group (UK) Ltd, Croydon

British Library Cataloguing in Publication Data:
  A catalogue record for this book is available from the British Library.

     ISBN-13: 978-1-906093-89-1 [paperback]
     ISBN-13: 978-1-907643-91-0 [hardback]
     ISBN-13: 978-1-909493-17-9 [PDF ebook]

'What they undertook to do
They brought to pass;
All things hang like a drop of dew
Upon a blade of grass.'

Gratitude to the
Unknown Instructors
William Butler Yeats

Contents

Foreword

Tim Smit
Eden Project, Cornwall, UK

There is an irony that the lexicon of sustainability and climate change should contain so many words loathed by the vast majority of people on Earth. 'Sustainability' itself, with its near mystical allusion to a body of knowledge that would enable us to both physically and spiritually occupy the planet with barely a trace of our footprint, serves as a red rag to a bull to many people. First for its perceived political bias and, second, for its arrogance! 'Biodiversity', which could just as easily be described as 'variety of life', is a word apparently not understood by 85% of visitors to London's Natural History Museum in 2012. 'Climate' versus 'weather' is another semantic nest of vipers, and then you come to the big one, the champion, the killer. The most hated word in our dictionary is 'change'. Yet we stubbornly hang on to it like a mantra. Be the change you want to be, is an invitation to self-loathing. Why?

We hate change ... and transformation is merely a stalking horse for change, like efficiency is for job cuts. The greatest problem is that there resides in our bosom a fairy tale we cannot give up—that somewhere there is a silver bullet, a cure all. Yet ... we all know that change, in the way we mean it, is slow in human, at least in present day 'I want it now' terms but, like a sapling planted in the garden, one day you suddenly notice that the little wispy trunk has girth and vigour and has become a tree.

We love doom and gloom. Our desire to save humanity from itself motivates us, unsullied by the frantic desire for distraction of the consumer society, our game is change, not fashion, but who is listening? Oh how we Cassandras shiver in excitement at the drought, the flood, the big freeze and thaw, the earthquake, tsunami and the hurricane. It makes us feel alive, threatened and vital. Our dearest wish is to give witness either to The End of Days or the dawning of a New Enlightenment. We, like those who cast doubt on us, need to be mindful of the Jon Stewart joke, 'Don't give me facts, I want the truth'. So ... what do we mean by 'transition' (a word, incidentally, that I love), and could it move any faster?

I have recently spent some time in China and while the naïve observations of a newcomer to a culture shouldn't carry much weight in a book of this substance, I was absolutely staggered by what I was being told. First, the meeting of the Politburo in November 2012 agreed to have the word 'sustainability' inserted into the Chinese Constitution—one of the first countries in the world to do so. I was told that the West believed China's GDP rates at its peril, with figures of annual growth of c. 12% until recently (8% at the time of writing), yet experts there say up to 4% of that represents a saved-up cost of medical care caused by environmental degradation. They told me that over the next five years the cultural narrative of China will have a story that revisits the Taoist ideal—China and its people living with the grain of nature. Finally, they told me how they were shocked at the short-sightedness of the West who used the environmental impact of China and India as an excuse for them to do nothing because their efforts would be but a blip in the ocean. They could not believe that the West couldn't see the intelligence of the Chinese and the Indians, and were not aware that the real revolution coming over the horizon at speed was to do with sustainable development in its most literal form. I may be blind, but I believe it. I was impressed by their desire to listen and to learn about what sustainable development might mean to them.

The transition to a new relationship between people and planet is underway all over the world, whether it is recognised or not. Governments are edging towards measuring wellbeing alongside economics, business knows that it must report on more than profits, and civil society—individuals globally—is maintaining pressure on all institutions to be more transparent and accountable. This is as true in Cairo and Beijing as it is in New York and London.

As a number of the authors in this brilliant, wide-ranging book note, humanity is at a turning point. For the entrepreneurs and creative thinkers among us this is a moment of great excitement and opportunity.

The evidence is that the climate is changing rapidly. Coupled to this are very serious issues of resource depletion, population growth, urbanisation, geopolitical destabilisation, consumerism and global inequity. We, the people, have been rubbish at giving politicians and business the signals they need to be brave; but look how far we have come in a short time when President Obama at his public inauguration on 21 January 2013 made addressing climate change a pillar of his presidency for the next four years.

Social media has given those of us with the technology the opportunity to find out what is going on and, as Paul Hawken has noted in his book *Blessed Unrest*, there are now over a million non-governmental organisations and pressure groups around the world, with no single leader. He makes a fabulous analogy that they act like antibiotics to a fevered body politic and environmental system. This is hugely exciting. For us to really create transformation we need to understand the power of story telling and the need to make our narrative feel personal, to tell stories where people are made not to feel powerless in the face of problems too big even to grasp, but powerful in the knowledge that, by getting together with others, attitudes and actions can be changed. We must be smart, we must be humble, we must actively build the new institutions and encourage the new economy.

I have been privileged to see a number of examples of transformation—Jack Sim and his World Toilet Organisation (WTO!), the Aravinda Eye Hospital, the Barefoot College in Rajasthan, the Grameen Bank, and there are thousands more. They all have something in common. They have created vast networks of people, culturally glued together by a story that makes sense to them. Jack Sim realised that poor people wouldn't buy a cheap toilet for health reasons, but they would when shamed at the disgrace they brought on their family by making family members defecate in public. Once purchased, they give the reason for buying as health! Grameen is about collective responsibility of small groups to repay microcredit; it works by peer group policing. Barefoot College trains Haridjan grandmothers to become solar and water engineers, giving them a valued trade and repositioning the wider view of women and caste, not to mention providing solar light for youngsters to take lessons at night after a day's work in the fields. The Aravinda Eye Hospital charges the rich to provide operations for the poor. And so on. If you want to understand behaviour change look no further than Aesop's Fables, don't look at World Bank or UN guidelines.

The philosopher Alain de Botton once wrote something along the lines of: from the dawning of mankind we have been in awe of nature, it held sway over life and death, then suddenly in the 1700s we fell in awe of ourselves and our magic to transform materials to the point where we began to look at nature as something washed up on the shores of our existence to be pitied and cared for as an act of charity. I do him a disservice in the paraphrasing, but the point is a good one. We need to fall in awe of nature once more.

Every chapter of this important book screams at us 'we must learn and adapt', it must be rapid for it is the necessary transition. Humans are wonderfully, fantastically successful; we have proved ourselves capable of solving many problems, our feats are awesome for a species that began on the savannahs, hunting in packs. There are now billions of us and the danger of our belief in our inventiveness may lull us into making a terrible mistake. It is the mistake of 'they'. 'They' will fix it, 'they' must do it. Ask ourselves, for a moment, who is 'they'? If not us, then who? I delight in the idea that, in an act of hubris, we, humankind, decided to call ourselves *Homo sapiens sapiens* (not just the wise hominid, but the wise wise hominid). If we fry to death we will have deserved it but, on the other hand, isn't it a pleasure to be living at a time when we can actually prove we are worthy of the name we gave ourselves?

If ever you want a justification for bringing smart people, vain yet humble people, fizzing, laughing hopeful people together to share their thoughts on the search for solutions to many different issues, you will find it here. For beating like a heart through this book is the intensity of hope that gives this book a reason for being. To encourage, incite and draw a picture of a future possible. Doom may make its presence felt like the cowboy in the black hat, but throughout you can hear the galloping hooves of the man in the white hat getting closer with every passing page.

Dame Barbara Ward once memorably said, 'We all have a duty to Hope'. By this she meant a positive, driven, muscular, vigorous, adaptive, primal howling-at-the-moon kind of duty.

The many authors of this book have, over the years, met at various venues around the world and have one thing in common—the book's co-ordinator and editor, Malcolm McIntosh, whose insight and dogged insistence on staying optimistic have long been an inspiration to me. They are each at the top of their professions and wouldn't normally work with each other, but have chosen to do so because professionally, and personally, they think it is important. Here are business strategists, climate scientists, social activists, educators, historians, public policy experts and business leaders all banging on about the same things—the absolute necessity to face the truth about the relationship between people and planet—and to tell it like it could be.

Tim Smit KBE is co-founder of the Eden Project.

Acknowledgements

This book, and the accompanying conference, The Necessary Transition 2012, held in Brisbane on 26–28 September 2012,[1] would not have been possible without a lengthy engagement with colleagues around the world who work in a global space which transcends national, ethnic and other boundaries to think hard about issues, risks, ideas, challenges and opportunities that present themselves to the world. So, to my fellow conspirators for social change on a human scale, thank you.

In particular I would like to thank all those who work at two places that every time I visit I am revitalised by their practical example, by energetic engagement, by their paradoxes, contradictions and challenges. These are learning places with the right values at their heart—the Eden Project in Cornwall, England, and the Sustainability Institute near Stellenbosch, South Africa. Like us all, neither are perfect, but both are places that shine a light on possible futures and the rivers we must cross.

I would also like to thank my colleagues at Griffith University in Queensland, Australia, for their help, loyalty and support in making many things, including this book and the conference, happen in a timely and well-organised manner.

To name a few people without whom the last few years and decades would have been less fruitful and less inspiring: Karen Brindley and all my colleagues at Griffith University; Mark Swilling, Eve Anneke and everyone at the Sustainability Institute; Caroline Digby, Tim Smit and everyone at the Eden Project; and John Stuart and Dean Bargh at Greenleaf Publishing.

Malcolm McIntosh, Brisbane,
January 2013

1 www.griffith.edu.au/conference/necessary-transition.

Introduction

Malcolm McIntosh

Asia Pacific Centre for Sustainable Enterprise, Griffith University, Queensland, Australia

The idea

That we are in the midst of a major transition in the history of humanity there is no doubt, but you can choose your transition point. For some, it is the cataclysmic effect of climate change, for others it is the depletion of natural resources, or the collapse of the international banking and finance system, or population and demographics, or the growing instability caused by nuclear weapons acquisition. For others, liberation and positive change is to be found in the growth of social media and the porosity of nation-state boundaries which have helped foment discussion in China, helped organise the Arab Spring, and given the Occupy movement life and made it global. So this transition point is also a moment to take stock of humanity's success and to celebrate our diversity, creativity, homogeneity, problem-solving and enterprising nature.

This book is about the transition that is necessary in order to move locally and globally to a socially-just sustainable enterprise economy. Life on Earth for humanity and our ecosystems is at a point of great change, and there is much to be learnt about previous great disruptions. The key words are 'learning', 'adaptation' and 'transformation'.

But if there is one thing that this book wishes to do it is to bring to the fore the fact that there are many transitions taking place—from high- to low-carbon economies; from gross inequality to egalitarianism; from massive human rights abuses to socially-just societies; and from high corruption to societies with high social cohesion and integrity. Most international companies operate across multiple social and environmental geographies so they have a grasp of this intellectual and practical landscape, and for many governments the challenges of social and environmental justice are also paramount, not least because equitable societies are best for business, and best for human wellbeing.

In bringing together experts from many different fields this book covers the necessary transition from many angles, but it also presents a problem in current knowledge development. The siloed nature of intellectual life, most particularly in our universities, means that it is rare that thought leadership crosses boundaries; but in this book we have worked in the space which the High-Level Group Report advising the UN Secretary-General for the Rio+20 Earth Summit called '"a new political economy" for sustainable development' (UN Secretary-General's

---

It is November 2012 and the new Chinese leadership team of seven men are paraded for the entire world to see in a heavily choreographed show of power, prestige, masculinity and assurance. We know that they will probably be in power in 2022. Headed by Xi Jongping, the new Secretary-General of the Chinese Communist Party, the seven dark-suited men are standing in a line. The audience is composed mostly of men and they are clapping in unison. For many, this is 'this century'—a world run by men over 50 in dark suits, members of the world's largest and most powerful organisation, the Chinese Communist Party, in charge of the world's largest totalitarian government, controlling the world's greatest agglomeration of natural resources and people, and many of the largest companies operating within the capitalist system. If you don't understand China, economics and sustainability you don't understand the 21st century.

Just a decade into the 21st century, it is so commonplace it is hardly worth mentioning that these events are unfolding on the BBC World News live from Beijing, apparently several worlds away if you are not there now, but in reality very much here and now.

Two days prior to this event in Beijing with the seven wise men of China, the world watched the election of 'the world's most powerful man': the US President, Barack Obama in November 2012. He will be in power until 2016, when this book of essays will still be relevant. In his acceptance speech President Obama twice made reference to the USA being the most powerful military nation the world has ever seen: he was obliquely referring to the fact that China launched its first aircraft carrier in 2012. And so the scene is set for the transition of economic and military power to the Asia Pacific region, with the USA remaining the pre-eminent global military power. But this is only one of many transitions that are taking place around the world and all of them are taking place under the shadow of humanity's triumphant point of destiny, by which we mean that humans have so shaped the world that the bipedal ape now has to decide what to do with its own future. We are in control, or are we?

High-Level Panel on Global Sustainability 2012: 12) because it is at the juncture of politics, economics and the environment that real understandings of sustainable development can be found. So here in this book are climate change scientists, political activists, social entrepreneurs, business leaders and educators. Political economy was founded in moral philosophy going back to Adam Smith, Karl Marx, Max Weber, Joseph Schumpeter, John Maynard Keynes and Karl Polanyi. Through combining bodies of knowledge and de-atomising intellectual compartmentalisation we will find the solutions to current world problems and face the challenges and opportunities of 'the necessary transition'.

> The transition we are necessarily talking about means no less than an irreversible shift to a new way of living on Earth (Sara Parkin).

This book, and 'the necessary transition', is concerned with those decisions and how we decide, if we are capable of deciding. In no way is this a nihilistic position; it is a statement that reflects the fact that, on reflection, there is much we can know and do, but there is also much that we do not know and can have no idea about. We are at the will of our own ability to adapt, to be flexible and to joyously learn day-by-day what it is to be human. The purpose of life is to strive, and to meditate on what has been, what is, and what could be. 'The necessary transition' posits that a transition is necessary, is already happening, and that it should happen. Hope is a central tenet of what it means to be human. And we keep moving along, on and on, on the road again. We cannot stop. You cannot step into the same river twice, you cannot forever live in the past, and last night's sunset will never be repeated. Hope springs eternal.

This set of essays is concerned with transition from a grand perspective, with a grand narrative in mind, with social and environmental justice being the goal. You, however, as the reader, may not recognise the authors' starting points or may be in some other place while reading this book. Where you are, here and now, is important—even though by the end of the page it may have changed and the world around you may have changed as well. It is not a conceit or a distraction to ask the reader: Have you eaten today? Do you have a roof over your head? Do you find it easy to read these words written in English? Have you just taken a bath or are about to go to sleep? And do you have a loved one snuggled up to you as you think about these questions? These things are important because it is difficult to put into any perspective the idea of a necessary transition of what might be if you are simply concerned with your next meal or the fate of your daughter who is out on the town and late back home tonight.

So where is your head? Is it important to think about the here and now, or next week, next year, the next ten years, the next 100 years or the next millennium? I ask because it matters to the writers in this book for whom the view from the window ranges from the immediate to the end of the century and beyond. This can be disconcerting. Are you more interested in watching the five-year-olds starting school, as described in Eve Annecke's essay on the Sustainability Institute and primary school in South Africa, or perhaps glorying in the copper roof of the Eden Project's new education centre in Cornwall, England, knowing that it has been tracked all the way from a mine in the USA to the UK?

But your interest might lie in looking back over millennia in order to look forward to the end of this century. In two chapters, Mark Swilling and Richard Cassels ask the question: given 'the necessary transition' and the hypothesis that humanity may have come to a fork in the road, what can be learnt from the past that might be useful for adapting to the future? As Mark Swilling says: 'Many writers cannot resist drumming up support from history to conjure images of the future to help influence the decisions taken today', but how helpful is this knowledge given that the situation today is different from all past turning points in human history? Or has that always been true for these moments in history? In this volume, Swilling unravels the debates: is this the fourth wave of revolution in human history, the sixth wave of change since industrialisation, and do Kondratiev's waves of prosperity make sense in a world that is subject to climate change scenarios? Or can we find a technical and social fix through the third wave of 'lateral power' distribution and redistribution of energy supplies and social connectivity? Or is this, as Swilling argues in his chapter, one of the many attempts to re-imagine a post-crisis landscape on terms that favour a relatively narrow set of elite actors?

Transitions can be peaceful, revolutionary and, sometimes, violent. Like an earthquake they can be expected, but not determined in time, and be very destructive, or, like a river flowing through sandstone, there can be a process of evolution. Peter Senge has argued elsewhere that we are in the midst of a 'necessary revolution' (Senge 2008), but some people in some political cultures see everything as dramatic, which may be the politics of affluence and inertia and a desire to stir up revolutionary and, perhaps, old testament images of theatrical turbulence, people on the streets, tyrants overthrown and new orders put in place. Paul Hawken's (2008) revolution comes from the streets in the form of the 'blessed unrest' of non-government and non-profit organisations. Both ideas ring true in this volume but from different places and perspectives. This is necessarily so because, as Karl Marx said, we all have our own histories and we all make our own futures. The multi-level perspectives approach to transition is based on a particular analysis of regime change and is, to some extent, useful for this diverse collection of essays on ideas of transition, but they (the chapters) do not fit neatly into any collective framework. Indeed, the only central theses are nods to learning, adaptation and change.

We may all be on the road together and the final utopia may be similar, but not the same, for two reasons. First, where we have come from and what we have been through has left a legacy of learning and, perhaps, some scars that can't be so easily removed by the idea of a single grand narrative, however persuasive it may be argued. We are, are we not, creatures of nature *and* nurture, of rationality *and* emotion, of the swamp *and* the mountain top, reptilian *and* transcendent?

The German apparel manufacturers described by Stefan Schaltegger and Erik Hansen in this volume deal at an everyday level with issues that are far removed from the extraction and delivery of coal, the black stuff, an elemental fossil fuel, to

China described in another piece in this book by Rio Tinto's Fiona Nicholls. And yet the clothing company and the energy provider are intimately connected through a natural web of life and through social systems that connect investments, energy use, sales and customers, consumers and governments. And yet both are apparently concerned with 'the necessary transition' as both authors were caught up by the idea of, and both speak eloquently about, the need to face up to one of the fundamental issues of the transition, namely adapting to and dealing with anthropogenically-induced climate change.

This set of essays is written by Germans, Americans, Japanese, Indians, Africans, English, Irish and Australians, all of whom came at the topic from different angles. At one point in a conference in Brisbane, Australia, that was held to share some of these diverse perspectives, on the stage were seven of the book's authors: several political and thought leader activists, a climate change scientist, a coal miner, a public policy analyst and activist, an educator and a politician. It is no small point that they were all there to sing different hymns from the same hymn sheet and that, rather than take up arms, they were present to bear witness to ideas and discussion.

The evolutionary psychologist Steven Pinker has said that, in the last few hundred years, we have learnt relatively rapidly to be peaceful.[1] The moral philosopher Jonathan Glover (2001) says the last century, the 20th, was the bloodiest. They are both correct—Pinker because the shape of our brains and our behaviour has changed for the better; and Glover because the scale of the last century's killing was on an unprecedented scale through the use of technology for and of war.

So is 'the necessary transition' inevitable or driven by our compulsion to change, for so-called progress? Almost all the authors in this book agree that this time it is different: that humanity is staring at its own history in the mirror and, if it is honest, knows that it is time for a rethink, for more than a face lift. It is time to take the road less travelled with all its uncertainties, challenges, opportunities and risks.

For the historians, such as Swilling and Cassels, the necessity for change is now; but, as history mostly tells us, change takes time. Some civilizations have come and gone in a few years, for others it has taken a generation or two. This time it is humanity itself that is up for change because of the nature of the global challenges now facing us.

For Kyoko Fukukawa and Sunil Manghani, even though the necessity for the transition may have come about because of the extent of the damage caused by a model of industrial capitalism and technological development that originated in the West (specifically, for various reasons, in the UK), this is no reason for Western philosophers to be so ignorant of 'the East' and, particularly, of ancient Asian cultures such as are offered by Japanese, Indian and Chinese history.

---

1 'At home: Steven Pinker', www.ft.com/intl/cms/s/2/a96b18bc-3ec6-11e2-87bc-00144 feabdc0.html#axzz2HuAzX8k9, accessed 13 January 2013.

A similar idea is presented by two very different contributions by Mark Swilling and Eve Annecke that the transition is very different depending on history, culture, affluence, politics, age and baggage. They write from post-apartheid South Africa where the transition to a peaceful, egalitarian society is taking a while longer than had been hoped. Some 15 years after apartheid ended, South Africa now has the distinction of being the most economically unequal society in the world, with the world's highest rape statistics and one of the highest rates of obesity. Swilling and Annecke have also created a safe place for research and teaching, at the Sustainability Institute between Cape Town and Stellenbosch, that reaches across intellectual, academic and institutional boundaries. In her chapter, Annecke observes: 'What has mattered most is creating space for new forms of transdisciplinary knowledge that is not just about working across disciplines, but letting real-world problems become the motive forces of applied research and learning'. Their transition is set, as Annecke says, '… within a country struggling with the challenges of a new democracy ravaged by its racist past'.

If you are in a favela or informal settlement you may just be more focused on a peaceful day than a peaceful planet. Similarly, if you are in Tohoku in the region of the Fukushima nuclear reactor, you may be more interested in the government not restarting the local nuclear reactors (Funabashi and Takenaka 2011). Kyoko Fukukawa and Sunil Manghani take the reader from South Africa to Japan with a plea to be more careful in 'the West' not to talk about 'Asian values' so glibly. They take as their target the prominent example, and currently fashionable, nihilistic philosopher Slavoj Žižek who talks of 'Chinese–Singaporean capitalism' as a casual catchall for anything that's not Anglo-Saxon capitalism. As Fukukawa and Manghani say in their chapter this is lazy 'journalistic shorthand' and not dissimilar to the way in which business text books, and often those on corporate social responsibility (CSR), talk of 'business', 'civil society' and 'the state' as if they constituted the same political economy around the world. How untrue this is, and how carefully we must all dig deeper into the complexities of diverse models of national, regional and global governance. As Fukukawa and Manghani say: '… this chapter evokes the prospects of a genealogical account of Japanese business ethics—i.e. not a teleological account of history, but one that unfolds in different directions and varying speeds'. For those hungry for other variants of capitalism than the Hayekian-Thatcher-Reagan model of neoliberalism, read on as this chapter explains just how Japan rose to become the second largest economy in a few decades after the end of World War II *and* built one of the most egalitarian and peaceful society's ever seen—with a strong sense of history and tradition. Developmental progress does not have to destroy all it sees as anachronistic, and can incorporate the best bits and build on them to create continuity and stability.

It is tempting to dichotomise the situation, as some of the essayists in this volume do. As Donella Meadows (2008) observes, although we know a great deal about the world, it is not enough; and it is often said that we know enough about economics, ecology and technology and the state of the world to solve our problems now without waiting for a new technological solution. One of the most frequently asked questions, especially from business audiences, is: 'Aren't we going to find a technological fix for this or that problem?' The answer is that there are three variables, or areas, of knowingness and non-knowingness:

- People and our social, psychological and biological development
- The planet with all its history, surprises and suppressed energies
- And, just as important, the unknown, a sense of the future

We cannot know, however hard we try with our apparently scientific, rational mindsets, the future. If there is one truth about the future it is to expect the unexpected—you can't step into the same river twice but we can seek a better future. As John Harris (2012: 38), Director of the Institute for Science, Ethics and Innovation at Oxford University, says: 'Enhancement was the last stage of human evolution and the one before that. By various random processes evolution has brought us to our present state'. Here and now, now.

But how? In this book, if Mark Swilling's sweep is magnificent in presenting a tour de force of theories of change and transition, then Richard Cassels is similarly so. He talks of 12 transitions, although he is careful, and honest, to say that he is talking about 'Western societies'. As a former museum director he is an expert at presenting information to the wandering but curious visitor, and his transitions start with stone making and finish with 'the sustainability revolution'. Read Chapter 3 to see what is in each transition that expands the often-used four part history of human development from agricultural, to industrial, to information, to living sustainably within the Earth's limits.

In Chapter 5, Sara Parkin introduces the reader to the idea that humanity has entered the 'Anthropocene', a term coined by Nobel Prize winner Paul Crutzen in 2011, but within a paragraph she references one of Adam Smith's friends and literary executors, James Hutton, who, in 1795, said that 'the purpose of life is life itself'. In the 1960s the world was encouraged to 'think globally, act locally' and this book has attempted to be grand in scale while dipping into case studies of places and ideas. As Parkin points out, states have to think locally while intelligent global governance develops at speed if we are to face the enormity of the global issues humanity, and the planet face. But how to reconcile the enormity of China with the low-lying and tiny Maldives around the same table thinking globally while acting locally? Parkin quotes Jeremy Greenstock (2008), former UK representative to the UN: 'Democratic accountability evaporates when we think globally ... culture, identity and politics are going local ... states must act locally in a globalised world'.

Parkin was at the heart of the European green 'velvet revolution' in the 1970s and 1980s which led to the downfall of numerous dictatorships and the Berlin Wall, and her chapter reflects the segue from 1989 into the Occupy movement in 2008–2010, with a comment from the then leader of the German Green Party (later to become Foreign Minister), Joschka Fischer, who 'for a moment ... heard the rustle of angels' wings'.

Peace, or the 'the rustle of angels' wings', is what Steve Killelea in Chapter 6 says lies at the heart of being able to manage the necessary transition, 'simply because peace creates the optimum environment in which the other activities that contribute to human growth can take place'. Quite so.

Arriving in Tokyo on a cold December day barely had I checked into my 30 storey hotel than there was a force seven earthquake which hit the building I was in and made it sway vigorously for about a minute. The previous year, on 3/11, as the Japanese know the mighty earthquake and tsunami of 11 March 2011, an offshore earthquake produced a tsunami that swept away whole towns, livelihoods and led to one of the world's greatest nuclear disasters (after the bombing of Hiroshima and Nagasaki 1945 and the Chernobyl meltdown in 1986). But also worthy of note is that the 3/11 earthquake struck Tokyo with a force of seven but almost no damage to infrastructure. This was despite people describing the floor turning to jelly and buildings swaying more than three metres. One resident who was on the 41st floor of her office building said: 'One moment I could see the adjacent office building where my husband was working, and the next I couldn't. That's how much the whole city moved'. The point of citing this incident is that in many poorer, more corrupt, cities the building standards and cement standards would have been compromised and the city would have been laid waste. The scientific, rational mind had triumphed over chaotic, corrupt societies and primitive minds and, for just this instance, come to terms with the natural world. That earthquakes occur we know. That some areas are more susceptible we know, but *when* they will occur we are less sure. One lesson for the future is that in order to marry people and planet, and to manage our ability to be the future (the triangulation that is progress), humanity needs to step back from a 'just in time', 'it'll be alright on the night', 'we can fix anything' culture and build resilience and hazard-adaptiveness into all our planning.

So the necessary transition has multiple entry points—from the state of the planet, to the new Chinese leadership, to US military might, to earthquakes, which in this volume are represented by the diversity of authors. One central question is: what can be learnt from history, or can anything be learnt at all given the apparent enormity of the situation. Given evolutionary randomness and the necessity to make rapid progress, what and how should we learn? Should we concentrate on social or natural systems? Can we overcome what author Tim Flannery (2010) says are the three greatest obstacles to planetary global governance: nationalism; tribalism; and misogyny?

Adapting to the necessary transition requires rapid learning. As bioethicist John Harris (2012: 38) says: 'We can no longer afford the millennia, the millions of years it's taken to evolve to our present state from our ape ancestors. The next stage of evolution has to be accelerated if we are to continue, if we are to survive … we will either be enhanced or die out … there is literally no alternative.' So, also, the necessary transition is a process of rapid evolution, of very rapid progress. Or, as biologist Paul Ehrlich put it in 1990, one of 'conscious evolution' (Ornstein and Ehrlich 1990).

For climate scientist Brendan Mackey, in this volume, the most pressing issue is adaptation to climate science, which is '… unlike any other environmental issue … (this) ethical concern for wellbeing of those yet to be born is the foundation of sustainability … it is essentially a moral position'. And for public policy and Indigenous land rights expert Ciaran O'Faircheallaigh, in Chapter 12, the most pressing problem is making public policy planning work for the planet and people. For business strategists Suzanne Benn and Cathy Rusinko it is the prism through which we see the issues that will determine how we tackle the situation and solutions. Thus, boundary objects '… beset the theory and practice of business sustainability … Boundaries are constructed by value judgements: they are temporal, spatial and both intra- and inter-organisational.' And we are back to the issue of looking at the necessary transition as political economy, integrating the length, breadth and wealth of politics, economy and society—and the natural environment.

According to academic and CSR thought-leader Jem Bendell, in Chapter 14, the route of all change must come through reforming the monetary system, but as he says 'modern humans are monetarily illiterate'. A corrupt and out of control financial system with its misallocation of funds and desire to find interest and rewards at whatever cost to the planet provides funding for Rio Tinto Coal's mines. But, as Rio Tinto's Fiona Nicholls argues here, developing economies need energy, and cheap energy at that, so why not allow them access to cheap coal: as far as Rio Tinto is concerned it is a human rights issue, and it also rewards shareholders who, for Rio Tinto, are mostly you and I through our investments, life insurance and pensions. Again, we are all part of the problem and we all have to be part of the transition, or rapid, radical evolution. As Nicholl's one time boss, the former chief executive officer of Rio Tinto, Tom Albanese, not a climate change denier in any way, put it in 2010: '… how do you devise policy for something that won't become reality for thirty or forty years?'[2] The problem is that the reality is all too real now for many people, it is not that far away.

If the entry points for the necessary transition are multiple then perhaps the action points are too. But this is belied by the commonality of concerns across the essays in this volume regarding climate change, resource depletion and the interface between people and planet, albeit with different emphases. The transition is already happening and, as Sara Parkin says, is 'a complex, muddled process'. There are however, she says, four frameworks to address: resilience; real capital growth; the psychology and sociology of change; and living in truth. These lead to five 'policies in transition': ecological demographic transition; extreme community energy; deep fair trade; sparse working, radical localism; and positive deviant leadership.

Climate change scientist Brendan Mackey declares that 'climate change is everyone's business' while Sandra Waddock, in Chapter 7, says that '… the existing social contract is badly broken … and much of today's business expertise, in fact, lends

---

2 www.riotinto.com/media/18435_presentations_19361.asp, accessed 2 April 2013.

itself to keeping the system as it is intact … through tactics of stalling, power and leverage, political action committees and campaign contributions'. So for much of the business world there is no 'necessary transition'. But for enlightened business leaders, with both morals and profits in mind, this is a Schumpeterian moment as 'sustainable entrepreneurship means creative destruction', according to Stefan Schaltegger and Erik Hansen in Chapter 11.

Joseph Schumpeter, a political scientist, drew on Karl Marx for his understanding and articulation of the process in free market capitalist economies of destruction and collapse that lead to new vistas for investment and progress. Sometimes this has been sectoral, as in the rapid transition from horsepower to the internal combustion engine, and sometimes geographical as in the collapse of gold mining in parts of North America and Australia. In the case of the necessary transition it is agreed that the current Schumpeterian gale is a global change point, and that the issues of climate change, resource depletion, population growth and global inequity have to be faced by the global community. The greatest challenge, and therefore the greatest opportunity, then, lies in the area of global governance. Global governance relates to local *and* personal identity. The necessary transition therefore requires a multi-level perspective with a single level objective—the delivery of human security to all.

If you are about to dip into this selection of essays, there is one truth that shines out. The authors exemplify the statement that is sometimes attributed to the Canadian author Margaret Attwood that 'we may be born somewhere, and we may die somewhere but this doesn't necessarily define our identity'. The authors are all global and local at the same time, as we all should be and sometimes are.

This book is divided into sections. Part 1 looks at history and transition theory through the eyes of Mark Swilling and Richard Cassels from their very different perspectives. Mark is a South African academic and an Ashoka Fellow and Richard is a former museum director who has lived and worked in the Middle East, UK and New Zealand, currently living in Australia, and who now speaks on climate change. Their contributions sandwich a case study of the inspirational Sustainability Institute between Cape Town and Stellenbosch in South Africa, which is where Eve Annecke and her partner Mark Swilling are based.

In this reflective part of the book Kyoko Fukukawa and Sunil Manghani, in Chapter 4, take us to Japan and how people in that country might see the fields of CSR and sustainability. Kyoko and Sunil are based in the UK but their life experiences have been shaped by their countries of origin. Just as Mark Swilling, Eve Annecke and Richard Cassels challenge us to think again about human 'progress' and development, so too Kyoko and Sunil ask us to start from somewhere new outside the hegemony of the Western mind.

Part 2 is called 'Re-seeing the World: Paradigm Shifts and Action' and begins with a tour de force by the political and social activist Sara Parkin. For many decades she has championed change which understands the state of the planet and, in her roles of agitator, activist, thinker and entrepreneur, she has helped bring many others to the state of anticipation. She is followed by Australian Steve Killelea who for many years stood atop a surf board, then trained in software development and made a fortune (every time you use an ATM you should think of Steve). He then decided that the best way to spend his money was on peace, as simple as that. His contribution to the debate on the links between economics and peace has been immense and often controversial on all sides. That peace is an essential for any of us to think carefully about the future seems a sine qua non, but we don't so often talk about it and how peaceful societies come into being.

Over the years, Sandra Waddock has written about mindfulness, corporate responsibility and sustainable enterprise. In this book she goes to the heart of the political economy, although she doesn't use the term, and tackles the necessity for a new contract or relationship between business and society. Given the globality of international business and the overarching impact of the market economy, Sandra's essay ties in with Jem Bendell's chapter at the end of the book on finance. Although both speak in different tongues they are both speaking the same language. Caroline Digby is Sustainability Director at the Eden Project, which the author of the book's Foreword, Tim Smit, co-founded. This project exemplifies in many ways the new social contract. The Eden Project is an educational charity that works closely with business and the local community and has so far inspired some 13 million people to visit it to marvel at the diverse and fascinating world of plants, and be wowed by a post-industrial development that is working hard to be more sustainable.

Political economy is multidisciplinary and Suzanne Benn is a professor not of corporate responsibility but of sustainable enterprise (CSR is so last century!), being what every organisation should be aiming for after it has climbed the foothills of corporate responsibility. Suzanne's and Cathy Rusinko's chapter, along with Chapter 7 by Sandra Waddock, lead to Part 3 of the book on sustainable development, climate change and business and finance, where climate scientist Brendan Mackey states what should be obvious, that climate change is everyone's business. Climate change, of course, is only one of the entry points for this collection on transition, development and change but it is fundamental. Climate change is probably more global and local at the same time than any other subject: everyone understands their own weather, but most people don't understand global climate issues or, to put more prosaically, Earth systems science.

Stefan Schaltegger and Erik Hansen work at Leuphana University Lüneburg in Germany and their chapter for this book is intensely practical, focusing, among other sectors, on the apparel industry. Germany has a lead in many areas when it comes to sustainable enterprise, particularly in industrial change and design. Indeed, it could be argued that German leads in this area and has developed a sophisticated, complex economy, unlike Australia where the reliance on mining has led to an overpriced dollar and an economy that lacks resilience because of its lack of complexity. Fiona Nicholl's chapter recognises that the move away from fossil fuels, and particularly from coal, is inevitable. But not yet, and not while new industrialising countries such as China and India are demanding easily usable energy reserves to provide electricity.

There is no denial of climate change on the part of intelligent companies such as Rio Tinto, but there is a difficulty in matching the necessity for the necessary rapid transition to a post-carbon world and the demands of new industrialising countries. The fossil fuel sector has joined forces with the pharmaceutical sector in arguing that denying cheap energy and cheap pharmaceuticals to people just coming out of poverty is a human rights issue, while failing to recognise that the rest of society has had to absorb the externalities created through using subsidised fossil fuels.

Ciaran O'Faircheallaigh's call for there to be changes in public policy is therefore where the debate should be. Until the bias towards the energy source that fuelled the industrial revolution is shifted towards energy sources that work at living on the interest, not the capital of planet Earth we will continue to leave mining holes in our planet home and threaten our existence.

References

Flannery, T. (2010) *Here On Earth: An Argument for Hope* (Melbourne, Australia: Text Publishing).

Funabashi, Y., and H. Takenaka (eds.) (2011) *Lessons from the Disaster: Risk Management and the Compound Crisis Presented by the Great East Japan Earthquake* (Tokyo and Osaka: The Japan Times).

Glover, S. (2001) *Humanity: A Moral History of the Twentieth Century* (New Haven, CT: Yale University Press).

Greenstock, J. (2008) 'States must act locally in a globalised world', *Financial Times*, 15 May 2008.

Harris, J. (2012) *Superhuman: Exploring Human Enhancement from 600 BCE to 2050* (London: Wellcome Trust).

Hawken, P. (2008) *Blessed Unrest* (London: Penguin).

Meadows, D. (2008) *Thinking In Systems* (London: Earthscan).

Ornstein, R., and P. Ehrlich (1990) *New World New Mind: Moving Towards Conscious Evolution* (New York: Simon & Schuster).

Senge, P. (2008) *The Necessary Revolution* (London: Nicolas Brealey Publishers).

UN Secretary-General's High-Level Panel on Global Sustainability (2012) *Resilient People, Resilient Planet: A Future Worth Choosing* (New York: United Nations).

Dr **Malcolm McIntosh**, FRSA, is Professor and Director of the Asia Pacific Centre for Sustainable Enterprise at Griffith University in Queensland, Australia, which he joined in 2009. He started teaching and writing on corporate responsibility and sustainability in 1990, has worked at the universities of Warwick and Coventry, and been a Visiting Professor at the universities of Bath, Bristol, Stellenbosch, Waikato and Sydney. He is the producer, author or co-author of more than 20 books and numerous articles, and has been a frequent commentator on television and radio around the world on social issues, business responsibility and sustainable enterprise. He has been a special adviser to the UN Global Compact and was the founding editor of the *Journal of Corporate Citizenship*.

1

Contested futures
Conceptions of the next long-term development cycle

Mark Swilling
Sustainability Institute, Stellenbosch University, South Africa

Introduction

This chapter will review some of the emerging *stories of the future* that have been generated by the global crisis. By drawing on the multi-level perspective (Grin *et al.* 2010), neo-Schumpeterian perspectives (Gore 2010; Köhler 2012) and a political ecology perspective on transitions (Lawhon and Murphy 2011), it will be argued in the first part of the chapter that these are attempts to re-imagine a post-crisis landscape in ways that, for some, will preserve the status quo (using, for example, market-oriented 'green economy' discourses) while for others quite significant changes in the patterns of production and consumption that have dominated the post-World War II period are envisaged. As such, these re-imaginings deserve attention because—thanks to the pervasive use of computer-aided scenario-building in recent times—images of the future do influence decisions that can shape these futures. However, the primary concern of this chapter is not just stories of the future, but also the kinds of real-economy conditions that could materially contribute to the possibility of a more sustainable and equitable future. In the second part of the chapter, it will be argued that rising resource prices have joined climate change and ecosystem services as a key landscape driver of change. After over a century of declining resource prices, the steady rise of resource prices since the turn of the millennium is clearly a game changer. It will be argued that the rise to prominence of the 'green economy' discourse reflects a growing recognition of this inflection point. This does not, however, automatically imply the unfolding of a sustainability transition precisely because the sociopolitical regimes and institutions of the post-World War II era remain dominant.

Re-imagining the landscape: crises, cycles and waves

According to the multi-level perspective (MLP) on sustainability transitions, the macro-level sociotechnical landscape provides the context for the relatively autonomous institutionalisation of sociotechnical regimes and the initiation of niche innovations protected somewhat from potentially hostile market and political dynamics (Grin *et al.* 2010). Regimes are institutionalised configurations of shared assumptions, technologies, regulations, market norms and consumer preferences that 'lock in' a particular mode of production and consumption. Niches, on the other hand, are loci for radical innovation that can either subvert or reform existing regimes depending on the dynamics and intensity of the landscape pressures. A regime can reform itself by tapping internal innovations and/or external knowledge that has evolved in niches, or it can deny/resist change and eventually collapse (Smith *et al.* 2005). If it collapses, a new regime is constituted from the knowledge sets that have evolved within the niches. The landscape includes:

> … environmental and demographic change, new social movements, shifts in general political ideology, broad economic restructuring, emerging scientific paradigms, and cultural developments. Landscapes provide an influential backdrop with ramifications across a variety of regimes and niches: providing *gradients and affordances for how to go about establishing socio-technical configurations* that service societal needs (Smith *et al.* 2010: 7, emphasis added).

Following Rotmans and Loorbach (2009), a key aspect of the transition management approach is the facilitation of engagements between actors to develop shared visions of the future. However, these actors—who are, as Lawhon and Murphy (2011) point out, largely drawn from corporate, scientific and policy elites—arrive at these engagements with preconceptions of the future that shape the discourse. These preconceptions are, in turn, influenced by a variety of academic, semi-academic and popular writing that construct imaginaries of future trajectories. What follows below is a review of a set of typical perspectives that all aim in one way or another to re-imagine the 'gradients and affordances' of a future sociotechnical landscape that transcends the present crisis-ridden landscape on terms that may, depending on who uses the ideas, challenge existing power structures.

Six key texts will be briefly reviewed, all of which systematise, in one way or another, a set of storylines about the future that are easily recognised in the diverse range of popular discourses about the future that have proliferated since 2007–2008. They represent, therefore, clusters of discursive and cultural ontologies of probable futures (Geels 2010). These texts are: Standard Chartered, *The Super-Cycle Report* (2010); Arun Motianey, *Supercycles: The New Force Transforming Global Markets and Investment Strategy* (2010); Allianz Global Investors, *The Sixth Kondratieff: Long Waves of Prosperity* (2010);[1] James Bradfield-Moody and Bianca Nogrady, *The Sixth Wave: How to Succeed in a Resource-limited World* (2010); Ernst Von Weizsäcker and colleagues, *Factor Five* (2009); and Jeremy Rifkin's *The Third Industrial Revolution: How Lateral Power is Transforming Energy, the Economy and the World* (2011).

Compiled by the research division of the global banking group Standard Chartered, the core argument of their report is that there have been two major 'super-cycles' plus a third which is current, namely: 1870–1913 when the global economy grew on average by 2.7% per annum; 1946–1973 when economic growth rates averaged 5%; and 2000–2030 when economic growth is expected to average out at 3.5% with the current recession seen as a relatively brief moment of 'rebalancing' (Standard Chartered 2010). The definition of a supercycle is 'a period of historically high global growth, lasting a generation or more' and which is characterised by a nation that becomes a dominant economic driver (Standard Chartered 2010: 1). For Standard Chartered, the shift in economic power from the 'West' to the 'East', rapid urbanisation and the massive future growth of the Asian middle class are seen as the key drivers of the next supercycle (2000–2030). Interestingly, the period between the 1970s and 2000 is seen as a period of weak debt-financed growth in the West, economic stagnation in Japan, collapse of the Soviet Union, debt and currency crises in Latin America, while China and India had not yet 'opened up'. As a result '[t]here was no dynamic driver for the world economy' during this period (Standard Chartered 2010: 3).

The key fact that is used to substantiate the argument that we are now well into a third supercycle is that the global economy in 2010 was almost twice the size it was in 2000 (i.e. a GDP of US$32 trillion in 2000, rising to US$62 trillion in 2010)—a trajectory driven mainly by growth in the East, a driver that is seen as lasting for at least two more decades. Yes, Standard Chartered admits, there are challenges today, but they have faith good policy decisions will sort out the economic problems in due course; and in a very short section it is argued that innovation will deal with the problems of climate change and rising resource prices (including rising oil prices which are specifically mentioned as an unpredictable threat). Global GDP is, therefore, confidently expected by Standard Chartered to be US$143 trillion by 2030 (in real terms) which is, of course, more than double what it was in 2010.

---

1 This particular report uses the 'Kondratieff' spelling, whereas usual practice is to use 'Kondratiev' which is the spelling used in the remainder of this chapter.

Arun Motianey worked for Citibank for 30 years which, he says, allowed him to experience first-hand the real workings of the booms and busts of the global financial system as it evolved during the period of globalised financialisation starting in the late 1970s (Motianey 2010). He concluded that how this system actually works contradicts the prevailing theories of how it should work. He sets out to debunk the notion that we can understand national economies as aggregations of individual/household transactions, and the global economy as aggregations of national-level economic dynamics. Instead, the globalised architecture of the financial, trade and production system has given rise to a sociotechnical landscape that he calls a 'supercycle' that has its own autonomous logic and 'laws'. He equates a supercycle to a large undulating integrated pipeline that is constituted at the level of the global economy unrelated to the specific dynamics of each national economy—a classic 'landscape' dynamic in MLP language. A supercycle starts with the extraction and processing of commodities, proceeds through to the production of intermediate goods, and ends with consumable goods and services that are bought and consumed by end-users (households, businesses). Waves of goods flow through the pipeline, expanding and contracting in line with the complex logics of price-regulated supply and demand. The problem is that in a world of nations comprising multiple currencies and exchange rates, as a price drops somewhere along the pipeline for whatever reason, this translates into higher profits and therefore over-investment in capacity, assets and expanded employment further down the pipeline. This would not be a problem if prices were a true reflection of economic value, but they are not because of institutional inefficiencies. Instead, the (frequently debt-financed) over-investment in capacity, assets and expanded employment translates into asset bubbles that end in crashes followed by deflation. This pattern starts at one end of the pipeline and gradually and steadily gets transferred down the pipe driving the booms and busts along the way that we now know so well. The hyper-financialisation of the global economy oiled the wheels of this roller coaster: fostered by the US Federal Reserve and the US Treasury, financialisation (made possible by the deregulation of financial institutions—what former UK Prime Minister Gordon Brown called the 'light touch' regulation) created the space for financial innovations that were used to accelerate and profit from transacting these booms and busts. Speculators and transactors made their profits, leaving behind a trail of economic devastation. As Motianey (2010: 23) puts it:

> Like a long snakelike balloon losing air, the pipeline begins to deflate at one end (the bust), which makes the next section closest to it on the balloon (the boom) appear to inflate. But then eventually the deflation travels through the entire length of the balloon.

For Motianey, once deflation has worked its way through the pipeline, the endpoint is either a great big crash due to policy failure (as happened after the 1929 crash), or a prolonged unproductive malaise similar to what has afflicted the Japanese economy since the 1990s. The Japanese malaise writ large is his metaphor for the future. Accordingly, therefore, he looks back and sees two great sociotechnical landscapes or supercycles. The first is what he calls the 'classical supercycle' which began with the adoption of the gold standard in the 1870s and ended in the early 1930s with the mass destruction of productive capacity as states held back from intervening after the 1929 crash until it was too late. The second supercycle is the 'modern supercycle', which began with the formation of what he calls the 'volcker fed' in 1979 and which is continuing well into the second decade of the 21st century. The deregulation of the global financial system that the US Federal Reserve promoted made it possible to create a gigantic pipeline of interlinked sovereign surpluses and debt that drove the booms and busts around the world—from the Latin American debt crises of the 1980s, transferred to the Asian crashes of the 1990s, and then on to the sovereign debt crises of developed economies in the 2000s. However, the key difference is that, unlike the end of the classical supercycle, states have learnt to respond with counter-cyclical measures that have transferred household and banking debts into sovereign debt coupled to austerity measures, while simultaneously keeping interest rates low in the hope of stimulating growth. Because monetary authorities are determined to also keep inflation low, the end result is what Motianey calls the 'great malaise'—a prolonged uncreative deflationary depression. The only alternative, in his view, would be to accept that a new era of inflation is needed to devalue the debt and realign the prices of production and consumption. But the resulting 'creative destruction' (to use Schumpeter's famous words) not only runs contrary to economic orthodoxy, it is also contrary to the interests of the banks who resist all attempts to devalue what they are owed by the governments of the world. So, contrary to the optimism of the Standard Chartered report, he concludes:

> We will not face the Second Great Depression; more likely we will face the first Great Global Malaise—where the whole world looks like Japan—or perhaps the Great Stagflation (Motianey 2010: 28).

As the global economy bumps along the bottom into its fifth year of recession, the combined impact of debt-constrained fiscal intervention, the limits to monetary policy imposed by ultra-low or even negative real interest rates and the build-up of unprecedented reserves of unspent cash by investors seems to confirm Motianey's profound pessimism. It must surely be more than a glitch in a long-term upward trend.

While reports like the one from Standard Chartered see a saviour in the birth of an Asian middle class, Motianey's perspective blames economic orthodoxy for the gutless opposition to the inflationary dynamics needed to flush out the deadwood of accumulated debt that is responsible for the great malaise. Both, however, ignore the question of sustainability; by contrast the next three perspectives directly link solutions to the global economic crisis to a transition to a more sustainable global economy.

The report published by the global asset management company Allianz Global Investors, *The Sixth Kondratieff: Long Waves of Prosperity*, argues that the current global economic crisis marks the beginning of the end of the fifth Kondratiev cycle and the start of the sixth Kondratiev cycle (Allianz Global Investors 2010). Following the tradition started by Kondratiev, the Russian economist who first thought of economic history in terms of long waves of 40 to 60 years (Kondratieff 1935), Allianz notes that during the first phase of the Kondratiev cycle interest rates go up as demand increases for capital to fund the investments in new technologies formulated by the alliances between innovators and entrepreneurs. However, this is not a problem because earnings from the new value chains that get created easily cover the costs of capital as profit margins soar. However, diminishing returns over time on investments in ever-maturing technologies reduces the demand for credit resulting, in turn, in a decline in real interest rates. Every major crisis, including the present one, has been brought on by this dynamic, the Allianz report argues. The conditions that lead to a new Kondratiev cycle include the exhaustion of the potential of mature technologies, an excess of financial capital versus physical capital, recessionary conditions and social/institutional transformation. Allianz argues that all these conditions pertain today. The obvious question, therefore, is what combination of technological innovations will become the focus of the next—the sixth—Kondratiev cycle. Their answer is as follows:

> While in the previous Kondratieff cycle the information age led to a tremendous increase in labour productivity, the key to a strong and sustainable economy in the next long cycle seems to lie in an increase in the *productivity of resources and energy* (Allianz Global Investors 2010: 12, emphasis added).

Figure 1.1: **Kondratiev cycles—long waves of prosperity**

Source: Allianz Global Investors 2010

Rolling 10-year yield on the S&P 500 since 1814 till March 2009 (in %p.a)

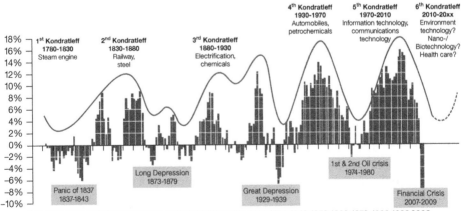

■ Rolling 10-year yield on the S&P 500

As reflected in Figure 1.1, by harnessing information technologies, innovations in the 'green tech', biotechnology, nanotechnology and health care (driven by aging populations) sectors will become the drivers of the next cycle. Significantly, they see the developed economies as the technology leaders of this new sociotechnical landscape because their levels of investment in innovation are higher than in developing countries where the focus is still on growth to meet rapidly expanding consumer demand. While developing economies are seen as the economic 'accelerator' of future global growth, developed economies benefit from being the lead innovators (i.e. owners of the intellectual property that the rest of the world will need)—this being an interesting coupling of quantitative (developing world) and qualitative (developed world) dynamics to imagine a future global sociotechnical landscape.

Bradfield-Moody and Nogrady (2010) also imagine a future sociotechnical landscape in terms of the dynamics of a 'sixth wave'. Written in a journalistic style for a business audience, it is an upbeat manifesto for those who want to believe that a sustainable world can be brought about by smart investors with sufficient vision to realise that the best returns will be generated by technological innovations that reduce waste, generate renewable energy, increase resource productivity and copy the organising principles of nature (biomimickry). The sixth wave is presumed to have started already because annual new investments in renewable energy have already overtaken new investments in fossil fuel-based energy. The fifth wave—the information and communication wave—is depicted as a response to the sclerotic bureaucratised business regimes that emerged during the inter-war years.[2] By the 1970s these highly inefficient regimes were pushing up transaction costs in a way that restrained the growth potential of expanding global markets. By massively reducing transaction costs, the information and communication technologies subverted the institutional architecture of the post-World War II boom and created the extraordinary business opportunities that became the drivers of the fifth wave. But the 'transaction cost revolution' drove down the costs of production as a new generation of information-driven regimes proliferated, accelerating global economic growth resulting, in turn, in rapidly rising prices of depleting natural resources, including climate space. The constraint now, therefore, is not transaction costs, but the resource costs generated by an entrenched set of resource- and energy-intensive regimes. It follows, therefore, that the sixth wave will be driven by innovations that will deploy the information technologies of the fifth wave to unleash a 'revolution that will see our world transformed from one heavily addicted to the consumption of resources, to a world in which resource-efficiency is the name of the game' (Bradfield-Moody and Nogrady 2010: 38). In short, they envisage a whole new generation of resource-efficient regimes that will have responded appropriately via the market to the rising resource prices created by accelerated resource depletion at the landscape level.

---

2 It may be worth noting that Bradfield-Moody and Nogrady date their five Kondratiev cycles very similarly to Allianz, but with subtle differences—the dates are: first wave: 1780s–1848; second wave: 1848–1895; third wave: 1895–1940; fourth wave: 1941–1973/7?; fifth wave: 1980–2001/2007–?; sixth wave: 2001/2007–?.

Led by well-known sustainability thought leader Ernst Von Weizsäcker, the co-authors of *Factor Five* tell a similar story to Bradfield-Moody and Nogrady, albeit in a less triumphalist business-manifesto kind of way, and with greater appreciation for the role of appropriately ambitious public policies to create the spaces for innovation (Von Weizsäcker *et al.* 2009). They repeat the familiar image of the five Kondratiev waves and suggest that a sixth 'innovation wave' is already emerging driven by technological innovations that can improve resource productivity by 80%.[3] What is significant about *Factor Five* is the systematic presentation of a wide range of empirical evidence from across the construction, heavy industry, agricultural and transport sectors to substantiate the claim that niche-level innovations have already generated the technologies that are needed to create fully-fledged economy-wide sociotechnical regimes that can improve resource efficiencies by 80% (i.e. by a factor of five). Put simply, by way of example, a five-fold increase in the energy efficiency of a house designed according to the German passivhaus standard will use 200 kWh/month instead of 1000 kWh. Likewise for many other innovations. What is significant about the current transition, they argue, is:

> … the availability of a wide range of fascinating new technologies promising to be roughly five times more resource efficient than those still dominating industry, households and the service sector. So we do not hesitate to call for and promote a new Green Kondratiev cycle (Von Weizsäcker *et al.* 2009: 14).

Significantly, Von Weizsäcker *et al.* clarify what they mean by resource productivity (used inter-changeably with resource efficiency) by equating it to the more familiar notion of labour productivity. They point out that labour productivity increased 20-fold over the past 200 years. Labour productivity improved by 1% per annum up until the mid-20th century, and thereafter by 2%–3% per annum (Von Weizsäcker *et al.* 2009: 15). This made rising real wages possible. Resource productivity, however, was never a priority, especially in light of the fact that real resource prices declined over the century ending in 2002 (Fischer-Kowalski and Swilling 2011). Labour, however, is no longer in short supply—the limiting factor now is depleting resources. It follows, Von Weizsäcker *et al.* argue, that: 'Resource productivity should become the main feature of technological progress in our days' (Von Weizsäcker *et al.* 2009: 17). Taking this to scale is the transformative driver of the emergent sociotechnical landscape that *Factor Five* sets out to imagine by drawing from actually existing resource efficiencies generated across a wide range of niches and regimes.

This brings us to Jeremy Rifkin's *The Third Industrial Revolution: How Lateral Power is Transforming Energy, the Economy and the World* (Rifkin 2011). Rifkin is a sustainability superstar with a long record of high-level policy involvement in

---

3   Some of the Australian co-authors of this book had already elaborated the core logic of the 'sixth wave' in an earlier work entitled *The Natural Advantage of Nations* (Hargroves and Smith 2005).

European policy-making circles. He writes, however, in an activist style for a broad popular audience about a 'brave new world' that can be brought about by those long-sighted enough to share his vision. Whereas Bradfield-Moody and Nogrady focus on entrepreneurial opportunities created by markets and Von Weizsäcker *et al.* put their faith in the potential of sustainability-oriented technological innovations, Rifkin is interested in the reconfiguration of socioinstitutional power relations brought on by the 'conjoining of Internet communication technology and renewable energies'. 'We are', he argues, 'in the midst of a profound shift in the very way society is structured, away from hierarchical power and toward lateral power' (Rifkin 2011: 28). It is this shift that is the distinctive mark of Rifkin's 'third industrial revolution'.[4]

Indeed, for Rifkin, the driving force of all major epochal shifts is the reconfiguration of conjoined energy and communication technologies that shape, in turn, the wider structures of economic and political power. The first industrial revolution, which commenced in the mid-19th century, began when steam-powered technology was introduced into printing which, in turn, revolutionised communications and education with the latter responsible for the creation of the literate workforce needed to 'organize the complex operations of a coal-powered, steam-driven rail and factory economy' (Rifkin 2011: 27). The second industrial revolution began in the first decade of the 20th century when 'electrical communications converged with the oil-powered internal combustion engine' (Rifkin 2011: 28). Long-distance power supplies, telephone lines and highways soon followed, creating the connectivity infrastructure that made possible the emergence of mass production and consumption in the 20th century. The third industrial revolution, which will come to dominate the 21st century, will emerge from the fusion of Internet and renewable energy technologies to create a new 'intergrid' of intelligent distributed electricity networks. This is what will subvert the 'conventional top-down organization of society' and replace it with 'lateral power'— 'distributed and collaborative relationships in the emerging green industrial era' (Rifkin 2011: 28).

Rifkin identifies five dimensions ('five pillars') of this future sociotechnical regime that will characterise this green industrial era:

1. Renewable energy will have replaced fossil fuel-based energy

2. Every building will becomes its own power station

3. Energy storage (including hydrogen) will be built into every building

4. Using the Internet, smart grids will be used to manage the infrastructures that conduct resource flows through socioecological systems (including trading between households and neighbourhoods)

---

4 For this reason, maybe Rifkin is to the sixth wave/third industrial revolution what Alvin Toffler was to the information revolution.

5. The combustion engine will have been replaced by vehicles with electric engines powered (via battery or fuel cell technologies as the storage mechanisms) by an interactive power grid connected to renewable energy generation

Standard Chartered and Motianey represent two ends of a spectrum of debate about long-term cycles that deal only with economic matters (with, at best, environment tacked on as a problem to be resolved by innovation): the former optimistically assumes that Asian demand is such a powerful landscape dynamic that it will continue to relentlessly drive global growth for another two decades, while the latter predicts a Japan-type grand malaise as deflation works its destructive way through the global economic pipeline reinforced by the all-pervasive fear of inflation.

In contrast to these two economistic narratives, the Allianz report, Rifkin, Bradfield-Moody and Nogrady and the *Factor Five* group all go beyond economic dynamics to identify wider environmental landscape factors (primarily resource depletion and global warming). They all envisage a sustainability transition by invoking long-term historical cycles to conjure up images of more sustainable long-term growth. They also warn that if major global environmental crises at the landscape level are to be avoided, investors and policy-makers will need to make sure the sixth innovation wave is aggressively accelerated by way of purposive policy interventions to upscale factor five technologies.

Making sense of the green economy

During the course of 2009 both Barack Obama and Gordon Brown began talking about a 'global green new deal'. Two substantial reports released in 2011 seem to substantiate this apparent ideological acceptance of the fact that the global economic crisis and the global environmental crisis are inextricably interlinked (Barbier 2009). The first is by the United Nations Environment Programme (UNEP) entitled *Towards a Green Economy: Pathways to Sustainable Development and Poverty Eradication* commonly referred to as the *Green Economy* report or *GER* (UNEP 2011); and the second is the United Nations' *World Economic and Social Survey 2011: The Great Green Technological Transformation* commonly referred to as the *UNWESS 2011* report (UN 2011). By mobilising insights from models and vast amounts of empirical information from across all economic sectors, both reports confirm that solutions to the current global economic crisis that do not address global warming and the underlying resource and ecological constraints are doomed to fail. In a remarkable opening statement, the *GER* cuts to the root of the problem:

> The causes of these crises vary, but at a fundamental level they all share
> a common feature: *the gross misallocation of capital*. During the last two

decades, much capital was poured into property, fossil fuels and structured financial assets with embedded derivatives. However, relatively little in comparison was invested in renewable energy, energy efficiency, public transportation, sustainable agriculture, ecosystem and biodiversity protection, and land and water conservation (UNEP 2011: 14, emphasis added).

Both the *GER* and *UNWESS* reports agree that a green economy is low carbon, resource efficient, restores ecosystems and is socially inclusive. Policy options for zero growth or an exclusive focus on population reduction to achieve environmental sustainability are ruled out because of the negative impact on poverty eradication programmes in developing countries. The only alternative is, therefore, 'reducing non-renewable energy and resource use, reducing waste and pollution, and reversing land degradation and biodiversity losses' (UN 2011: vi). Both explicitly set out to transcend the 'myth' that there is a trade-off between economic growth and sustainable resource management. And both emphasise the vital importance of public policy and the leading role of governments—as the *UNWESS* report puts it: 'The needed acceleration of technological innovation and diffusion is unlikely to occur if left to spontaneous market forces' (UN 2011: 22-23).

The analysis and policy prescriptions of both reports relate to three dimensions: the traditional concerns with climate change mitigation (reducing carbon dioxide); reducing biodiversity losses and the need to restore degraded ecosystem services; and what is generally referred to as resource and energy efficiency. Surprisingly, and in contrast to some of the texts reviewed in the previous section, rising resource prices and related innovations are not given much emphasis. Instead, carbon reduction and biodiversity restoration are clearly seen as more significant drivers than rising resource and energy prices.

The *GER* model analyses the potential impact of investing 2% of global GDP on an annual basis (about US$1.3 trillion/year) to 2050 into green economy sectors, and compares this to a business-as-usual scenario. Half of this investment is allocated to energy efficiency (buildings, industry and transport) and renewable energy measures that will achieve global carbon reduction targets by 2050 (mitigating the rising cost of oil is not emphasised). The remainder is devoted to waste management, public transport infrastructure and the restoration of ecosystem services across a range of natural capital-based sectors (agriculture, fisheries, forestry and water supplies). The results show that a green investment of approximately US$1.3 trillion/annum 'delivers long-term growth over 2011–2050 that is at least as high as an optimistic business as usual case, while avoiding considerable downside risks such as the effects of climate change, greater water scarcity, and the loss of ecosystem services' (UNEP 2011: 500). Other than the explicit modelling of energy prices, it is not clear whether or not the *GER*'s macro-economic model implicitly takes into account rising resource prices.

The *UNWESS* report confirms that the kind of 'fundamental technological and structural transformation' envisaged by a long-term investment in the building up of a green economy can only happen if the following five objectives can be achieved (UN 2011: 11):

- Reduction of resource requirements in general and of energy requirements in particular, in both absolute terms and relatively, per unit of output

- Substitution of renewable for non-renewable resources, given the total resource use

- Substitution of biodegradables for non-biodegradables, at any given level of output or waste

- Reduction of waste (including pollution), at any given level of resource use

- Protection of biodiversity and ecosystems

Although both the *GER* and *UNWESS* reports envisage a radical transformation of the global economy that takes into account the poverty challenges of developing countries, it is surprising that despite explicit reference to resource efficiency in the *GER* and the need for resource reduction in the *UNWESS* report, the potential space for sustainability-oriented innovations created by the market dynamics of—and policy responses to—rising resource prices is under-emphasised.

UNEP's International Resource Panel (IRP),[5] however, explicitly fills this gap. It was established in 2007 to deal with global material flows, resource depletion and decoupling. The IRP distinguishes between four categories of resources: biomass (everything from agricultural products, to clothing material like cotton, to forest products); fossil fuels (oil, coal and gas); construction minerals (cement, building sand, etc); and ores and industrial minerals.[6] By the start of the 21st century the global economy consumed between 47 and 59 billion metric tonnes of resources (which is equal to half what is physically extracted from the crust of the Earth). Between 1900 and 2005 total material extraction increased over this period by a factor of eight. The strongest increase was for construction minerals, which grew by a factor of 34, ores and industrial minerals by a factor of 27, fossil fuels carriers by a factor of 12 and biomass extraction increased by only 3.6-fold. Taking into account population growth, what this means is that although global resource use increased 8-fold, average resource use per capita only doubled from about 4.6 tonnes/capita in 1900 to between 8.5 and 9.2 tonnes/capita by 2005. More significantly, while global resource use increased 8-fold, GDP increased by a factor of 23 for the same period (Fischer-Kowalski and Swilling 2011). As reflected in Figure 1.2, the result is relative decoupling between rates of resource use and global growth rates.

As the IRP report shows, rising global resource use during the course of the 20th century (including the metabolic shift that took place from mid-century onwards as non-renewables grew and dependence on renewable biomass declined)

---

5 www.unep.org/resourcepanel, accessed 27 March 2013.
6 Note that water and land resources are excluded from this categorisation of global material flows—for a justification see Fischer-Kowalski and Swilling (2011: 8-9).

Figure 1.2: **Global metabolic rates 1900–2005, and income**

Source: Fischer-Kowalski and Swilling 2011: 12

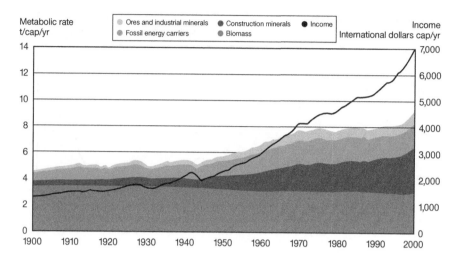

corresponded with declining real resource prices—a trend that came to an end in 2000–2002. Since 2000–2002, the macro trend in real resource prices has been upwards (notwithstanding dips in 2008–2009 and again in 2012).

The McKinsey Global Institute report, *Resource Revolution*, which was published after the IRP report, generally confirms the trends identified by the IRP report (McKinsey Global Institute 2011). The McKinsey report calculates that resource

Figure 1.3: **Composite resource price index (at constant prices, 1900–2000)**

Source: Fischer-Kowalski and Swilling 2011: 13

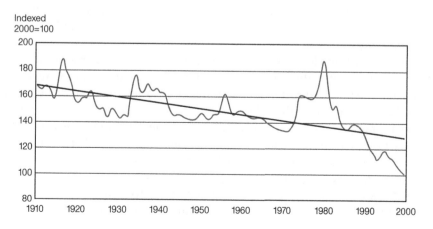

Figure 1.4: **Commodity price indices**

Source: Fischer-Kowalski and Swilling 2011: 13

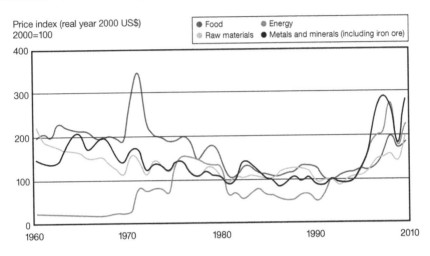

prices increased by 147% in the decade since 2000 and that this cannot be separated from the fact that up to US$1.1 trillion is spent annually on what they call 'resource subsidies'. McKinsey argues that if resource subsidies are reduced and an additional US$1 trillion per annum is invested in resource efficient production systems to meet growing demand (an amount similar to what the *GER* has in mind), the result will be the creation of a whole new set of 'productivity opportunities' with an internal rate of return of 10% at current prices. In other words, from a long-term perspective, increasing resource productivity is a viable business opportunity for its client base. The top 15 business opportunity areas (that represent 75% of the potential resource savings) include, in order of potential: energy efficient buildings; large-scale farm yields; food waste; municipal water leakage; urban densification; energy efficiency in iron and steel production; smallholder farm yields; transport efficiency; electric and hybrid vehicles; land degradation; end-use steel efficiency; oil and coal recovery; irrigation techniques; road freight shift to rail; and power plant efficiency.

In short, the IRP and McKinsey reports confirm the arguments reviewed in the first section of this chapter, that resource depletion may well drive up resource prices over the long term. As a direct input into production rather than a negative environmental impact (such as carbon dioxide), the cost of resources will unsurprisingly drive a wide range of responses from downsizing through to innovations that enlarge existing—or open up new—markets. It follows that this is a factor that deserves much greater attention when it comes to modelling green economy pathways.

According to conventional economic logic, to reduce deficits and debt, developed and some developing economies desperately need economic growth. However, high debt levels constrain stimulatory fiscal interventions and ultra-low interest rates (in many places) mean monetary policy can achieve very little. Putting aside for the moment the politically challenging alternative of lowering wage levels, there is really only one other alternative, namely investment to stimulate growth. However, investment has steadily dropped as confidence has eroded. Instead of taking risks, more and more spare funds have been squirreled away in safe low-interest solvent sovereign bonds (such as Germany where the bond rate even went negative during the course of 2012).

By 2011 Gross Domestic Investment dropped to 16% of GDP in the USA, which is below what it was in the early 1960s and way below the 1979 peak of 23%; and in the UK Gross Fixed Capital Formation dropped to just above 14%, which is below what it was in 1960 and way below the 1990 peak of 22% (Zhengelis 2012). In plain English this means investors are not spending the profits they are making. *The Economist* reported on 31 March 2012 that the profits of American companies by early 2012 were higher than at any time in the past 65 years. In simple numbers, this amounted to over US$1 trillion of unspent cash. In South Africa, the Minister of Finance moaned that in 2012 there was over R500 billion of unspent cash held by corporates while poverty levels got worse as economic growth rates remained lower than what was required to absorb enough labour to reduce unemployment.

So if fiscal and monetary policies are ineffective, do green economy investments, as proposed by the *GER* and the *UNWESS* report (or investments in resource productivity opportunities as proposed by the McKinsey report) really offer an investment pathway that can end the global investment strike? Dimitri Zhengelis from the London School of Economics and senior adviser to Cisco recently published a paper that makes a credible macro-economic case in favour of this proposition (Zhengelis 2012). Zhengelis disagrees with Paul Krugman's unreconstructed Keynesianism which allows him to argue that debt constraints are overstated and that fiscal spending holds the key to economic recovery (Krugman 2012). He is also critical of the view that austerity measures will rebuild the levels of confidence needed to drive a sustainable global economic recovery. Unlike the Keynesians and austerity economists, his faith lies in the creation of new 'additive' investment opportunities in green growth. For Zhengelis, there are two compelling reasons why investments in green growth can unlock unspent investment funds in ways that could stimulate growth: they can go to scale rapidly (decentralised renewable energy plants, for example); and they will be responsive to credible multi-year policy interventions that limit uncertainty and build confidence over time. In his words:

> It is precisely the overwhelming and growing long-term need to address numerous market failures [such as climate change] through transformational investment and innovation that has the potential to make the opportunity from intervention so credible. 'Green' investment is also large-scale and offers potentially profitable markets for decades. It can therefore leverage in serious private money. As a result, much of this private investment should be additive (rather than displaced from elsewhere), helping to break out of the deflationary confidence spiral, much as Roosevelt's New Deal did in the United States from 1933 (Zhengelis 2012: 18).

Green growth, from this perspective, provides the most credible and viable way of unlocking the mountains of unspent cash chasing the diminishing pool of solvent sovereign bonds as fiscal and monetary policies fail to revive confidence in the unsustainable business-as-usual policies that prevailed in the bulk of Organisation for Economic Co-operation and Development (OECD) countries in 2012. Unless a credible long-term investment programme of this kind can be formulated and adopted by governments around the world, the optimistic projections of the *GER* and *UNWESS* report have little chance of being realised in practice. This, then, brings the discussion back to the dynamics of the current interregnum and what it will take to catalyse a transition to a more sustainable global economy.

Conceptualising the next long-term development cycle

The perspectives reviewed thus far need to be understood as a response that may satisfy a deep cultural desire to make sense of seemingly chaotic dynamics by invoking the logics of historical trends, but it may also be a reasonable response to what Edgar Morin has referred to as the 'polycrisis'—a nested set of globally interactive socioeconomic, ecological and cultural–institutional crises that defy reduction to a single cause (Morin 1999: 73). Instead of seeing the crisis as a black swan event, long-wave theory provides a set of heuristic conceptual framings that make it possible to depict the crisis as a particular moment in a much wider and deeper set of historical trajectories that have not only occurred before but can be expected to unfold in future in more or less predictable ways. But before proceeding to elaborate this framework, it is necessary to recognise the critiques of long-wave theory (for reviews of these debates see: Rosenberg and Frischtak 1983; Fagerberg 2003; Verspagen 2005; Broadberry 2007) and the relationship between long-wave theory and the MLP (Köhler 2012).

Whether one refers to the more classical Kondratiev cycles used by development economists (for a lead example see Gore 2010), or the S-curves at the centre of the MLP (Grin *et al.* 2010) and the structural evolutionary approaches (Freeman and Louca 2001; Perez 2002), the obvious danger is that they are prone to techno-economic determinism: technological innovations do the 'acting' and sociopolitical institutions do the 'reacting'. One solution to this problem offered by the 'co-evolutionary framework' is to analyse the co-evolution of socioeconomic, institutional and ecological systems and their causal interactions (Foxon 2011). Foxon and Pearson argue that long-wave theorists:

> ... are keen to stress that these attributes of technologies do not 'determine' wider socio-economic change, but they enable co-evolutionary changes in institutions and practices that, together with technology changes, give rise to significant macroeconomic impacts (Pearson and Foxon 2012: 121).

Some writing from within the MLP school has given greater emphasis to institutions. By analysing the capacities for accessing new knowledge and managing change, it becomes possible to assess whether particular sociotechnical regimes will adjust or be replaced by new regimes formed from alternative niche innovations (Smith *et al.* 2005). Furthermore, it is problematic to assume that there is a grand wave of economic development that somehow takes hold simultaneously everywhere and—using language from neoliberal ideology—'lifts all boats'. Instead, innovations originate in particular countries for quite specific well-documented reasons related to institutions, culture, labour markets and economic dynamics (Pearson and Foxon 2012). They then radiate outwards absorbing others into mutually reinforcing new economic and financial circuits, while still others get excluded from innovations and investments in human capital and institutional reform, or subordinated to providers of primary materials (for the uneven development impact of the information revolution see Castells 1997). As radical geographers have argued for decades, it needs to be accepted that uneven development has been intrinsic to all the different phases of capitalist development since the start of the industrial era (Smith 2008)—contrast, for example, how rising resource prices deepens Africa's dependence on resource extraction/exports (Collier 2010) while Germany, South Korea and China are becoming 'green tech' innovation leaders to offset the negative implications of rising prices (Jänicke 2012).

Accepting the critiques of long-wave theory and the strong arguments in favour of co-evolution and uneven development, a framework is needed that differs from existing approaches because it deals with three interactive long-wave dynamics that operate at different temporal scales and with reference to different units of analysis:

- 'Sociometabolic transitions' that focus on the flow of materials and energy through socioecological systems across the pre-industrial, industrial and (potentially more sustainable) post-industrial epochs (Fischer-Kowalski 2011)

- 'Technological revolutions' comprising the evolution of the five main clusters of 'general purpose technologies' (Lipsey *et al.* 2005) that have partially driven and shaped the fundamental changes in production and consumption during the industrial era (Perez 2002)

- 'Long-term global development cycles' that focus on cycles of economic growth, prices, crises and 'creative destruction' (Gore 2010)

While admitting that any discussion of future trends are merely conjectures rather than certainties, it remains constructive to contribute to the storylines that could be considered by many who build future scenarios that often guide the decisions to be made today.

The substantial body of work by Venezuelan economist Carlota Perez has deeply influenced those who write about technological cycles. She identified five 'transitions' that she associates with specific technological innovations that emerged at particular historic moments since the dawn of the industrial era in the 1770s (Perez 2002). These transitions were roughly 50-year cycles that began with technological innovations (steam, then steel, followed by oil and, finally, information) that were funded initially by high-risk investors, enticed by the profits that revolutionary new processes could generate. As reflected in Figure 1.5, after disrupting the previous structure of industrial organisation over two or even three decades, these innovations were themselves displaced after enjoying fairly long periods of technological dominance during a 'deployment period' that could last for two to three decades (Perez 2002, 2007).

Figure 1.5: **Industrial transitions since 1771**

Source: Adapted from Perez 2007

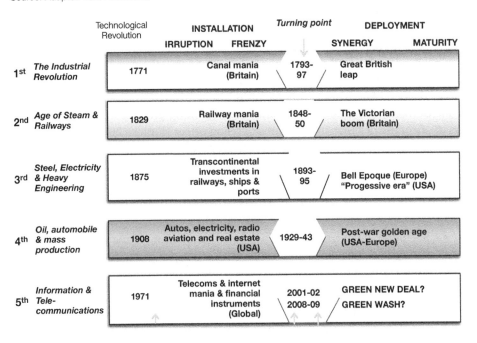

In the words of UN Conference on Trade and Development (UNCTAD) economist Charles Gore, each of these transitions is characterised by:

> … the introduction of a few leading sectors which provide cheap inputs to a wide range of economic activities; the installation of large-scale transport, communications and energy infrastructures; induced investment and innovation in economic activities, which are related to the leading sectors and the new infrastructures through forward and backward linkage effects; and the creation of new organisational and managerial practices (Gore 2010: 719).

Each of the five periods resulted in unique configurations of primary resource inputs, infrastructures and associated innovations in order to consolidate the hegemony of the lead sectors that had become the focus of financial investment. This can only be achieved by designing and establishing an appropriate set of institutions to direct, manage and monitor capital flows, up-skilling and infrastructure development.

Significantly, Perez demonstrates that each transition goes through distinct periods, starting off with an 'irruption' phase during which the innovations are generated, followed by a phase of 'frenzy' as investors rush for a stake in the businesses spawned by the innovations. After this crowding-in of investments in search of capital gains triggers a bubble and associated financial crisis (devaluation), the state steps in to reorganise institutions to absorb the new technologies, leading to a phase of 'synergy' during which there is a generalised global dispersion of production systems across the economy as a new 'golden age' (of steady growth and long-term profitability from dividends rather than capital gains) sets in. The transition ends with a 'mature' phase during which the new technologies reach saturation point and production systems are stabilised with diminishing returns on investment.

In each case, significantly, the financial crisis is followed by massive state interventions aimed not only at managing the crisis, but also at fundamentally restructuring the institutional and moral orders of society to prepare the way for the mass deployment of the new technologies and production systems. As power shifts from financial capital that drove the 'installation phase', to productive capital that drives the 'deployment phase', innovations get embedded in newly structured regimes of accumulation and governance, that are often seen as the 'golden ages' that follow the crisis period as solutions are introduced to 'resolve' the problems that are seen to be causes of the crisis. Without new roles for the state and the establishment of a new set of institutions, such a transition would be impossible. Although in each case the ideological language of interventionism was different ('Keynesianism' after 1920 and 'free-market economics' in the 1980s), the goals and modalities of the interventions were similar.

The obvious question, therefore, is whether the analytical framework developed by Perez helps us to understand the global economic crisis that began with the sub-prime financial crisis in the USA in 2007. What makes this a tricky question is that the 'information age' has, in fact, experienced what Perez has called a 'double bubble'—the so-called 'dot com' bubble of 1997–2000, followed by the financial bubble of 2004–2007. Perez has argued that these 'two bubbles of the turn of the century are two stages of the same phenomenon' (Perez 2009: 780). She argues against the Keynesian argument that explains the financial crisis as a 'Minsky moment' in terms of which debt markets have an in-built tendency towards financial instability, which can only be mitigated by increased state spending (Krugman 2012). Instead, she argues that the most significant crises are triggered by the financial opportunities created by new technologies that result in 'major technology bubbles' (MTBs) that eventually burst. This is what the Internet mania of 1997–2000 was all about. However, instead of triggering an economic recession that would have necessitated extensive state intervention to prepare the way for productive capital to take over from financial capital after the bubble burst in 2000–2001, the post-crisis recession was mitigated by the rapid financialisation of the global economy that deregulation combined with the IT revolution made possible. Accessing Chinese exports not only brought down the cost of mass consumer goods (which effectively raised real wages), it also became the world's largest lender of cash to developed world consumers (as debt securitised against domestic property) via the purchase of massive quantities of US Treasury bonds. Indeed, the preference for liquid assets and quick operations within the paper economy that this created generated skyrocketing capital gains between 1996 and 2000, while profits in the real economy remained flat or even negative (Perez 2009: 787). After the 'dot com' crash, instead of interventions to restrain financial capital, the opposite happened as various interventions by the Federal Reserve and neoliberal governments around the world effectively allowed the paper economy to mushroom into a gigantic unregulated global casino (Gowan 2009)—what former Prime Minister Gordon Brown called 'light touch' regulation. The resulting bubble was not, according to Perez, another MTB, but rather a Ponzi-type 'easy liquidity bubble' (ELB) driven by massive concentrations of investments in paper assets (or what Warren Buffet famously called 'financial weapons of mass destruction') that eventually lost their value in the crash of 2007–2009 (Perez 2009).

Striking a possibly over-optimistic note, in 2009 Perez wrote:

> What came after the Internet bubble was not the restructuring of the real economy that tends to occur in the aftermath but a casino revival that only fulfilled part of that task. There can be, however, little doubt that this second major bust and its consequences are likely to follow the script and facilitate the necessary institutional recomposition to unleash the deployment period of the current surge (Perez 2009: 800).

While pointing out that a spate of mergers and acquisitions brought on by the crisis has put in place the conditions for productive capital to take the lead, Perez admits that this time round it will not be easy to discipline financial capital. *The Stiglitz Report* has described, in practical terms, what it might take to restructure the global financial system without dismantling capitalism in order to prepare the way for the re-emergence of the 'real economy' as the centre of global economic gravity (Stiglitz 2010). However, by 2012 there was little evidence of any fundamental restructuring of the global financial system. Instead, the evidence suggests an interregnum between the old, which has not died, and the new waiting to be born: we have the rivalry between China and the USA about the value of the Chinese currency; the ongoing financial instabilities in the EU, exacerbated by the multiple sovereign debt crises; the de facto bankruptcy of the USA masked by 'quantitative easing' (i.e. printing money); the relatively unfettered flow of speculative finance through global markets despite the Dodd-Frank regulatory reforms in the USA; the hoarding of cash as investors wait for short-term capital gains opportunities to return, instead of looking for long-term productive investments in the real economy; and national governments who, having experienced massive devaluations in the past, continue to build up currency reserves to counteract financial shocks, thus keeping much-needed investment capital away from productive investment.

To make the links between the sociotechnical cycles that Perez has identified and long-term economic growth waves, we turn to the work of UNCTAD economist Charles Gore. He has located the sociotechnical cycles described by Perez within the Kondratiev-like 'global development cycle' that took off in the 1950s and ended with the global economic contraction of 2009. For Gore, a Kondratiev cycle cannot be equated to a technological cycle. While technological cycles follow the typical S-curve used by the MLP and Perez of irruption-crisis-deployment (see Fig. 1.6B), as Figure 1.6A suggests the global economic development cycles adhere to a very different logic: growth-plus-price-inflation during the spring–summer period ending in a stagflation crisis; followed by another growth-with-limited-inflation during the autumn–winter period ending in deflationary depression.

Figure 1.6: **The synchronisation of growth cycles, price cycles and the life-cycles of technological revolutions. A, Growth cycles and price cycles in the Kondratiev long wave (based on USA). B, The life-cycle of technological revolution**

Source: Gore 2010: 718

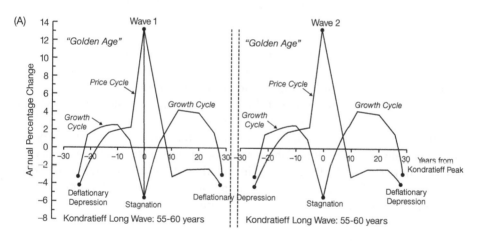

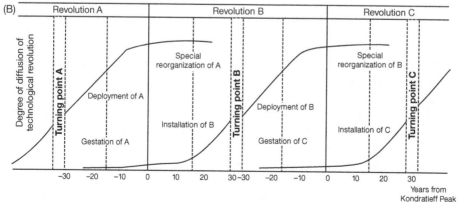

As Gore points out, the post-World War II, long-term development cycle (1950s–2009) does not correspond to the sociotechnological cycles that Perez describes. Although Perez tried to link technological cycles to economic growth, in her later work she gave up this effort. Gore has completed the picture. His first key insight is that the post-1970s growth phase was driven *both* by the deployment phase of the fourth cycle or 'age of oil' ('Revolution A' in Fig. 1.6B) and the installation phase of the fifth cycle or 'information age ('Revolution B' in Fig. 1.6B), with the mid-point crisis of the fifth cycle marking the break between the post-World War II Kondratiev cycle and the next Kondratiev cycle. His second key insight, then, is that it follows that the next Kondratiev cycle will again be driven by *two* technological cycles—the deployment phase of the information age (fifth cycle) and the installation of the sixth cycle which may be over-determined by technologies that address climate change, rising resource prices and the consequences of ecosystem breakdown.

Table 1.1 summarises the synthesis of these approaches to sociometabolic transition, technological revolutions and global development cycles. Rows 1, 2 and 3 capture the Kondratiev-like price and growth cycles, while rows 7 and 8 depict moments of crisis and periods of inclusion/exclusion. Rows 4 and 5 summarise Perez's technological revolutions, revealing their non-alignment with the rhythms of the global price and growth cycles referred to in row 1 (read together with rows 2 and 3). Row 6 factors in the sixth ('green tech') technological revolution and how this is not just a necessary driver for the spring–summer period of the next global development cycle (rows 1 and 3), but is also a necessary condition for the sociometabolic shift anticipated in rows 9 and 11 (assisted by the dynamics of resource prices—row 10). Obviously, none of the projections here for the 2010s–2030s are inevitable. While they are dependent entirely on policy choices that must still be made by a wide range of actors, they do reflect patterns of what may be possible. Specifically, the initiation of the next global development cycle, driven by the deployment period of the fifth and the installation of the sixth technological revolution, could provide the conditions required for a fundamental sociometabolic transition that could also be more equalising and inclusive.

Gore's argument provides the connection we need between macro-economic growth cycles, sociotechnical cycles as described by Perez, and the discussions reviewed in this paper about transition to a more sustainable or green economy as anticipated by the *GER* and *UNWESS* report. If Gore's application of Kondratiev cycles to the current crisis is correct, it means that the spring–summer period of the next (post-2009) long-term development cycle will need to be powered by the deployment phase of the information age (fifth industrial transition in Perez's terms) *and* the sociotechnical imperatives of the transition to a green or more sustainable global economy (sixth wave). But this is by no means inevitable. Like Gore, in her recent work Perez is concerned about the logics of the global financial system that could block the shift in power from finance to productive capital that is the defining feature of a successful transition (Perez 2009). The persistence of austerity suggests that finance capital has not been dislodged. At the same time, the interests of the global energy complex are already blocking the transition to a low-carbon

Table 1.1: **The global development cycle, 1950s–2030s**

Sources: Compiled and adapted from Fischer-Kowalski and Swilling 2011; Gore 2010; Haberl *et al.* 2011; McKinsey Global Institute 2011; Perez 2010a; Swilling and Annecke 2012; UNEP 2011; UN 2011

		1950s	1960s	1970s	1980s	1990s	2000s	2010s	2020s	2030s
1	Phase of Kondratieff cycle (Gore)	Spring		Summer	Autumn		Winter	Spring??		Summer?
2	Price cycle	Rising price inflation			Falling price inflation				Rising price inflation (driven by rising resource prices, debt devaluation & capital demand/interest rates)	
3	Growth cycle	Growth acceleration		Growth deceleration	Growth acceleration		Growth deceleration	Stagnation	Growth acceleration beginnings of deceleration from late 2030s?	
4	4th industrial transition (Perez)	Deployment phase			Maturity, but persistence of socio-technical regimes		Oil Age	Decline?		
5	5th industrial transition (Perez)			Irruption	Frenzy		Crisis	Synergy		Maturity
6	6th industrial transition (Perez)						Irruption		Frenzy, start of crisis by late 2030s?	
7	Nature of financial crisis			Stagflation crisis			From 2007: deflationary crisis			Start of stagflation crisis from late 2030s?

		1950s	1960s	1970s	1980s	1990s	2000s	2010s	2020s	2030s
8	Pattern of economic development	Equalising (welfarism, Keynesianism, actually existing socialism, decolonization)			Unequalising (globalization, privatization, deregulation, markets)			Equalising? (rise of the BRICs, return of Keynesianism, developmental states, etc.)		
9	Resource flows (Fischer-Kowalski and Swilling)	Mainly biomass, 10-20bt/yr	Doubling of non-biomass materials, 20-30bt/yr	Non-biomass materials become dominant, increase to 50bt/yr				Two thirds non-biomass, 60bt/yr, relative decoupling	Relative and absolute resource reduction?	Absolute resource reduction?
10	Resource prices (IRP/McKinsey)	Declining resource prices				Rising resources prices			Stable/declining resource prices?	
11	Socio-ecological regime (Fischer-Kowalski)	Industrial socio-ecological regime					(Transition to) sustainable socio-ecological regime?			

economy by defending their right to subsidies that are now running well over the US$1 trillion mark and attempts to re-regulate the financial institutions are either ineffectual or consciously (and often illegally) subverted by the financial institutions. It therefore follows that the next long-term development cycle will only emerge when ways are found to reconcile the rapidly evolving information technologies that are moving into a deployment phase in the social and real economies (following Perez 2010b; Rifkin 2011), the sustainable use of resources to counteract rising resource prices (following Bradfield-Moody and Nogrady 2010; McKinsey Global Institute 2011; Von Weizsäcker *et al.* 2009), and a set of institutional and financial arrangements that make it possible to deploy the expanding amount of unspent investment capital on the best long-term needs of the economy, society and the environment (following UNEP 2011; Zhengelis 2012).

Conclusion

This paper started out by reviewing the stories of future landscapes encapsulated in a range of recent influential texts. Except for Motianey's dystopian grand malaise, these texts all draw on long-wave theory to represent the complex dynamics of transition to a post-global crisis future. Significantly, they recognise—in weaker and stronger ways—that there are natural limits to long-term future economic growth and development trajectories. For Standard Chartered this is a minor irritation that will be overcome by innovations. For the others, these natural limits—especially resource depletion and rising resource prices—will become the primary catalysts for the next wave of sustainability-oriented innovations that will, in turn, transform the global economy. Indeed, they all, in one way or another, argue that this wave has already begun by referring to a wide range of niche-level innovations and even some regime-level reforms. But they all call for greater urgency and more policy-level commitments to accelerating these processes. A recently released set of reports seem to confirm these stories of future landscapes. The *GER, UNWESS,* IRP and McKinsey reports all provide vast amounts of empirical and modelling-based evidence to directly or indirectly support the notion that the next Kondratiev cycle could indeed be coterminous with a transition to a 'green economy' if economic growth can in reality be reconciled with sustainable resource use and social inclusivity.

To conceptualise these apparently converging lines of argument about the dynamics of a global sustainability transition, it was necessary to draw on long-wave theory and, in particular, the institutional implications of the information technology revolution for niche- and regime-level innovations. A synthesis was developed which suggested that the potential for a 'sustainability-oriented transition' during the 'spring–summer' phase of the next long-term development cycle certainly exists, especially if factors such as resource depletion and rising resource prices are recognised. However, the length of the interregnum during the 2010s will depend, to a large extent, on whether a new generation of institutions emerges that make possible a very different set of capital and resource flows to those that were reproduced by the globalised corporate and financial institutions built up during the course of the 19th and 20th centuries. These institutions (and the constellation of sociotechnical regimes they entailed) managed unprecedented levels of material accumulation that benefitted a billion or so über-consumers while externalising the costs of resource depletion, environmental degradation and greenhouse gas emissions. The shift in power from finance to productive capital will be a key marker that the interregnum is ending and the fifth wave is moving into its deployment phase; so too will be acceptance of the need for inflation to reduce the debilitating effects of the sovereign debts that ballooned after governments nationalised private banking debts after 2008. A policy regime to direct the growing mountains of un-invested cash into real-economy investments directly linked to the primary green economy goals would signal that financial capital and sustainability-oriented innovations had finally connected and converged to drive the installation period of the sixth wave. The combined impact of the deployment phase of the fifth and the installation phase of the sixth waves could well accelerate the consolidation of a new generation of labour-absorbing sociotechnical regimes generating significant returns on capital. Both waves, however, will be held back if the global institutional structure of financial and resource extractive power is left intact.

References

Allianz Global Investors (2010) *The Sixth Kondratieff: Long Waves of Prosperity* (Frankfurt, Germany: Allianz Global Investors).

Barbier, E.B. (2009) *A Global Green New Deal*, report prepared for the Economics and Trade Branch, Division of Technology, Industry and Economics, UNEP.

Berry, B.J.L. (1991) *Long-wave Rhythms in Economic Development and Political Behaviour* (Baltimore, MD and London: Johns Hopkins University Press).

Bradfield-Moody, J., and B.T. Nogrady (2010) *The Sixth Wave: How to Succeed in a Resource-limited World* (Sydney, Australia: Vintage Books).

Broadberry, S. (2007) *Recent Developments in the Theory of Very Long Run Growth: A Historical Appraisal* (Warwick, UK: Warwick University, Warwick Research Paper No. 818, Department of Economics Research Papers).

Castells, M. (1997) *The Information Age Volumes 1, 2 and 3* (Oxford, UK: Blackwell).

Collier, P. (2010) 'The Political Economy of Natural Resources', *Social Research* 77.4: 1105-32.

Fagerberg, J. (2003) 'Schumpeter and the Revival of Evolutionary Economics: An Appraisal of the Literature', *Journal of Evolutionary Economics* 13.2: 125-59.

Fischer-Kowalski, M. (2011) 'Analysing Sustainability Transitions as a Shift between Socio-metabolic Regimes', *Environmental Innovation and Societal Transitions* 1: 152-59.

Fischer-Kowalski, M., and M. Swilling (2011) *Decoupling Natural Resource Use and Environmental Impacts from Economic Growth* (Paris: UNEP, report for the International Resource Panel).

Foxon, T.J. (2011) 'A Coevolutionary Framework for Analysing a Transition to a Sustainable Low Carbon Economy', *Ecological Economics* 70: 2258-67.

Freeman, C., and F. Louca (2001) *As Time Goes By: From Industrial Revolutions to the Information Revolution* (Oxford, UK: Oxford University Press).

Geels, F. (2010) 'Ontologies, Sociotechnical Transitions (to Sustainability), and the Multi-level Perspectives', *Research Policy* 39: 495-510.

Gore, C. (2010) 'Global Recession of 2009 in a Long-term Development Perspective', *Journal of International Development* 22: 714-38.

Gowan, P. (2009) 'Crisis in the Heartland', *New Left Review* 55: 5-29.

Grin, J., J. Rotmans, J. Schot, F. Geels and D. Loorbach (2010) *Transitions to Sustainable Development: New Directions in the Study of Long Term Transformative Change* (New York: Routledge).

Haberl, H., M. Fischer-Kowalski, F. Krausmann, J. Martinez-Alier and V. Winiwarter (2011) 'A Socio-metabolic Transition Towards Sustainability? Challenges for Another Great Transformation', *Sustainable Development* 19: 1-14.

Hargroves, C., and M. Smith (2005) *The Natural Advantage of Nations: Business Opportunities, Innovation and Governance in the 21st Century* (London: Earthscan).

Jänicke, M. (2012) '"Green Growth": From Growing Eco-industry to Economic Sustainability', *Energy Policy* 48: 13-21.

Köhler, J. (2012) 'A Comparison of the Neo-Schumpeterian Theory of Kondratiev Waves and the Multi-level Perspective on Transitions', *Environmental Innovation and Societal Transitions* 3: 1-15.

Kondratieff, N.D. (1935) 'The Long Waves in Economic Life', *Review of Economics and Statistics* 27.1: 105-15.

Krugman, P. (2012) *End This Depression Now* (New York and London: W.W. Northon & Company).

Lawhon, M., and J.T. Murphy (2011) 'Socio-technical Regimes and Sustainability Transitions: Insights from Political Ecology', *Progress in Human Geography* (8 December 2011; phg.sagepub.com/content/early/2011/12/07, accessed 27 March 2013). DOI: 10.1177/0309132511427960

Lipsey, R.G., K.I. Carlaw and C.T. Bekar (2005) *Economic Transformations: General Purpose Technologies and Long Term Economic Growth* (Cambridge, MA: MIT Press).

McKinsey Global Institute (2011) *Resource Revolution: Meeting the World's Energy, Materials, Food, and Water Needs*, McKinsey Global Institute (www.mckinsey.com/client_service/sustainability.aspx, accessed 6 December 2011).

Morin, E. (1999) *Homeland Earth* (Cresskill, NJ: Hampton Press).

Motianey, A. (2010) *Supercycles: The Economic Force Transforming Global Markets and Investment Strategy* (Columbus, OH: McGraw-Hill).

Pearson, P.J.G., and T.J. Foxon (2012) 'A Low Carbon Industrial Revolution: Insights and Challenges from Past Technological and Economics Transformations', *Energy Policy* 50: 117-27.

Perez, C. (2002) *Technological Revolutions and Financial Capital: The Dynamics of Bubbles and Golden Ages* (Cheltenham, UK: Edward Elgar).

Perez, C. (2007) *Great Surges of Development and Alternative Forms of Globalization*, Working Papers in Technology Governance and Economic Dynamics (Oslo, Norway and Tallinn, Estonia: The Other Canon Foundation and Tallinn University of Technology).

Perez, C. (2009) 'The Double Bubble at the Turn of the Century: Technological Roots and Structural Implications', *Cambridge Journal of Economics* 33: 779-805.

Perez, C. (2010a) *The Advance of Technology and Major Bubble Collapses: Historical Regularities and Lessons for Today* (Cambridge and Sussex, UK and Estonia: Universities of Cambridge and Sussex, and Tallinn University, unpublished monograph).

Perez, C. (2010b) *The Financial Crisis and the Future of Innovation: A View of Technical Change with the Aid of History* (Oslo, Norway and Tallinn, Estonia: The Other Canon Foundation and Tallinn, University of Technology, Working Papers in Technology Governance and Economic Dynamics, 28).

Rifkin, J. (2011) *The Third Industrial Revolution: How Lateral Power is Transforming Energy, the Economy and the World* (New York: Palgrave MacMillan).

Rosenberg, N., and C.R. Frischtak (1983) 'Long Waves and Economic Growth: A Critical Appraisal', *American Economic Association Papers and Proceedings* 73.2: 146-51.

Rotmans, J., and D. Loorbach (2009) 'Complexity and Transition Management', *Journal of Industrial Ecology* 13.2: 184-96.

Smith, A., A. Stirling and F. Berkhout (2005) 'The Governance of Sustainable Socio-technical Transitions', *Research Policy* 34: 1491-510.

Smith, A., J.P. Voss and J. Grin (2010) 'Innovation Studies and Sustainability Transitions: The Allure of the Multi-level Perspective and its Challenges', *Research Policy* 39.4: 435-48.

Smith, N. (2008) *Uneven Development: Nature, Capital, and the Production of Space* (Athens, GA: The University of Georgia Press).

Standard Chartered (2010) *The Super-cycle Report* (London: Global Research Standard Chartered; available from Gerard.Lyons@sc.com, accessed 15 March 2012).

Stiglitz, J.E. (2010) *The Stiglitz Report: Reforming the International Monetary and Financial Systems in the Wake of the Global Crisis* (New York: New Press).

Swilling, M., and E. Annecke (2012) *Just Transitions: Explorations of Sustainability in an Unfair World* (Cape Town, South Africa and Tokyo, Japan: UCT Press and United Nations University Press).

UN (United Nations) (2011) *World Economic and Social Survey 2011: The Great Green Technological Transformation* (New York: UN).

UNEP (United Nations Environment Programme) (2011) *Towards a Green Economy: Pathways to Sustainable Development and Poverty Eradication* (Nairobi, Kenya: UNEP).

Verspagen, B. (2005) 'Innovation and Economic Growth', in J. Fagerberg, D.C. Mowery and R.R. Nelson (eds.), *The Oxford Handbook of Innovation* (Oxford, UK: Oxford University Press): 487-513.

Von Weizsäcker, E., K.C. Hargroves, M.H. Smith, C. Desha and P. Stasinopoulos (2009) *Factor Five: Transforming the Global Economy Through 80% Improvements in Resource Productivity* (London: Earthscan).

Zhengelis, D. (2012) *A Strategy for Restoring Confidence and Economic Growth Through Green Investment and Innovation* (London: Grantham Research Institute on Climate Change and the Environment; and Centre for Climate Change Economics and Policy, London School of Economics).

Professor **Mark Swilling** is Programme Co-ordinator, Sustainable Development Programme in the School of Public Leadership, Project Leader of the Centre for the Transdisciplinary Study of Sustainability and Complexity, and Academic Director of the Sustainability Institute (www.sustainabilityinstitute.net). He is co-author, with Eve Annecke, of *Just Transitions: Explorations of Sustainability in an Unfair World* (2012), which was runner up in the Harold and Margaret Sprout Award for 2013.

2

Radical openness and contextualisation

Reflections on a decade of learning for sustainability at the Sustainability Institute

Eve Annecke
Sustainability Institute, Stellenbosch, South Africa

Introduction

French philosopher, Edgar Morin, ends *Homeland Earth—A Manifest for the New Millennium* with his uncanny dance in paradox:

> The task is huge and unassured. We cannot eschew either hope or despair. Both holding of, and resignation from, office seem equally impossible. We must have a 'passionate patience' (Morin 1999: 149).

The unique experience of combining an ecovillage with a learning capability has generated insights into what it means to build up from below the foundations of a more sustainable world. What has mattered most is creating space for new forms of transdisciplinary knowledge that is not just about working across disciplines, but letting real-world problems become the motive forces of applied research and learning.

Context

Thirteen years ago, a radical shift in uprooting our family from Johannesburg, South Africa, and beginning a life on the Spier Wine Farm, Lynedoch, Stellenbosch, saw my husband and myself deeply immersing ourselves within our new local context, and finding the rhythms within a space contorted by centuries of violence through colonisation, slavery, massive ecological degradation and apartheid. The underpinning melody of our work, heard long before we knew the words—an international living and learning centre for studies and experience in ecology, community and spirit—started in understanding the etymology of the word 'radical'. For the inherent challenge in the Latin 'radix' meaning 'root', meant to us that the justice we hungered for as activists within a country struggling with the challenges of a new democracy ravaged by its racist past was never going to happen unless transformative action took place at the very roots of the microcosm of our new and fragmented community.

First, the context showed almost instantly the attention demanded by the lack of prioritisation of children of poverty-ridden farm workers—too frequently evicted off white farmers' land without access to tenure. The highest documented prevalence in the world of foetal alcohol syndrome caused by the so-called 'dop' (tot) system whereby wages have, for decades, been paid in part with alcohol; violence in homes linked to substance abuse; teenage pregnancy; aspiration to gang life; and unaffordable Western style consumption are but some of the still-present patterns. Without any form of early childhood development, preschool or crèche, the local primary school was housed in a threadbare, prefabricated building on a local white farmer's land, again without tenure. Our way in to figuring out a wider process of contextual development was to provide the facilitation that looked to build sustainable futures with children at the heart.

Second, and parallel to this, emerged the crisis of soil and land reform. Finding ways of feeding communities looked remote without fertile soils, complicated by the state of land reform remaining to this day bafflingly slow. Chemically-treated and fertiliser-reliant soil over decades had eradicated the intricate living networks of microbes, organic matter and soil organisms that make healthy and fertile soil. Linked to Spier was 100 ha—known as 'commonage'—a portion of land that the white-controlled Stellenbosch Municipality had leased to white landowners with cheap 50-year contracts shortly before the democratic elections in 1994 in a bid to prevent land reform. A painful and ongoing process of knitting together restoration of soils, access to land and dignity began at the same time as starting to build community through putting children first.

These fragile and small beginnings have taken root and, over the past 13 years, one quiet articulation of a radical openness has manifested as spirit-in-action. Not content with a mere dry roll-out of a strategic project plan that holds little joy and fertility, our approach has held a kind of exuberance in one of the core values made explicit by one of our closest colleagues, a young African woman—'lerato'

(Southern Sotho)—'work is love made visible'. Creating a sense of place has meant to us paying attention to the traces of energy within the Lynedoch Valley at a multiplicity of levels. These initial traces have translated into:

- The first mixed-income ecological village in South Africa

- Replanted indigenous gardens with over 1,000 new trees and uncountable shrubs

- Partnership with an organic land reform farm

- Vegetable gardens for a 'farm-to-fork' approach to food at the SI

- Baby centre for 12 infants, and Montessori crèche for 42 farm worker children

- Lynedoch Primary School—a government primary school for 400 mainly farm worker children (a free school serving one of the poorest rural communities)

- Junior and senior aftercare facilities for nature-based learning for 50 children and adolescents

- Twenty-four, soon rising to 30, ecologically designed houses, half of which are for subsidised homeowners

- Renewable energy through solar water geysers, solar roof tiles, wind chimneys and rock store

- Water and solid waste recycling

- Collection of storm-water

- Measurement systems in place for monitoring use of energy and water

- Vocational skills—Earning for Sustainability Further Education and Training College for accredited courses in early childhood development, sustainable communities and youth sustainability skills (the first of its kind in South Africa)

- Home to the SI, a non-profit trust

- Partnership with Stellenbosch University's School of Public Leadership on a master's level degree in sustainable development planning and management

- Partnership with Stellenbosch University in the TSAMA hub—a Centre for the Transdisciplinary Study of Sustainability and Complexity with the first transdisciplinary PhD programme in South Africa linked in with a network of six African universities

- Home to ongoing applied research through projects such as incremental upgrading in local informal settlements, learning partner to the National Department of Human Settlements, policy development, etc

Using an interpretive lens many years later, it is probably no coincidence that making sense of our own personal uprooting created space for exploring new roots with an emerging community. Inspired as we were by creative leadership provided within Spier, our entanglement with transformation and renewal demanded authentic engagement with a context left devastated by generations of exploitation. This was a far cry from conventional academic journal articles 'on' a particular aspect of the Lynedoch Valley or a non-governmental organisation professional approach to providing assistance 'to' specific aspects of wrecked community life, or surveying grassroots life in the valley and cultivating progressive policy debates, or creating some interesting cases for students to visit and interview. It meant becoming the context. And, finding within ourselves first the points of messy damage directly connecting us in this context, rather than assuming a safe and untrue 'healed' stance which would have enabled us to stand apart. Children and soil—in retrospect, they seem one and the same. Images of birth, infancy and strong childhoods creating different adulthoods and futures in the present intermingled with the fertility of soils, textured patterns of beauty within food grown locally by farmers deeply connected with the rich processes and rhythms of nature. Always difficult to find the words to describe, our community meant to us the community of all life—not only human life. And the identity that has emerged is a result of, and constituted from, the interconnectivities and differences that make up the ongoing journey of an ever-thickening meshwork of relationships.

Learning for sustainability

The complex wrestling emerging from slowly falling in love with, and building, a sense of place has resulted in an imperfect integration of ecology, equity and beauty, and recognising that the underpinning question for over a decade now is really about leadership. What kind of leadership is required in order for all life to flourish?

One of the ways we have attempted to answer this question is through the crafting of our master's level degree in partnership with the School of Public Leadership, Faculty of Economic and Management Sciences, Stellenbosch University—an MPhil in sustainable development. The first cohort began in 2003 with 19 participants. This, the tenth year of running the programme, sees 45 post-graduate diploma participants from over 200 international applicants, and 25 MPhil participants taught by an international faculty. With four areas of specialisation possible—in sustainable development, renewable energy, sustainable agriculture and development planning—the core modules include sustainability, complexity theory, environmental ethics and leadership. In our quest to create space for transformation at a multiplicity of levels, it seems that there are three key strands that, woven together in the constant and dynamic tension between individual and learning community, have built a learning process that unlocks possibilities for unexpectedness. These are: place as teacher; an integrated approach to learning; and creative disruption and discomfort.

Place as teacher

Rooted in the most unequal country in the world, embedded in systematised poverty and knowing more than we had words for, it was an intuitive choice to make the location of the degree programme at the SI in the Lynedoch EcoVillage, sharing the ecologically renovated main building with the Lynedoch Primary School. Not only do the students seldom (if ever) go to main campus, but they arrive every morning at the same time as groups of farm children tumble out of buses and as the farmers' trucks that drop them off daily. A fast game of soccer before school for the boys, age-old skipping and hopping games for the little ones, quick coffee for bleary-eyed students, start the day. The SI students, however, do not go straight to class. They start with a short morning group meeting in the huge hall, with poetry or meditative reading and doing breath-work, yoga or tai chi. From here, working in small groups, they contribute to the Lynedoch community through morning work—gardening, tree planting, working on the organic farm, cleaning the SI, preparing food from the gardens for the crèche, aftercare, SI students and visitors. This way, through purposeful activity, the students too become one with their context. And, in their experience of engaging in these ways, there seems to evolve a relationship with the place in its capacity to teach without words. Not only does this manifest in the ongoing dialogue between students, community and nature but, in particular, the students have opportunities to engage the tensions and contradictions inherent in making sense of sustainable living. Navigating postcolonial, indigenous research methodologies with the scientific method, technical engineering wizardry with community ownership, extreme poverty in malnourished children with middle-class attempts to live without excess, and building soils through organic farming with little access to capital investment required to make small farming commercially viable are but some of the areas in which the students have practice in making sense of ecological living in a post-apartheid South Africa where there is little room for grandiosity, over-claiming successes or mere intellectual curiosity.

Prior to commencing with his sustainable development studies in 2010, Andreas Keller was working as a hedge fund accountant in Cape Town with assets under administration of R1.1 billion. His personal transformation has focused his MPhil thesis topic as: 'Conceptualising a sustainable energy solution for in situ informal settlement upgrading'. He responded to my query in the following way (my emphases): [1]

1 Personal communication, 1 July 2012.

Without a question, my experience has been that Lynedoch is a teacher in its own right! I am a practical person by nature and really benefited from having the classroom grounded within a living sustainability space (Lynedoch EcoVillage). This meant that my academic studies were continually complemented *and challenged* by real life experiences, such as learning about ecologically-designed housing, talking to residents about living in a mixed-income community, watching sun-backed adobe bricks being made, planting vegetables organically, seeing a biogas digester in operation, eating lunch prepared with a solar cooker or learning about biological water treatment. Combining living and learning experiences into one space gave me a deeper, more informed experience of sustainability challenges and opportunities *and, in particular, forced me to question my own ways of being and thinking.*

Integrated approach to learning

Morin has blamed the failure to address our complex problems on disciplinary reductionism:

> Intelligence that is fragmented, compartmentalised, mechanistic, disjunctive, and reductionistic breaks the complexity of the world into disjointed pieces, splits up problems, separates that which is linked together, and renders uni-dimensional the multi-dimensional. It is an intelligence that is at once myopic, colour blind, and without perspective; more often than not it ends up blind. It nips in the bud all opportunities for comprehension and reflection, eliminating at the same time all chances for a corrective judgement or a long-term view. Thus, the more problems become multi-dimensional, the less chance there is to grasp their multi-dimensionality. The more things reach crisis proportions, the less chance there is to grasp the crisis. The more problems become planetary, the more unthinkable they become. Incapable of seeing the planetary context in all its complexity, blind intelligence fosters unconsciousness and irresponsibility (Morin 1999: 128).

A gritty and integrated approach to transformative learning creates for participants the space for becoming entangled in the complexities at Lynedoch—a microcosm of the 'planetary context' to which Morin refers. Each of the compulsory eight modules sees a certain rhythm emerge. This includes morning community work and group work. Group work entails a specific angle on which each small group is expected to present at the end of a module, as part of formal assessment. Ranging from the technicalities of specific solar water geysers and comparing these, or exploring the rationale behind the different sustainable building methodologies used in the ecovillage, through to engaging the governance of the homeowners association or exploring the multiple strands of sustainability education for children, the students have a web of options and lenses through which to navigate, critique and propose innovations in a safe place, open to scrutiny.

Good old fashioned rigour in the reading demanded within each module, to be demonstrated by written summaries of articles, along with a 6000 word individual assignment, are counter-balanced by a personal journal which can be submitted in the form of prose, poetry, YouTube clip, or any creative form that is able to make explicit the experience of the individual participant in that module.

Creative disruption and discomfort

> Sustainability is not about giving up on development as the environmentalists have done, or simple 'greening' development as ecological modernisers do; rather it is about agonistic engagements across diverse paradigms, disciplines and interests to help redefine what is generally understood by the notion of progress. Progress can be meaningful only if it includes the entire web of all life in ways that deal directly and boldly with the imbroglios that have engulfed modernity as we know it (Swilling and Annecke 2012: 25).

In many ways, creating a challenging holding space for learning for sustainable futures means constant opportunity for dialogue, disruption and disequilibrium. Often, we have been quietly astonished at the questions from colleagues that intimate pushing boundaries too far. In our experience, it is our students themselves who strongly challenge conventional boundaries forced by collisions of consumerism, the crash of the financial markets and ecological crises the world over. For this new generation of activist–academics, these questions seem constantly underpinned by those of other ways of knowing and being. The roles of intuition, consciousness, spirituality, mindfulness, dreaming and indigenous wisdom are easy companions in explorations of what it might mean to participate in innovations not simply from spaces of conventional, or 'known', knowledge.

However, the 'agonistic engagements' are not to be under-estimated in the learning journey the students undertake when they sign up for this degree. There are times of existential questioning, emotional outpouring, self-doubt and nagging discomfort with the lack of tried and tested recipes for a grand narrative with clear-cut solutions. What does seem evident, is that the closing off too early of discomfort and disruption is counter-productive, removing from the students the very practice that appears to be useful in navigating uncertainty (i.e. building a stomach for disequilibrium, living with vertigo and immersing oneself deeply in paradoxes).

The often unexpected space for creativity that is constituted from rich engagement of the students in the complexity within the multiplicity of pathways of the SI learning approach seems too to generate unexpected creativity in the topics of their assignments and theses. A smattering of thesis topics focuses a lens on the diversity and scope:

- 'The Role of Indigenous Governance Systems in Sustainable Development: The Case of Moshupa Village, Botswana', Segametsi Moatlhaping, 2007

- 'Applying Corporate Social Responsibility Principles to the Church: A Case Study of the Interface Between the Indian Pentecostal/Charismatic Church in the Phoenix Community, Durban North (KwaZulu Natal) and Social Responsibility', Virginia Francis, 2008

- 'Spaces for Enchantment and the Unknown: Fairy Tales, Complexity Thinking and a Search for New Ways of Dreaming: Child-centred Sustainable Development', Amelie Guyot, 2009

- 'Exploring the Factors Influencing Non-participation of Women Living with HIV/AIDS in Empowerment Projects Attached to Primary Healthcare Clinics, Tembisa, South Africa', Kgomotso Papole, 2010

- 'Solar Roof Tiles: A Macro-economic Model', Ben Mokheseng, 2010

- 'An Investigation of Natuurboerdery (Natural Farming) Approach: A ZZ2 Case Study', Silent Taurayi, 2011

- 'Integrating the Poor Into the Fibre of the City in Housing and Urban Policies in Post-apartheid South Africa', Walter Fieuw, 2011

- 'A Case Study from a Gold Mining Company: A Call for Leadership Towards More Sustainable Futures', Hlombe Makuluma, 2011

- 'Just Facilitation: Facilitating Sustainable Social Change in Contexts of Injustice', Rebecca Freeth, 2011

- 'Spirituality and Nature in the Transformation to a More Sustainable World: Perspectives of South African Change Agents', Helen Lockhart, 2011

- 'Acid Mine Drainage in the Gauteng Province of South Africa: A Phenomenological Study on the Degree of Alignment Between Stakeholders Concerning a Sustainable Solution to Acid Mine Drainage', Timothy Ewart, 2011

- 'A Critical Review of the Development of Sustainability Indicators for the City of Cape Town: A Focus on Environmental and Socioeconomic Sustainability', Eunice Ndeke, 2011

Conclusion

While it is clear from the students' engagement with the Lynedoch EcoVillage that they are inspired and challenged, it must also be said that the ecovillage dwellers and work participants are intrigued and encouraged by the responses of the students to their stories. A key way to understanding the identity of the Lynedoch EcoVillage is as constituted through story telling over the last decade.

The SI in the Lynedoch EcoVillage, with mindful attention to an unfolding web of processes, is a place where potentialities for transformation are created through the intricate weaving together of equity, ecology and innovation. Our experience of integrating an ecovillage with leadership building and learning capabilities seems to have generated insights into what it means to develop from below the possibilities of more sustainable futures. Perhaps what has mattered most is the realisation that transdisciplinary knowledge is not just about working across disciplines, but letting real-world 'wicked' problems become the imperatives of learning. The different levels this explores is best expressed in a poem by a student in the master's programme (who has an under-graduate degree in chemical engineering), which he read one morning to our motley gathering in the hall: [2]

Nature is like Africans

We live our lives through rhythm and dance,

Like the pulsating dances of the Earth around the sun, giving birth to the seasons and to time itself.

We breathe one air with our ancestors and our progeny, all at once.

Like the never birthed and immortal elements that form the cell that gave us the mighty elephant.

Our songs guide us through hostile terrains and hold the dance of our hearts in their pitch and tone.

Like the magnificent whales of the wondrous seas speaking secretly across the seven seas.

Nature is like Africans.

We carry the weight of the world on our broad shoulders, asking only to be greeted as you pass us by, lumela.

Like the howling Katrina yearning for man to hear Earth's cries.

We shed tears that give life from our death.

Like the torrents that flood modern cities, filling our feeble gutters and weakly guts with the Earth's bitter tears.

We endure suffering with a passivity unknown even to prehistoric glaciers.

Like the magical rivers of this world, rolling on in barren emptiness, longing for life that lived for life itself.

Nature is like Africans and it will die the same death.

We will all take our share, say sorry and walk away.

But nature is like the African, she will awaken and forgive all.

Maloba G Tshehla

While a decade is absurdly short in which to place any stake in the ground at all on success, many of the children who seemed so small when we began are now matriculating, and heading for tertiary education. For most of their families this is a first. Our soils are beginning to show signs of increased carbon. We have a long way to go, but the glimpses of the first green shoots are encouraging.

2 Read at the Sustainability Institute, 14 June 2012.

References

Morin, E. (1999) *Homeland Earth: A Manifesto for the New Millennium* (Cresskill, NJ: Hampton Press).

Swilling, M., and E. Annecke (2012) *Just Transitions: Explorations of Sustainability in an Unfair World* (Claremont, South Africa: UCT Press).

Eve Annecke is Founding Director of the Sustainability Institute, and co-founder of Lynedoch EcoVillage. She leads the SI focus on child-centred sustainable communities, and teaches at master's level on sustainability, leadership and environmental ethics.

3

The devil is in the synergy
The exhibitions at MOSET: a hypothetical museum of human transitions

Richard Cassels
Climate Leadership, Brisbane, Australia

Introduction

Like passengers in an aircraft heading into turbulence, we know there is a bumpy ride ahead. Annie Leonard, creator of *The Story of Stuff,* said at a conference in Brisbane, 24–26 October 2011: 'We have only one choice: to change by design or to change by disaster'. How proactive will we be? How can we prepare ourselves? What parts of our lives will change? Will the 'sustainability revolution' (Edwards 2005) finally happen? What can history tell us?

This chapter proposes that a key to understanding transitions is that 'the devil lies in the synergy' (a phrase coined by Mantyka-Pringle 2011).

The museum exhibition genre

A creative way to explore an issue is to imagine how one might create a museum exhibition about it. What is the storyline, what are the key objects, images and sound effects? This paper adopts the scenario of a hypothetical museum of human transitions and the exhibitions it might contain.

Museum exhibitions (Falk and Dierking 2000) provide an enjoyable way to visualise the past, present and future. They isolate, present and juxtapose images and objects to suggest new connections or understandings, or to provoke new enquiry. Objects and exhibits stimulate visual learning, perhaps the most powerful learning tool of all. Openness to different meanings encourages creativity and lateral thinking. While founded on scholarship, exhibitions are not an exercise in scholarship. They seek to engage a wide range of visitors, all of whom may arrive with fundamentally different prior knowledge and values.

So join me now as we explore the exhibitions of a hypothetical museum of the future—MOSET—the Museum of Social and Environmental Transitions. Let us imagine that the idea of MOSET was conceived in 2005, just before the publication of Al Gore's *An Inconvenient Truth* (Gore 2006). After a long gestation period that included planning, fundraising and construction, the museum finally opens to the public in the year that the United Nations declares that the 'sustainability revolution' is complete—society has achieved sustainability!

Our branch of MOSET is located in Australia. As with the Guggenheim Art Museum franchise, other branches are being built elsewhere in the world, each adapting a global story to its local context.

The exhibition galleries at MOSET

There are 13 exhibition galleries: the principles gallery and 12 chronological galleries.

The principles gallery

The key exhibit in the principles gallery is a diagram showing the invention of the motor car (Fig. 3.1).

The invention of the motor car is an instructive model when analysing transitions. Systemic change takes place, not when something first occurs or is first invented, but when a number of developments coincide, create positive feedback between each other, and trigger a new transition. A previously inert combination suddenly transforms the system into a new state as one new element is added to other pre-existing and evolving components. Positive feedback loops transform the system These moments are the tipping points of history, when whole systems tip from one state to another (Clarke 1968: 273; Gladwell 2001; Ball 2004).

From a systems view of change, it is difficult (and may be impossible) to distinguish cause from effect or stimulus from consequence. This is also the case for those living through the changes, or even for historians of recent events (Randers 2008).

Figure 3.1: **Inventions leading to the patenting of the motor car**
Source: Clarke 1968: 282

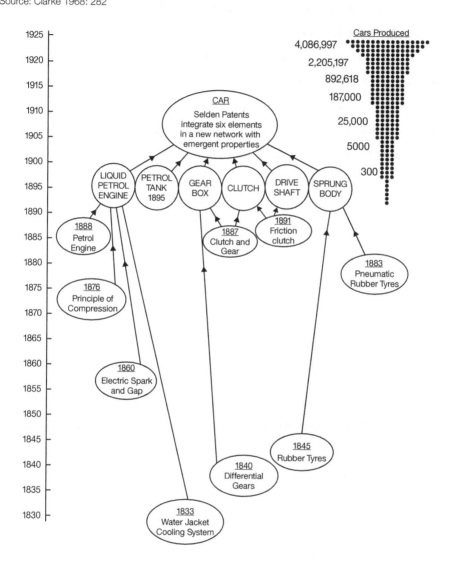

The chronological galleries

The 12 remaining galleries are dedicated to 12 global systemic transformations which are considered most relevant to Western history in general (Christian 2004; Wright 2004; Ponting 2007; Scarre 2009; Morris 2010) and Australian history in particular:

- The tool-making revolution (from 2.5 MYBP)
- The second human revolution (from 100,000 BP)
- The first agricultural revolution (from 10,000 BCE)
- The first urban revolution (from 4,500 BCE)
- The first imperial revolution (from 2,500 BCE)
- The reinvasion of the Americas (from 1450)
- The Western scientific revolution and the Enlightenment (from 1600)
- The first Industrial Revolution (from 1750)
- The age of oil (from 1920)
- The nuclear age (from 1950)
- The digital revolution (from 1980)
- The sustainability revolution (from 2005)

There is a standard format for the exhibition brief of each gallery:

- Name of the transition
- Brief description of the transition
- Stimuli for the transition
- Nature of the new society
- Technological innovations
- Organisational innovation
- Innovations in communication
- Social consequences
- Environmental consequences
- Iconic exhibits—artefacts, objects or images

The tool-making revolution: African ape to tool-making proto-human (from 2.5 MYBP)

Iconic exhibit: 2.5 million-year-old Oldowan stone chopping tool, an example of the earliest stone tool tradition yet discovered.

Other exhibits: casts of early hominin skulls; artist's impressions of early hominins on the African savannah; photographs of bonobos and chimpanzees (humans' closest relatives), living in forest.

The first gallery features the appearance in Africa of tool-making, upright, intelligent, proto-human ancestors, 2.5 million years ago (MYA). Tool use and tool-making evolved in conjunction with a bigger brain, upright posture, freed hands, opposable thumbs, intelligence, social organisation and a climatic shift favouring grasslands over forests. These developments enabled the migration of human ancestors out of Africa into Asia and southern Europe. The exhibition draws attention to the variety of explanations for this success.

Interestingly, it now seems that human ancestors had been bipedal (walking upright) for some millions of years previously. What seems to have occurred around 2.5 MYA was a geologically instantaneous addition of some ingredient into a mix of pre-existing adaptations. Paleoanthropologist Tim White (quoted in Shreeve 2010: 13) suggested that: 'Bipedality is the frame. Technology is the body. Language is the engine, dropped in at the final stage'. Whatever the catalyst was, the resulting synergy catapulted humans to a whole new level of capability.

One of the synergies evident in this transition continues throughout human history: the co-evolution and mutual symbiotic relationship between humans and grasses. In the later successes of *Homo sapiens*, we see human use of fire as furthering this partnership. It continues through the invention of agriculture and the rise of civilisation to the present day. To paraphrase Margulis and Sagan (quoted in Christian 2005: 123): 'Grasses don't need legs, brains or chemicals when they have humans'. As with all feedback systems, it is impossible to say whether humans or grasses are 'in charge' (BBC Two 2012).

Labels in this gallery explain why the museum never uses the term 'The' environment, a phrase that immediately externalises environment. Environment simply means surroundings, so it is always necessary to specify whose surroundings we are talking about. Humans are permeable: any chemical and many physical elements in our surroundings are often also inside us (Suzuki 2010). Environment is always personal (Wickson 2012).

All of our past revolutions have ramifications that are still with us today. The adoption of upright posture and bipedal gait, at least as long ago as 6 MYA, still poses problems for women in childbirth today. And, from this time onwards, technology became hard-wired into the human response to problems.

Exhibition concept. The tool-making revolution

Stimuli for transition: increasing aridity in Africa expands grassland habitats and reduces forest, providing new challenges and opportunities for already bipedal, omnivorous human ancestors.

New technology	*New organisational ability*
First stone and bone tools (wooden tools presumed).	Unknown but presumed significant.
Increased access to meat as a result of hunting large prey by running it down in the heat of the day.	
Tools and knowledge to dig up deep tubers and process starch foods.	

Exhibition concept. The tool-making revolution

New society	New communication ability
Family-based societies. The first human societies are presumed to combine elements of ape, carnivore and traditional human societies. Proto-language presumed.	Proto-language presumed.

Social adjustments	Environmental consequences
Unknown but presumed significant.	Co-evolution with grassland. Competition with, and elimination of, contemporary hominins, some terrestrial primates and specialised carnivores (e.g. sabre-tooth cats). Dispersal out of Africa to Asia and southern Europe—significant ecological impacts in newly invaded ecosystems which had no prior experience of tool-making apes.
Critical synergy	Natural spread of grasslands + evolution of bipedalism, freed hands, tool-making, hairlessness, ability to sweat and intelligence.

The second human revolution: the great expansion of Homo sapiens (from 100,000 BP)

Iconic exhibit: finely-crafted stone spear points produced by pressure-flaking.

Other exhibits: skeletons of extinct megafauna (mammoths, sabre-tooth cats and Australian giant kangaroos); an Inuit kayak; an Australian Aboriginal string bag; and photographs of Aboriginal people burning their country.

The second human revolution sees the second or third great human expansion out of Africa—that of modern humans, *H. sapiens*. This wave reinvades Eurasia and colonises Australia and the Americas for the first time. There are competing theories about what gave these humans the competitive edge over other contemporary human types.

This great migration seems to have occurred as much as 100,000 years after the first appearance of the physical form of *H. sapiens*. While the archaeological evidence is scant, considerable technological innovation is presumed to be a key factor in the success of this migration. This included the ability to make composite artefacts such as clothes, boats, houses, baskets and stone-tipped spears. The control of fire created new grasslands and enabled humans to increase the productivity of ecosystems and manage resources such as large herbivores (Gammage 2011). The use of cooking may have greatly increased the number and value of foods accessible to humans. Bill Bryson (Bryson 2010) attributes success to the invention of 'string'—the use of fibre and sinews to make composite artefacts. For whatever reasons, our cooking, hunting, 'string technologist', ancestors were able to replace or overwhelm the existing human populations of Eurasia and to colonise Australia, Japan and the Americas for the first time.

McBrearty and Brooks (2000) argue that the long ancestry of some of the traits of this human transition proved that this transition was not a revolution. They miss the point—it is not when things first occur that matters, it is when they combine with other things that makes the difference. A very potent new synergy was created around 60,000 years ago.

The extinction of megafauna, both in Eurasia and in newly colonised lands, was one of the consequences of this expansion. While these extinctions were clearly partly linked to the extraordinary climate changes of the time (notably the last glaciation and its abrupt termination), we can also clearly see at work the hand of humans, now the world's most dangerous predator and newest habitat shaper.

As the undisputed top predator of the natural world, human populations probably required little time to reach environmental carrying capacity in their newly-colonised territories. For example, Joseph Birdsell (Birdsell 1977) calculated that once a group of 25 Aboriginal people reached Australia, it would take them only 2,000 years to populate the continent. The implication is that for the remaining 48,000+ years of their history, they were living more or less sustainably around environmental carrying capacity. Further, given that their society and intelligence seems to be pretty much identical to modern humans today, we can assume that they were consciously coping with 'sustainability' issues from this time onwards. Every human society ever known has some method of population control, so it is almost certain that by this time every human society had became aware of the need to control their own populations and had developed their own ways of doing this. The real success of humans has probably been more to do with their ability to limit their impact on their resources, rather than their ability to find ever more ingenious ways to extract them. We should celebrate *H. sapiens sustainabililis* not *H. sapiens extractor*!

The exhibition addresses a common misconception that early humans lived in isolation from each other. This is ecologically unrealistic. All animals live in constant contact with, and defend their territories against, their neighbours (Wynne-Edwards 1962).

Exhibition concept. The second human revolution

Stimuli for transition: opportunities created by development of superior intelligence, technology, control of fire, knowledge of cooking and advanced social organisation. Challenges and opportunities created by extreme climatic variation during the last glacial period, including 100-metre lowering of sea levels at the last glacial maximum.

New technology	New organisational ability
Construction of composite tools, development of fibre and textile technology (e.g. for making clothes, bags, tents and boats), architectural skills (to make substantial huts and other forms of shelter), cooking; habitat management by fire. Possibly dog domestication.	Presumed to include the essential elements of every known traditional human society, such as kinship rules, long-term planning, cooperation, abstract thought and regulation of fertility. Long-distance exchange networks for precious goods.

Exhibition concept. The second human revolution	
New society	*New communication ability*
Tribal societies. First artistic creations. First evidence of spiritual beliefs.	Modern language presumed; also permanent iconic communication through 'art'.
Social adjustments	*Environmental consequences*
Unknown.	Extinction or absorption of other human species—*H. erectus*, Neanderthals etc, and, possibly, relict *H. habilis*.
	First human colonisation of Americas, Australia, Melanesian and Japanese Islands.
	Megafaunal extinction, particularly in newly colonised lands, also in Eurasia in conjunction with environmental changes at the end of the last glaciations.
	Deliberate use of fire for habitat and resource management. Humans accelerate expansion of grasslands.
Critical synergy	Superior technical skills + use of fire for cooking and habitat modification + presumed superior communication, planning and social organisation.

The first agricultural revolution (from 10,000 BCE)

Iconic exhibit: earliest pottery from the Middle East.

Other exhibits: artists' reconstructions of early towns, villages and religious structures; examples of domesticated crops and animals showing evolution over time from small wild ancestors to larger, domesticated forms; model of Polynesian voyaging canoe; Easter Island statue.

Following the end of the last Ice Age, the agricultural revolution (from 10,000 BCE) saw explosive human development associated with the 'invention' of agriculture. The significance of this revolution is probably matched only by the first Industrial Revolution. Humans were now able to colonise every major landmass and islands as remote as Easter Island.

The rise of agricultural economies hinged on various successful combinations (or synergies) of plant and animal foods. In Western Eurasia the combination was wheat + barley + beans + sheep + cattle + pigs; in Southeast Asia it was rice + 'greens'+ fish + chickens + pigs; in the New World, maize + beans + squash. These combinations were ecologically, nutritionally and economically complementary.

Even 9,000 years ago, we see the first evidence of overexploitation of habitats and exhaustion of soils by cultivators and their herds. No major new food crops have been domesticated since this first agricultural revolution. While productivity has increased almost inconceivably, the diversity and hence the resilience of the human food base has remained fundamentally the same.

The colonisation of even the remotest islands of the Pacific was made possible by superb seafaring technology and skills, understanding of natural energy systems (especially winds and currents), and highly adaptable horticulture and fishing economies. Often, these first human populations had catastrophic impacts on island ecosystems, ultimately degrading the societies themselves, for example on Easter Island (Diamond 2005).

Agricultural revolutions continued long after this initial transition. The development of draught animals and the deep plough expanded pre-industrial agrarian economies. In the 1970s the 'green revolution' was based on genetic modification of the same staple crops.

Exhibition concept. The first agricultural revolution

Stimuli for transition: environmental change (new, warmer, stable climate) creates pressures and opportunities. Agriculture leads to huge productivity increases. Enhanced ability to access or store food over long periods. Social, technological and ecological innovation.

New technology	New organisational ability
Domestication of crops and (Old World only) animals.	Walled towns reflect more intense warfare.
'Permanent' houses, villages and small towns. Pottery.	Extensive trade networks, increased travel and communication beyond tribal boundaries.
Many food storage solutions. Monumental architecture.	Ability to preserve large quantities of seed and grain for long periods.
Long-distance voyaging canoes reach Madagascar and Pacific islands.	

New society	New communication ability
Tribal societies with new levels of stratification, including chiefs, craftspeople and religious specialists.	Learning other languages to increase trade and support networks.
First towns and villages, sometimes walled towns.	Communication through artistic expression in buildings and on artefacts.
First religious constrictions.	

Social adjustments	Environmental consequences
Major social changes to societies abandoning mobility and choosing to live in close proximity to each other.	Evolution of winning ecological/economic combinations.
Emergence of mobile pastoralist societies (Old World), co-operating and, at times, battling with settled societies.	New disease ecologies resulting from new proximities—intra-species (human–human) and inter-species (human–non-human animal).
	Displacement of wild animal and plant populations.
	Soil erosion and exhaustion.
	Human colonisation of remote islands (Pacific, Madagascar, North Atlantic, etc).

Critical synergy	
	Agriculture (increased productivity) + storage technologies + new crafts and construction abilities + new social stratification and specialisation + commitment to fixed settlements.

The first urban revolution (from 4,500 BCE)

Iconic exhibit: Sumerian cuneiform writing on baked clay tablet.

Other exhibits: Egyptian hieroglyphics and Chinese oracle bone pictograms; artist's aerial view of early Sumerian city showing city walls, dense housing, streets and irrigated fields; example of early plough and model of wheeled vehicle.

The first urban revolution (from 4,000 BCE), has been defined (Childe 1950) by the appearance of writing, monumental architecture, full-time specialists and cities with populations over 5,000 people. The first known cities are in what is now southern Iraq. Writing enables the communication of information to occur beyond face-to-face, communication that is not reliant on human memory and is capable of harnessing mental powers greater than that of an individual. Increases in population density leads to an increase in the size and variety of information networks, which in turn leads to exponential increase in the accumulation of knowledge.

Since the terms 'urban revolution' and 'agricultural revolution' were coined by V.G. Childe (1950), archaeologists (e.g. Scarre 2009:196-97) have used dating evidence that shows gradual change to argue that these were not 'revolutionary' changes. They miss the point—the time-frames may not be revolutionary, but the social and ecological implications of the new synergies certainly were. City-based societies rapidly evolved into empires, as a result of a kind of inevitable arms race.

Urban revolutions are still with us today—the accommodation of billions of new humans into the huge urban concentrations of the 21st century will be one of the greatest challenges humanity has ever faced, although in principle the ancient Sumerians faced the same social and organisational issues 6,000 years ago!

Exhibition concept. The first urban revolution

Stimuli for transition: population pressure, technological innovation such as irrigation, advantages and need for greater co-operation.

New technology	*New organisational ability*
Cities (some walled) and monumental ceremonial centres.	Urban society, writing, record-keeping, taxation and armies.
Writing and counting systems.	
Irrigation systems.	
In the Old World, bronze metallurgy, ploughs, wheeled vehicles and draught animals.	

New society	*New communication ability*
Stratified, urban societies, including rulers, priests, specialist craftspeople and administrators.	Writing and counting systems.
Taxation and government.	

→

Exhibition concept. The first urban revolution	
Social adjustments	*Environmental consequences*
Major social changes, appearance of rulers, full-time specialists, religions, warfare, co-operation over irrigation/water sharing.	First major salinity problems e.g. in what is now southern Iraq.
Dense human concentrations stimulate innovation.	Urban diseases.
Critical synergy	City power + superior social organisation + specialisation + irrigation + writing and records.

The imperial revolution: appearance of pre-industrial, agrarian civilisations (from 2,000 BCE)

Iconic exhibit: statues of pharaohs at Abu Simbel, Egypt.

Other exhibits: images of the architectural remains and artistic triumphs of the great ancient civilisations—Rome (Italy), Angkor Wat (Cambodia), Machu Picchu (Peru) and Chichen Itza (Mexico).

The great pre-industrial agrarian empires range from Greece, Rome and Han China to the Aztecs, the Maya and the ancient Khmer. The rise and fall of pre-industrial empires was almost continuous from 2,000 BCE and continued, in some cases, until the Industrial Revolution around 20,000 years later. To lump them together as one transition does some historical injustice to this long and complex period, but they have much in common. The energy sources of all these empires were human power (including both slaves and tribute-payers), animal power and water power. Ships were powered mainly by rowing and rarely ventured far out to sea. All major trade routes were overland.

Above all, these empires resulted from massive improvements in human organisation, including communication. This organisational ability is reflected today in the remains of many extraordinary engineering achievements, from the aqueducts, bridges, harbours, roads, temples and concrete domes of ancient Rome to the flawless perfection of the pyramids of Giza, the perfectly fitted stone blocks of the Incas and the huge scale of the Grand Canal in China. Also attributable to this era are innovations such as the concept of zero and the alphabet.

Thanks to the existence of written records, we now have insights into what these ancient empires understood, or failed to understand, about sustainability. There is an extensive literature on the rise and fall of the ancient civilisations, the cycles of Dark Ages and Golden Ages (e.g. Elvin 2004; Homer-Dixon 2006; Chew 2007; Morris 2010), a pattern reflecting the universal struggle between order and entropy.

Regular ecological overshoot triggered collapse and the arrival of so-called 'horsemen of the apocalypse' (e.g. Morris 2010: 392 and passim)—the deadly synergies of famine, disease, war (especially civil war), state failure and unmanageable environmental change. Perhaps it was these experiences that lead to another distinctive achievement of these ancient civilisations- the development of the all world's major religions! Morris (2010) notes the transition from religions strongly associated with rulers' divine status, to current religions based on the principle of 'Compassion is Revolution' (Morris 2010: 256).

None of these empires lasted indefinitely, with Egypt being perhaps the longest lasting, probably due to the inherently sustainable nature of the Nile River's floods. What is now southern Iraq was abandoned due to salinity caused by over-irrigation (Wright 2004). Even the ancient civilisations based on 'sustainable' human and natural energy sources were unable to sustain themselves indefinitely.

As important as the imperial cities were, contemporary societies such as the agriculturalists, nomads (in the Old World) and hunter-gatherers, were often in some form of symbiotic relationships with the empires.

Several authors identify the late medieval periods of both western Europe and China, and even precocious fossil fuel 'industrialisation' in China, as deserving the status of a major transition (White 1940; Elvin 2004; Langdon 2004; Morris 2010). In western Europe, White (1940: 156) identified the synergy between the evolution of much more productive land use systems, better wind-powered ships and greater human freedom, a synergy she summarised as between 'the labor-saving power machines of the late Middle Ages and the implicit theological assumption of the infinite worth of even the most degraded human personality'. This new synergy led to the explosive development of societies in northern and western Europe, eclipsing the previously dominant societies of the Mediterranean.

Exhibition concept. The imperial revolution

Stimuli for transition: population pressure, desire and need ('arms race') to increase control of people and resources; ability to harness human energy (including slavery).

New technology	*New organisational ability*
Iron metallurgy (Old World) for ploughs and weapons. Major engineering achievements— aqueducts, roads, bridges, ports, fortifications. Human-powered ships.	Administrative achievements include maintenance of armies, tribute and tax systems, sanitation, medicine, education, irrigation, public health, roads, water management systems, baths and public order.
New society	*New communication ability*
Emperors, armies, conquest, tribute, slaves, citizen rights. All the world's major religions develop during this phase.	Many independent writing and counting systems and technologies.

→

Exhibition concept. The imperial revolution

Social adjustments	Environmental consequences
Cyclical rise and fall of civilisations; conflict between nomads and settled societies. Civil wars over political control. Transition away from theocratic control to more secular power systems. Limited 'democracy' in some cases (e.g. Greece and Rome).	Major environmental damage including soil exhaustion and erosion and over-hunting of animals. Abandonment of cities and some regions due to salinity, deforestation, desertification and state failure. Cycles of rise and fall of these civilisations. Vulnerability to synergistic collapse—'horsemen of the apocalypse'—disease, famine, state failure, invasion and environmental calamity.
Critical synergy	Superior organisation, including massive use of human power and ability to control and exploit huge territories + technical innovation + commitment to large city populations.

Reinvasion of the Americas: western maritime expansion and the European Renaissance (from 1450)

Iconic exhibit: painting of Spanish conquistador with armour, sword and horse.
Other exhibits: model of the Copernican solar system; compasses, early printing press and Bible; models of Christopher Columbus' ships; Aztec codices and Renaissance portraiture; replicas of potatoes, tomatoes, maize, tobacco and sugar cane.

The Renaissance, the western maritime expansion and the reinvasion of the New World should be treated as different faces of one major transition. Western Europeans reinvaded the New World, and expanded their commercial activities throughout the Old World. Their success was based on new maritime technology, and on military and epidemiological superiority, a combination that Diamond summarised as 'guns, germs and steel' (Diamond 1999). Sailors in capacious ships, exploiting their new knowledge of the circulating trade winds of the Atlantic and Pacific oceans, rewrote the map of global communication and transport. Conquistadors and settlers poured across the Atlantic into the Americas. They seized a continent abounding in many of the natural resources that had been so depleted in the Old World. They devastated Indigenous populations and initiated the 'Columbian exchange' of foods, plants and animals (potato, maize, tomato, horse, cattle, pigs, sheep), and of diseases and ideas between the Old and New Worlds (Crosby 2004). Crucial to all of this was the rise of commercial entrepreneurs backed by sophisticated capital-raising systems, such as the Dutch and English East India Companies.

Crosby (1986: 105-107) described five prerequisites for this expansion: the desire to undertake imperialistic adventures overseas; adequate vessels; the right equipment and techniques (e.g. for navigation); superior weaponry; and knowledge of how to harness a new source of energy—the trade winds—the gigantic 'wind wheels' of the Atlantic and the Pacific. He described the critical synergy as: 'Christian square sails, Muslim lateen sails, Chinese compasses and European ship owners, bankers, monarchs and nobles, cartographers, mathematicians, navigators, astronomers, masters, mates and ordinary seamen'.

Ironically China, from whom much of the West's maritime technology originated, abandoned its maritime exploration of the world at this very moment in history, thus isolating itself from much of human development for some centuries (Morris 2010).

Each revolution has its own new communication technology (Davidson 2007). In this case, the printing press (and, arguably, the invention of eye-glasses, see White 1940: 143) revolutionised communications and broke the monopolistic control of the Church and rulers over information.

The period saw revolutionary social change as reflected in the cultural and scientific 'Renaissance' of Europe. The 'paradigm wars', which inevitably accompany social transformations (Kuhn 1970), are well exemplified in the battles of this period between Church, state and science, reaching an extreme point with the savagery of religious oppression by the Spanish Inquisition.

Arguably, the sudden availability of huge areas of land in the Americas, so rich in natural resources, set back the progress of sustainable development in the West by three centuries. The 'frontier mentality' (Tim Flannery's [2001] ecological history of North America was titled *The Eternal Frontier*) that developed in the societies of the 'new worlds' of America and Australia can be seen as a reversion to a more primitive kind of human response, last experienced when *H. sapiens* invaded their 'new worlds' thousands of years previously.

Exhibition concept. Reinvasion of the Americas

Stimuli for transition: technological and scientific innovation in the West. Population pressure. Military superiority of the West.

New technology	*New organisational ability*
Capacious, ocean-going sailing ships with hinged rudders, lateen sails and magnetic compasses.	Commercial entrepreneurship—ability to raise capital by share markets, leading to commercial empires such as the Dutch and English East India Companies.
Improved ship-building techniques.	
Swords, gunpowder and guns.	
Scientific advances (e.g. the telescope and microscope).	
New horse technology—iron shoes and harnesses.	

➜

Exhibition concept. Reinvasion of the Americas

New society	*New communication ability*
The European Renaissance—commercial entrepreneurs and individualist artistic expression. Increased individual freedom.	Invention of the printing press enables mass access to knowledge previously held only by the elite.

Social adjustments	*Environmental consequences*
Conflict in Western Europe between Church, state and science, and worldwide between invaders/colonisers and Indigenous populations.	Devastation of Indigenous societies. Global exchanges of animal and plant foods, weeds and diseases. Ecological impact of worldwide expansion of Western societies.

Critical synergy	
	New maritime technology + military superiority + epidemiological advantage + commercial entrepreneurship and political innovation + scientific advances.

The Western scientific revolution and the Enlightenment: discovering science and liberty (from 1600)

Iconic exhibits: Harrison's chronometers (Sobel 1996) and art works from both the French Revolution and the American War of Independence.

Other exhibits: a musket; a portrait of Thomas Jefferson; a facsimile of the American Declaration of Independence; a copy of Isaac Newton's *Philosophiae Naturalis Principia Mathematica* and a replica of his telescope; a model of Captain Cook's ship *Endeavour* and Hawaiian headdress collected by him (MacGregor 2010: 566); and a canal boat.

This fruitful coming together of science, philosophy and discovery, both in the West and in China, has been labelled variously (and presumptuously) as 'The Enlightenment', the 'Age of Reason' and the 'Age of Scientific Discovery'. The English Civil Wars and, later, the French and American revolutions created capable new democracies that replaced old, less adaptable, monarchies and theocracies. Europeans explored the entire world, including the fringes of the Arctic and Antarctic. Europeans invaded Australia and colonised parts of Africa. Commerce drove the new colonial empires. The transatlantic slave trade grew to enable the exploitation of the Americas. Explorers and scientists interpreted and classified the amazing biological and cultural diversity they found. Their new discoveries stimulated science and the humanities and prepared the way for the Industrial Revolution. The last great free-living resources of the planet—whales, seals, bison and the temperate forests—were ruthlessly exploited (Ponting 2007).

Exhibition concept. The Western scientific revolution and Enlightenment

Stimuli for transition: advance of science and notions of freedom; exploration of the whole world and encounters with cultural and natural diversity.

New technology	*New organisational ability*
Scientific advances (e.g. Newton, Halley and Linnaeus). Formation of scientific societies. Voyages of exploration (e.g. Cook). First accurate chronometers (Harrison). Engineering inventors (e.g. Newcomen and Watt). Canal construction.	Worldwide exploration and colonisation by Europeans. East India Companies (Dutch and English).
New society	*New communication ability*
New democracies and American Independence.	Expansion of printed publications.
Social adjustments	*Environmental consequences*
American War of Independence, French Revolution.	Displacement of Indigenous populations, spread of Western agriculture.
Critical synergy	Scientific progress and discovery + advance of notions of freedom and democracy + colonisation of 'New Europes'.

The first Industrial Revolution: coal power (from 1750)

Iconic exhibit: photograph of Isambard Kingdom Brunel standing in front of the *Great Eastern* steamship.

Other exhibits: portraits of Karl Marx, Charles Darwin, Bishop Wilberforce and Abraham Lincoln; photographs of Victorian cities, factories, slums and pollution; of great engineering feats like bridges, dams and the Suez and Panama canals, of the US Civil War; models of *SS Great Eastern* and the Great Western Railway; a telegraph morse code transmitter; a telegram; an early camera; newspapers; a rifle and a machine gun; flags of the new empires of the industrial nations (Britain, France, Germany, Belgium, Netherlands, USA and Japan).

The first Industrial Revolution started in the UK and clearly had its origins in the preceding scientific revolution. Technological leadership moved from Britain to the USA and Germany. Some authors (e.g. Landes 2003) distinguish a second Industrial Revolution that began with Bessemer steel production in the 1860s and culminated in mass production and the production line. In Chapter 1 of this book, Mark Swilling discusses the three 'Kondratiev waves' that can be discerned in the period 1780–1930.

Technological superiority enabled a new wave of Western imperialism, colonisation and exploitation of the rest of the world. Steam ships, railways and telegraphs transformed the patterns of global communication and trade, replacing the circular trade-wind routes of the sailing age with direct routes across land and sea.

In the West this was the time of the explosion of industry and industrial cities, of factories, railways, steam ships, and of huge engineering feats such as bridges, tunnels, canals, the telephone and the wireless. A high environmental price was paid for this astounding progress. As well as being an age of technical change, it was also one of immense social change in the industrialising countries themselves, as reflected in enormous social disruption and devastating wars, notably the American Civil War and, much later, the Russian Revolution.

The 'paradigm wars' of the Enlightenment continue. Ferocious debates about evolution followed the publication of Charles Darwin's *On the Origin of Species By Means of Natural Selection,* and have an uncanny similarity to the debates over the role of humans in climate change in the early 2000s.

Exhibition concept. The first Industrial Revolution

Stimuli for transition: technical innovation linked with depletion of natural resources (e.g. timber and easily accessible coal deposits); invention of coal-coking technology and methods of industrialised production.

New technology	*New organisational ability*
Steam engines (for industry, mining, railways, ships and agricultural operations).	Industrial imperialism.
Coal-based energy production for countless new machines; photography; gas lighting.	

New society	*New communication*
Huge new industrialised cities.	Instant global communication by telegraph, morse code, telegrams; mass publications and photography.
New prosperity, dispossession of rural peasantry, migration to the cities; creation of the working class, urban slums and factories.	
Public health initiatives in new cities.	
New imperialism based on industrialisation.	
Colonisation to control the natural resources of the empires.	
Photography.	

Social adjustments	*Environmental consequences*
New urban populations and lifestyles.	Decimation of natural resources such as whales, seals, bison.
US Civil War (slavery, industrialisation).	Industrial pollution in slums.
Great debates (e.g. evolution versus creationism).	Human impacts extend to the atmosphere.

Critical synergy	
	Coking technology/coal power + factories + industrialised cities + scientific progress + industrialised new imperialism + global resource extraction.

The age of oil: the modern age (from 1920)

Iconic exhibits: Ford tri-motor aeroplane, Ford model T automobile; 1920's women's fashions; a photograph of the Empire State building in New York and of art deco buildings in Australia.

The power and transportability of oil made cars and aeroplanes possible. Stimulated by World War I, modern industry and industrial chemistry developed in the USA and Germany. Nitrogen was artificially synthesised, providing almost inexhaustible supplies of fertiliser. Skyscrapers, the Hoover dam and the Golden Gate bridge were created. Cars started to shape our living environments—in America suburbia appears, in Australia car-dependent Canberra is created. The aeroplane gives limited access to remote regions. 'Modern' society and fashions appeared, reflecting post-World War I disillusionment with old imperial institutions and values. Worldwide decolonisation movements commence.

Environmental disasters included the North American dust bowl, the Great Depression and the introductions of cane toads and prickly pears in Australia.

Exhibition concept. The age of oil: the modern age	
Stimuli for transition: oil technology; competition between industrialised nations exemplified by World War I; depletion of natural resources.	
New technology	*New organisational ability*
Oil powered cars and propeller-driven aeroplanes. Production of fertiliser by nitrogen synthesis (Haber-Bosch method).	League of Nations. Pan American World Airways.
New society	*New communication*
'Modern' society and fashions, greater personal freedoms and erosion of class systems. Expressionist and Surrealist art; art deco architecture. Construction of skyscrapers. Creation of suburbia.	Radio. Domestic telephone.
Social adjustments	*Environmental consequences*
Great Depression, Wall Street crash. Decline of British Empire. Post World War I politics—Weimar Republic. Rise of fascism.	Great dust bowl in the USA. Disastrous cane toad and prickly pear introductions to Australia.
Critical synergy	Oil energy + cars + artificial fertiliser + social change following World War I.

The coming of the nuclear age (from 1950)

Iconic exhibit: photograph of thermo-nuclear bomb test Castle Romeo on Bikini Atoll 1954.

Other exhibits: include the Comet 1, the first commercial jetliner, representing the era of national hubris and industrial competition between Western nations (as well as the price paid by pioneers of new technologies); the 1969 American moon lander and the photograph of 'Earth rise' from the moon; a 1964 Cadillac, complete with enormous tail 'wings' and the text of Buddy Holly's song 'No particular place to go', reflecting the era of cheap fossil fuel energy; an enormous mainframe computer—cutting edge in its time; Chairman Mao's *Little Red Book*; the contraceptive pill; the first antibiotics; and Beatles songs reflecting both a flirtation with oriental philosophies and the 'free love' revolution; a domestic television, representing the communication revolution of the time; Rachel Carson's book *Silent Spring* (Carson 1962) and a genetically-improved wheat specimen, created as part of the 'green revolution'.

Other names given to this era include the 'space age' and the 'jet age'. A new intellectual paradigm—postmodernism—appears. Human exploration reaches the moon and resource extraction extends to the deepest oceans and the remotest wildernesses. The motor car dictates the shape of urban expansion. The world decolonises. New nations struggle. India is riven by religious, and China by political, schisms.

Environmentally, 1950 is the turning point at which the global environmental impact of industrialisation becomes unmistakable. At this moment many identify the beginning of the 'Anthropocene', the era in which human activity becomes the dominant geological and biological force on the planet (Syvitski 2012). Almost every negative environmental indicator accelerates.

Exhibition concept. The nuclear age	
Stimuli for transition: competition between industrialised nations; World War II and the Cold War.	
New technology	*New organisational ability*
Nuclear energy and weapons.	New international organisations such as the World Bank (1944), IMF (1944), United Nations (1945), World Health Organisation (1948).
Space rockets and use of space for military and commercial ends.	
Jet aircraft.	
Genetic modification of crops.	Global corporations such as Coca Cola.
Contraceptive pill.	
First computers.	
Advances in medicine include antibiotics.	

→

Exhibition concept. The nuclear age	
New society	*New communication ability*
Postmodernism.	Television.
Women's liberation.	
'Free love' and 'flower power'.	
Elvis Presley and the Beatles.	
Cheap fuel and large cars.	
Domestic television.	
Social adjustments	*Environmental consequences*
Cold War and proxy wars (Korea, Vietnam, Middle East, Cuban Crisis).	Exponential increase in all environmental impacts of industrialisation.
Oil crisis.	Nuclear accidents.
China's 'cultural revolution'.	Poisoning and shrinkage of freshwater bodies such as the Aral Sea.
	End of Atlantic cod industry due to over-fishing.
	Rise of environmentalism, publication of *Silent Spring, Man's Role in Changing the Face of the Earth* and *Prehistoric Overkill*.
	'Earth rise' photo from the moon promotes concept of 'Planet Earth'.
Critical synergy	Cheap fossil-fuel energy + nuclear weapons + decolonisation + contraceptive pill + medical innovation + car dependency.

The digital revolution and global industrialisation (from 1980)

Iconic image: an early personal computer (Commodore); a mobile phone made in China.

Other exhibits: aerial photographs of motorways; images of urban traffic conges-tion; airline advertisements; images of mining and media billionaires; photographs of climate refugees in African camps; a credit card (MacGregor 2010); and a video clip of the Hollywood Oscars (chosen as a symbol of global and non-religious val-ues, and as a reflection of this period of American cultural dominance).

Communication is revolutionised by digital, wireless, Internet technology. It is accompanied by, and feeds into, the global spread of the Industrial Revolution. Despite growing evidence of its dangers (Rockstrom *et al.* 2009), the rest of the world rushes to get aboard the 'fossil fuel express' that has so enriched the first industrial societies. Society is locked into fossil-fuel dependency and mobility addiction, a form of living that is increasingly set in concrete as new roads, motorways and sub-urbs are built. Wireless digital communication and the worldwide construction of airports expand the spread of communication routes far beyond those that were established in the 19th century on imperial axes.

The poorer nations of the world continue to pay a high price for the prosperity of the wealthy nations.

Exhibition concept. The digital revolution and global industrialisation	
Stimuli for transition: technological innovation; spread of fossil-fuel-based industrialisation; birth of capitalism in China.	
New technology	*New organisational ability*
Digitisation technology, Internet, computer chip and miniaturisation technology, mobile phones, personal computers.	Credit revolution (credit cards, international banks).
New society	*New communication ability*
Rise of BRIC nations, especially semi-capitalist China. Digital connectedness. Most people live in cities. Spread of various forms of democracy.	Internet and wireless technology, new international communication protocols established.
Social adjustments	*Environmental consequences*
Rise of the global citizen. Terrorism culminating in 9/11 attack on New York in 2001. Rwandan genocide linked to overpopulation. Famines in Africa and accompanying social collapse. China integrates capitalism and communism. Collapse of Russian communism.	Rising population, soaring energy and resource consumption putting major pressure on world resources and ecosystem services. Depletion of ozone layer and start of international action. Exacerbated environmental damage in the poorer nations.
Critical synergy	Success of capitalism, end of communism + spread of industrial technology + new, global, communication technology.

Conclusions from the 11 previous transitions

This cursory examination of 11 major transitions of the past highlights some common principles of system transformations in history:

- It is all about synergies. It is not what comes first that matters, it is when new and pre-existing conditions coalesce. It is not about cause and effect, it is about tipping points at which whole systems transform themselves into new states (e.g. Walker and Salt 2006)

- Synergies work both ways. For long periods they prevent change and then, at critical moments, they trigger revolutionary change

- With systemic change it is hard for both historians and for those living through periods of transformation to discern what caused what

- The key synergies in human history are technology, society and its values and paradigms, organisational ability (including communication technology) and environmental dynamics. They all reinforce each other and they cannot be considered independently of each other. The great human transitions involved all of them

- The hard part of change is social change. Humans persistently hope that technological innovation or political change will spare them the need for social change

- After episodes of transformation there is, characteristically, a period of rapid growth. Soon a new threshold is reached. Society then bumps around at this new threshold for a long period of time as it comes to terms with the new system dynamics. Eventually, it either invents a way to raise the threshold, or it overshoots and lowers the threshold or carrying capacity

- The catalyst for transformation may be quite minor if a system is already close to a tipping point

- Regrettably, it seems that wars (such as World Wars I and II) may often be drivers of transformation

- Human history exhibits some consistent trends: there has been unrelenting increase in environmental damage and continuous reduction of planetary resilience. At the same time, there has been continuous increase in human productivity, ability to distribute resources over space and time, and in knowledge and capacities

- The pace of change gets faster, and the periods of relative stability between major transformations become shorter and shorter

- The planet's ecosystems have had insufficient time to readapt to the changes that we have imposed on them over the last 20,000 years, let alone the last 300

- As human productivity has been ratcheted up, the option of 'winding back' has steadily diminished

- All transitions produce winners and losers, in a cyclic process where today's innovative winners are tomorrow's conservative losers (Morris 2010)

- The rapid changes of the last 300 years are all based on the exploitation of a finite and toxic natural resource—fossil fuels. It is by no means certain that the riches and benefits of the fossil fuel civilisations can be sustained indefinitely. Humanity may have wasted the opportunities offered by this extraordinary, one-off windfall

- Even the ancient civilisations based on 'sustainable' human and natural energy sources were unable to sustain themselves indefinitely

- The environmental struggles of the ancient civilisations tell us, in principle, nearly much of what we need to know about the challenges of sustainability, of the battles between short-term self-interest and long-term co-operation

- History tells us that ecological overshoot is very serious. Millions of people die (McMichael 2011)

- Perhaps the greatest achievement of our species, *H. sapiens*, has been its ability to regulate its own population. It has probably practised this consciously for over 100,000 years

While humans have always been aware of their environmental impacts, the present era is the first time we have had information about our long ecological history (Diamond 2005: 525). This gives us a unique advantage over previous societies. Today, we are at the beginning of a period of exponential growth and environmental impact, not at its apex, as is often imagined (AtKisson 2009). If we think that past environmental damage was bad, we haven't thought about what is coming.

Gallery 13 the sustainability revolution: clean reindustrialisation (from 2005)

Let us now imagine the exhibition brief for gallery 13—the sustainability revolution—as it might be written in 2060. The premise for this scenario is that global sustainability was achieved by 2060. We can use this opportunity to scrutinise various theories about how a more sustainable society might be achieved. What might success look like? Is the vision realistic? What might the transition be like? How big a transition is required? (compare Randers 2012, Charlton 2012 and Gilding 2011).

Exhibition concept. The sustainability revolution

Stimuli for transition: competition for increasingly scarce resources; decline of the old industrialised countries; collapse of many ecosystem services; the third and the fourth global financial crises; widespread social breakdown; political, economic, scientific and technical innovation; the new honour and wisdom social and spiritual movement.

New technology	New organisational ability
Clean, renewable energy sources stabilise emissions and end fossil fuel dependency. Global communication technology. Molecular and ecological engineering. Green chemistry, clean reindustrialisation.	Increased international co-operation including new treaties and conflict resolution bodies. United Nations renamed United Humanity Organisation. Increase in social responsibility by international corporations. Sustainable and equitable global financial system.

➔

Exhibition concept. The sustainability revolution

New society	*New communication ability*
The new honour and wisdom movement. Economists cost externalities. Wellbeing measures replace GDP. International Justice Commission resolves major injustices. Greater localisation and greater internationalisation. Global citizenship and elections. Global urbanism. Universal education for women. World population starts to reduce, increase in smaller family sizes and rise of the one-child family.	Universal hyper-connectedness—affordable, secure, mobile communication devices. Global inter-human text language. Global inter-computer language. Automatic translation software and the spread of English, Spanish and Mandarin effectively create universal language. 3-D, multisensory, wireless, digital communication technology—'just like being there'.
Social adjustments	*Environmental consequences*
State failure in developing countries (Mexico) and undeveloped countries (e.g. African Sahel). Tumultuous social conflict over values in developed countries. Strong social innovation in 'periphery' societies. Rise and fall of nationalistic 'new right wing' attitudes, fundamentalist beliefs, and attempts to selectively accept science and technology.	Environmental catastrophes of mid-21st century, including those resulting from global warming, climate destabilisation and oceanic acidification. Start of remediation of ecosystems and remediation of toxic legacies, including removal of plastic waste from world environments. Genetic and geo-engineering technologies create new challenges. Huge new biosphere reserves created. Growth of the science of the 'new biodiversity'. Cities as national urban parks.
Critical synergy	Reform of capitalism and democracy to incorporate long-term and inter-generational values + environmental and social catastrophes + resource constraints and competition + technological innovation + global hyper-communication

The 'brief' above assumed that the sustainability revolution did occur. Some of the main features were:

- The nature of democracy and capitalism had to change (Klein 2011)

- The challenge was to instil long-term thinking and to develop international co-operation at a time of resource competition

- Among the universal drivers for change were environmental disasters, social conflict, state failure and international competition

- The greatest innovations occurred in 'fringe' societies not locked into the dirty industrialism of the first Industrial Revolution

- In developed economies change were driven by the military (D'Estries 2012), accountants (Gittins 2012), insurance companies, technological innovators, conscience-driven consumers and progressive governments who priced externalities and future costs

- Serious impacts were experienced personally by the citizens of the developed countries. Regrettably, however, the pace of social change was not fast enough to avoid further environmental and social catastrophe (Four Degrees Conference 2011; Stager 2011)

- Features of this new society included 'green' chemistry[1] (Moody and Nogrady 2010: 165), cradle-to-cradle industrial processes (McDonough and Braungart 2002), success in resolving injustice, steady-state economics (Daly 1997, 2008; Jackson 2009),[2] measuring society by wellbeing rather than GDP, gender and inter-generational equity, new paradigms and new values, population growth reduction, and more vibrant local communities

- The change was made easier by worldwide hyper-connectedness and almost universal urbanism

Conclusions

The current transition is one of 12 major transformations in Western human history. The scale of social change entailed in this 'sustainability revolution' has been underestimated. It may be as profound as the transition from the agrarian subsistence economies of Europe 200–300 years ago to the current industrial society (Haberl 2012). Based on the pace of change of the last century, we should expect at least two major transitions in the period 2005–2055. Sustainability is unlikely to be the catch-cry of this revolution. This revolution is more likely to be called 'global clean reindustrialisation' or even 'post fossil fuel enlightenment'!

The drivers of history are the great synergies (based on positive feedback loops). Historical examples include the co-evolution of humans and grasses, the emergence of successful agricultural combinations, the appearance of the first empires (built on writing, administration, cities, armies and irrigation), and the expansion of Western societies in the 15th and 16th centuries (based on 'guns, germs and steel' (Diamond 1999), Chinese compasses and boat-building techniques, Islamic sails, and Western technological innovation and commercial entrepreneurship).

A powerful set of synergies grip our society today—fossil fuel dependency, mobility addiction, settlement patterns and communication routes set in concrete, and selfish, short-term political and financial systems. Dangerous synergies await

1 See Warner Babcock Institute for Green Chemistry, www.warnerbabcock.com, accessed 15 August 2011.
2 See Centre for the Advancement of the Steady State Economy, steadystate.org, accessed 15 August 2011.

us, such as carbon dioxide levels and climate tipping points, or ocean acidification combining with plastic pollution leading to the devastation of marine ecosystems. A sustainable society is one that has achieved a working synergy between its ecological and economic realities, its technology, its politics and its ideology. Ideological conflicts, such as the Renaissance battles between religious belief and scientific evidence or the recent confrontations over climate science, exemplify the difficulties when values and evidence are no longer congruent. History shows that we are engaged, not in a 'necessary' transition, but in many inevitable transitions. Change is upon us, whether we like it or not. Our only choice is the extent to which we proactively try to shape these forces towards a more benign outcome.

So, is there more to transitions than the timeless ebb and flow of entropy and orderliness, simplicity and complexity, between the 'Dark Ages' and the 'Golden Ages' (Christian 2005: 79-80)? There seems to be a force at work that I have called 'synergy', a force that continually seeks congruence between society's structures, paradigms and values, its technology, organisational and communication systems, and its ecological relationship with the dynamics of our planet. We seem to be on a planet that strives for congruence.

How to tip a system

The nature of systemic transformations means that almost any positive action can help to tip society to a better state. As the *Bioneers* (www.bioneers.org) newsletter on 21 June 2012 puts it:[3]

> As the world situation heats up both literally and figuratively, each of us faces a profound choice—and collectively we face the same choice: life and hope—or resignation and decline. Both are self-fulfilling prophecies. The real tipping point is the consciousness we cultivate and our actions that flow from it. In every system, the hardest thing to change is the paradigm, but it can happen fast. As the great systems thinker and ecologist Donella Meadows advised: 'Keep pointing at anomalies and failures in the old paradigm. Keep speaking loudly and with assurance from the new one. Insert people with the new paradigm in places of public visibility and power. Don't waste time with reactionaries; work with active change agents, and the vast middle ground of open people'.

References

AtKisson, A. (2009) 'A Song About Exponential Growth', *AtKisson Group* (5 January 2009; (www.youtube.com/watch?v=aDkRHY16Py4, accessed 20 June 2012).

Ball, P. (2004) *Critical Mass: How One Thing Leads to Another* (New York: Farrar, Strauss and Giroux).

3 myemail.constantcontact.com/The-Real-Tipping-Point-Is-The-Consciousness-We-Cultivate.html?soid=1011074386079&aid=kSdF8jTlYko, accessed 2 April 2013.

BBC Two (2012) 'The Challenger: Episode 3', *How to Grow a Planet* (www.bbc.co.uk/programmes/b01ckw5g, accessed 26 March 2013).

Birdsell, J.B. (1977) 'The Recalibration of a Paradigm for the First Peopling of Greater Australia', in J. Allen, J. Golson and R. Jones (eds.), *Sunda and Sahul* (London: Academic Press): 113-68.

Bryson, B. (2010) *At Home: A Short History of Private Life* (London: Transworld Publishers).

Carson, R. (1962) *Silent Spring* (Boston, MA: Houghton Mifflin).

Charlton, A. (2012) 'Man-made World: Choosing Between Progress and Planet', *Quarterly Essay* 44, 2011 (Collingwood, Australia: Black Inc Books): 1-72.

Chew Sing, C. (2007) *The Recurring Dark Ages: Ecological Stress, Climate Change and System Transformation* (Lanham, MD: AltaMira Press).

Childe, V.G. (1950) 'The Urban Revolution', *The Town Planning Review* 21: 3-17.

Christian, D. (2005) *Maps of Time: An Introduction to Big History* (Berkeley, CA: University of California Press).

Clarke, D.L. (1968) *Analytical Archaeology* (London: Methuen).

Crosby, A.W. (2004) *Ecological Imperialism: The Biological Expansion of Europe, 900–1900* (Cambridge, UK: Cambridge University Press).

Daly, H.E. (1997) *Beyond Growth: The Economics of Sustainable Development* (Boston, MA: Beacon Press).

Daly, H.E. (2008) 'A Steady-State Economy', paper for Sustainable Development Commission (24 April 2008; www.sd-commission.org.uk/data/files/publications/Herman_Daly_thinkpiece.pdf, accessed 15 December 2011).

Davidson, I. (2007) 'Scales and Balance: Archaeology, Cultural Heritage and Sustainability', *Australian Academy of Humanities Proceedings 2007* (Canberra: Australian Academy of Humanities, www.humanities.org.au/Portals/0/documents/Publications/Proceedings/Proc2007.pdf): 113-43.

D'Estries, M. (2012) 'The Military Sets Ambitious Goals', *Ecoimagination* (www.ecomagination.com/operation-sustainability-us-military-sets-ambitious-environmental-goals, accessed 31 August 2012).

Diamond, J. (1999) *Guns, Germs and Steel: The Fates of Human Societies* (New York: Norton).

Diamond, J. (2005) *Collapse: How Societies Choose to Fail or Survive* (London: Allen Lane).

Edwards, A.R. (2005) *The Sustainability Revolution: Portrait of a Paradigm Shift* (Gabriola Island, Canada: New Society Publishers).

Elvin, M. (2004) *Retreat of the Elephants: An Environmental History of China* (New Haven, CT and London: Yale University Press).

Falk, J.H., and L.D. Dierking (2000) *Learning from Museums: Visitor Experiences and the Making of Meaning* (Lanham, MD: AltaMira Press/Rowman and Littlefield).

Flannery, T. (2001) *The Eternal Frontier: An Ecological History of North America and Its Peoples* (Melbourne, Australia: Text Publishing).

Four Degrees Conference (2011) *Four Degrees or More? Australia in a Hot World*, Melbourne, 12–14 July 2011 (www.fourdegrees2011.com.au, accessed 15 August 2011).

Gammage, B. (2011) *The Biggest Estate On Earth* (Sydney, Australia: Allen and Unwin).

Gilding, P. (2011) *The Great Disruption: How the Climate Crisis Will Transform the Global Economy* (London: Bloomsbury).

Gittins, R. (2012) 'Environmental Accounting is Closer to Reality', *Sydney Morning Herald* (23 June 2012; www.smh.com.au/business/environmental-accounting-is-closer-to-reality-20120622-20tgl.html, accessed 25 June 2012).

Gladwell, M. (2001) *The Tipping Point: How Little Things Can Make a Big Difference* (London: Abacus).

Gore, A. (2006) *An Inconvenient Truth: The Planetary Emergency of Global Warming and What We Can Do About It* (London: Bloomsbury).

Haberl, H. (2012) 'Addicted to Resources', *Global Change: International Geosphere–Biosphere Programme* 78 (March): 20-23.

Homer-Dixon, T. (2006) *The Upside of Down: Catastrophe, Creativity and the Renewal of Civilisation* (Melbourne, Australia: Text Publishing).

Jackson, T. (2009) *Prosperity Without Growth: Economics for a Finite Planet* (London: Earthscan).

Klein, N. (2011) 'Capitalism vs. the Climate', *The Nation* (28 November 2011; www.thenation .com/article/164497/capitalism-vs-climate?page=0,0, accessed 15 August 2011).

Kuhn, T. (1970) *The Structure of Scientific Revolutions* (Chicago, IL: University of Chicago Press, 2nd edn).

Landes, D. (2003) *The Unbound Prometheus: Technical Change and Industrial Development in Western Europe from 1750 to the Present* (New York: Cambridge University Press, 2nd edn).

Langdon, J. (2004) *Mills in the Mediaeval Economy: England 1300–1540* (Oxford, UK: Oxford University Press).

MacGregor, N. (2010) *A History of the World in 100 Objects* (London: Allen Lane).

Mantyka-Pringle, C. (2012) 'The Devil is in the Synergy: Interactions Between Climate Change and Habitat Loss', *Decision Point, Monthly Magazine, Environmental Decision Group 57*, (6–7 March 2012; www.decision-point.com.au/images/DPoint_files/DPoint_57/dp57%20mantyka-pringle%20cc%20%20hab%20loss%20p67.pdf, accessed 3 August 2012).

McDonough, W., and M. Braungart (2002) *Cradle to Cradle: Remaking the Way We Make Things* (New York: North Point Press).

McMichael, A.J. (2011) 'Insights From Past Millennia Into Climatic Impacts on Human Health and Survival', *Proceedings of the National Academy of Sciences* (www.pnas.org/cgi/doi/10.1073/pnas.1120177109, accessed 1 May 2012).

McBrearty, S., and A.S. Brooks (2000) 'The Revolution That Wasn't: A New Interpretation of the Origin of Human Behaviour', *Journal of Human Evolution* 39: 453-563.

Moody, J.B., and B. Nogrady (2010) *The Sixth Wave: How to Succeed in a Resource Limited World* (Sydney, Australia: Random House).

Morris, I. (2010) *Why the West Leads—For Now. The Patterns of History and What They Reveal About the Future* (New York: Farrar, Strauss and Giroux).

Ponting, C. (2007) *A New Green History of the World: The Environment and the Collapse of the Great Civilisations* (London: Vintage Books).

Randers, J. (2008) 'Global Collapse—Fact or Fiction?', *Futures, the Journal of Policy, Planning and Future Studies* 40: 853-64.

Randers, J. (2012) *2052: A Global Forecast For the Next Forty Years* (White River Junction, VT: Chelsea Green Publishing).

Rockström, J., W. Steffen, K. Noone, Å. Persson, F.S. Chapin, III, E. Lambin, T.M. Lenton, M. Scheffer, C. Folke, H. Schellnhuber, B. Nykvist, C.A. De Wit, T. Hughes, S. van der Leeuw, H. Rodhe, S. Sörlin, P.K. Snyder, R. Costanza, U. Svedin, M. Falkenmark, L. Karlberg, R.W. Corell, V.J. Fabry, J. Hansen, B. Walker, D. Liverman, K. Richardson, P. Crutzen and J. Foley (2009) 'Planetary Boundaries: Exploring the Safe Operating Space for Humanity', *Ecology and Society* 14.2: 32 (www.ecologyandsociety.org/vol14/iss2/art32, accessed 21 June 2012).

Scarre, C. (ed.) (2009) *The Human Past: World Prehistory and the Development of Human Societies* (London: Thames and Hudson, 2nd edn).

Shreeve, J. (2010) 'Middle Awash. The Evolutionary Road', *National Geographic* (July 2010; ngm.nationalgeographic.com/2010/07/middle-awash/shreeve-text/13, accessed 21 June 2012).

Sobel, D. (1996) *Longitude: The True Story of a Lone Genius Who Solved the Greatest Scientific Problem of His Time* (London: Fourth Estate).

Stager, C. (2011) *Deep Future: The Next 100,000 Years of Life on Earth* (Melbourne, Australia: Scribe Publications).

Suzuki, D. (2010) *The Legacy: An Elder's Vision for a Sustainable Future* (Vancouver, Canada: David Suzuki Foundation).

Syvitski, J. (2012) 'Anthropocene: An Epoch of Our Making', *Global Change: International Geosphere–Biosphere Programme* 78 (March): 12-15.

Walker, B., and D. Salt (2006) *Resilience Thinking: Sustaining Ecosystems and People in a Changing World* (Washington, DC: Island Press).

White, L. (1940) 'Technology and Invention in the Late Middle Ages', *Speculum* 15.2: 141-59.

Wickson, F. (2012) 'Why We Need to Forget About the Environment', *The Conversation* (30 August 2012; theconversation.edu.au/why-we-need-to-forget-about-the-environment-8818?utm_medium=email&utm_campaign=The+Weekend+Conversation&utm_content=The+Weekend+Conversation+CID_59e01a964e57f9f5c7730f24a19d0e11&utm_source=campaign_monitor&utm_term=Why+we+need+to+forget+about+the+environment, accessed 31 August 2012).

Wright, R. (2004) *A Short History of Progress* (Melbourne, Australia: Text Publishing).

Wynne-Edwards, V.C. (1962) *Animal Dispersion in Relation to Social Behaviour* (London: Oliver & Boyd).

Richard Cassels is Director of Climate Leadership, a community group in Brisbane promoting more sustainable living. Previously, he has been a museum director and curator in Australia and New Zealand, following his position as Senior Lecturer in Prehistory at the University of Auckland, New Zealand where he studied the impact of prehistoric people on island ecosystems.

4

Transformations and translations of Japanese business–society

Kyoko Fukukawa
Bradford University School of Management, University of Bradford, UK

Sunil Manghani
Winchester School of Art, University of Southampton, UK

> The master said, He who by reanimating the Old can gain knowledge of the New is fit to be a teacher (Confucius).

In the wake of the global banking crisis of 2008, and with ongoing financial instability in world markets, capitalism has come under renewed scrutiny. Of course critics of capitalism are nothing new, and the idea of 'capitalism with a conscience' dates back before 2008 (cf. Goodpaster 2007). Yet the phrase, if lacking in substantive meaning, has gained traction. It is suggestive of the emergence of a genuinely new perspective, which is neither anti- nor pro-capitalism, but searching somewhere in-between. The critical theorist, Slavoj Žižek, in his book *Living in the End of Times* (2011a), offers a somewhat pessimistic view of the global capitalist system, as 'approaching an apocalyptic zero-point'. In interview, he notes both a desperate need and a growing desire for a 'real alternative':

> I think today the world is asking for a real alternative. Would you like to live in a world where the only alternative is either Anglo-Saxon neoliberalism or Chinese–Singaporean capitalism with Asian values? I claim if we do nothing we will gradually approach a kind of a new type of authoritarian

society. Here I see the world historical importance of what is happening today in China. Until now there was one good argument for capitalism: sooner or later it brought a demand for democracy [...] What I'm afraid of is with this capitalism with Asian values, we get a capitalism much more efficient and dynamic than our Western capitalism. But I don't share the hope of my liberal friends—give them ten years, [and there will be] another Tiananmen Square demonstration—no, the marriage between capitalism and democracy is over (Žižek 2011b).

Žižek does not adequately enunciate what is meant by 'Chinese–Singaporean' capitalism and so-called 'Asian values'. At best such journalistic shorthand creates a binary opposition; at worst, it perpetuates an essentialist myth about how capitalism is formulated in different contexts. Nonetheless, Žižek's account marks an important transition in our thinking about capitalism. The collapse of communism, symbolised by the fall of the Berlin Wall in 1989, seemingly brought to fruition the neoliberal doctrine that, as Žižek puts it, 'sooner or later [capitalism] brought a demand for democracy'. Fukuyama's (1989) 'end of history' thesis is the most well-known statement proffering this view. He argues, for example:

[The] state of consciousness that permits the growth of liberalism seems to stablize in the way one would expect at the end of history if it is underwritten by the abundance of a modern free market economy. We might summarize the content of the universal homogenous state as liberal democracy in the political sphere combined with easy access to VCRs and stereos in the economic (Fukuyama 1989: 8).

The 'problem' of Fukuyama's thesis, for the Left, was always the lack of an adequate alternative to liberal capitalism. Indeed, it is quite possible to update the end of history thesis to include easy access to smartphones and wide-screen TVs. Žižek, however, makes the argument that the 'end of times' while remaining (for now) capitalist, is heading in a direction that is not stable, universal or indeed democratic. We might usefully accept a decoupling of capitalism and democratic ideology, and the subsequent acceptance of different forms of capitalism. At the same time, however, we can attempt to restore greater complexity to what Žižek pointedly refers to as so-called 'Asian values'. The point here is not to argue for or against capitalism, nor to prop up an essentialist notion of 'Asian values', but instead to thicken the picture to consider 'difference' within capitalism not as a mere fact of cultural difference, but as a quality inherent to the functioning of capitalism in the first place; as embedded in our already existing structures of business and society. Žižek's evocation of 'Asian values' is skewed by a thinly veiled criticism of China as a totalitarian regime, undermining significant points of interest, not least the relationship between Eastern religious philosophies and commerce.

This chapter looks away from the example of China, and instead considers the Japanese context—which, following the 'economic miracle' since World War II, has long been aligned with the most prosperous global capitalist economies. Nonetheless, after the bubble burst leading to a 'lost decade' (1991–2000), Japan went through a period of introspection and reassessment. It has reinvented the relationship between business and society, both as a result of the external demands of global corporate governance, and by having reconnected with its tradition of closely integrating business and society.

Japan has long benefited from a form of democratic capitalism, yet equally demonstrates its own 'Asian values'. Following the catastrophic East Japan earthquake in 2011, the private sector has readily played a strong role in both remedial work and future planning. The Japanese Business Federation, Keidanren, recently put forward a statement regarding the building of a 'resilient society', which immediately evokes strong business–society relations, but also, importantly is articulated through both an international and national business perspective:

> Building a resilient society that is more robust against natural disasters is indispensable and is also a major premise for recovering international trust and attracting investment. Keidanren shall contribute to building a more resilient society with the world's highest level of disaster prevention by fully utilizing the private sectors' technology and the wisdom (Keidanren 2012).

This chapter considers how, in the context of Japan, the idea of 'Asian values' maps onto and re-fashions issues of contemporary business ethics in particular ways. Following an account of contemporary business–society relations, the chapter turns attention to three key periods of Japan's past, not so much as to provide a sense of continuity and origin for Japanese business ethics, but rather to bring to light a more complex history. In circling historical points of transition, this chapter evokes the prospects of a genealogical account of Japanese business ethics—that is, not a teleological account of history, but one that unfolds in different directions and at varying speeds, which nonetheless inform the contemporary Japanese context. In providing this account, the chapter opens up critical awareness of our seemingly urgent concerns with 'new' agendas for social responsibility, sustainability and security.

History and progress

Japan famously remained cut off from the world system from the early 1600s through to the end of the 1850s, when an American fleet of ships arrived to force the opening of various shipping ports. The legacy of this dramatic opening, as imposed by the West, is that Japan is often characterised as being a latecomer to the world system and, indeed, a laggard in the face of change and new possibilities. The stereotypical view is demonstrated with the 1958 film classic *The Barbarian and the Geisha*, starring John Wayne as Townsend Harris, the US Consul General to Japan (who in reality, in the 1860s, managed to secure the treaty with Japan). During a critical scene in which Harris is being interrogated by the Imperial Council—the Shogunate—he argues the need for mutual understanding, since only in this way can 'the world hope to progress'. A council member then asks: 'What is progress [*shinpo*]?' Harris' response is revealing: 'It can mean many things', he suggests, yet offers a specific example: 'Among them', he says, 'not having to kill girl babies in time of famine'. This drastic example works to position America (who Harris represents) as being 'ahead' in its management of society; yet, crucially, what gets left unsaid is the far more interesting line that 'progress can mean many things'. We never get to see what other things progress can mean and whether there are alternative forms, rather than just one kind of progress. Does it include Japan's own sense of progress—would that be allowed within the 'many things' that Harris suggests progress can mean?

The view of Japan as a laggard is certainly rather short-sighted, both in cultural and economic terms. As Lambourne (2005: 7) notes:

> We have come to realize more and more that Japan's relations with the outside world were the result of a gradual, complex process. The fall of an imaginary 'bamboo curtain' in 1858 has analogies with the breakdown of the Iron Curtain and the fall of the Berlin Wall in our own time. In each case curiosity concerning events in the outside world provided the motivation that eventually led to the fall of restrictions and prohibitions.

It is easily forgotten, for example, that while Japan did remain closed off to much of the world's emerging markets, it nonetheless chose to maintain controlled trading with China, Korea, Holland and the neighbouring islands, Ainu and the Ry ky Kingdom (both now part of modern Japan). Robertson (1992: 85-96), in his study on globalisation, goes against the received view to suggest we view Japan's 'isolation' as a 'globally oriented gesture'. As a period of 'world watching', he argues, the Tokugowa period (1603–1868) can be reappraised as a time of 'preparation for the extensive global involvement of the twentieth century and beyond'.

Robertson is writing at a time, in the early 1990s, which had seen Japan's dramatic economic boom, making it the focus of a great deal of attention. Of specific interest was Japan's 'virtual uniqueness' in maintaining a 'high degree of careful selectivity concerning what is to be accepted or rejected from without' (Robertson 1992: 90). Robertson's (1992: 20) critical interest is in how a country—'the epitome of insularity and post-primitive mechanical solidarity'—had become such a key player on the world stage *without* relinquishing its specific characteristics. Yet, by the year 2003, a year named by Japanese business commentators as the first year of corporate social responsibility (CSR)—*CSR gannen*—this interest in the country's 'virtual uniqueness' appeared to have waned (Fukukawa and Teramoto 2009). Japan is seen more readily to be a late adopter of CSR practice. One might correlate this view with the fact that a number of high profile scandals were being exposed from the late 1990s onwards (see Tsalikis and Seaton 2008), leading to the view that Japanese corporations held no firm moral compass and that it would only be the adoption and auditing of CSR practices that might revive the business world. Arguably, however, this is an overly simplistic view, with business ethics having been deeply woven into the running of business–society in Japan over centuries.

This chapter looks towards a genealogical method, which in philosophy refers to a historical technique concerned with the *grounds* upon which beliefs, narratives and discourse in any given period are both held together and resisted. In trying to account for the wider scope or breadth of meaning (or ideology) within a given time period, the genealogical method presents a critique of singular or dominant ideologies. More particularly, drawing on the work of Michel Foucault, genealogy relates to a critical task, to look *beyond* a given ideology, for the conditions of possibility:

> … if [the genealogist] listens to history, he finds that there is 'something altogether different' behind things: not a timeless and essential secret, but the secret that they have no essence or that their essence was fabricated in a piecemeal fashion from alien forms. […] What is found at the historical beginning of things is not the inviolable identity of their origin; it is the dissension of other things. It is disparity (Foucault 1984: 78-79).

To illustrate Foucault's conception of history, and historical analysis, we can consider an image evoked by the photographer and theorist Victor Burgin (1996: 184). He describes the phenomenon of joining or (mis)layering histories as 'the assembly of simultaneously present events, but whose separate origins and durations are out of phase, historically overlapping'. This, he suggests, is the 'imbricated time of our global lived space'. He takes the metaphor from Freud, who used it as a warning against explaining one part of the manifest dream by another 'as though the dream had been coherently conceived and was a logically arranged narrative' when, on the contrary, it is 'like a piece of breccia, composed of various fragments of rock held together by a binding medium, so that the designs that appear on it do not belong to the original rocks imbedded in it' (cited in Burgin 1996: 178). Imbricated time is another way of alerting us to the dilemmas of historiography. In order to better understand our history/change, we need to get past the all too obvious narratives that pull things together and instead get in amongst the original 'rocks', to dislodge what so readily binds them. The propensity to see transitions and transformations (as if we are leading to a kind of final development or progress) needs to be tempered.

Contemporary Japanese business–society

As noted, 2003 is generally regarded the first official year of CSR in Japan—apparently alerting us to another (if less dramatic) 'opening up' of Japan to the West. In looking at the transition period 2002–2003 leading up to the so-called *CSR gannen*, Fukukawa and Moon (2004) investigated the extent and character of CSR in Japan through analysis of CSR reporting on websites of the top 50 corporations in autumn 2002. The study showed significant growth in the interests and engagements in CSR activities among Japanese multinational enterprises (MNEs), a marked increase in comparison to an earlier study by Yamagami and Kokubu (1991). One of the driving factors for Japanese corporations engaging in CSR practices was a relationship between business and society specific to the Japanese context. Experiences of corporate scandals and corporate environmental damages weakened confidence in the society's perception of the business community. This led corporations to need to announce their (re-)commitment to 'co-habitation' [*kyōsei*] with society. As the then head of Keidanren described in one newspaper report: 'Companies are a member of society, and without trust of the society they cannot exist' (cited in Fukukawa and Moon 2004: 58).

As early as 2000, the wider societal and corporate governance norms on 'good corporate behaviours' were more explicitly pronounced by a series of authoritative bodies including governmental ministries, business associations and universities, all helping to drive and shape CSR practice. This added strength in promoting the close co-ordination of corporate strategy and national government policy (Fukukawa and Moon 2004: 47-48). Demand for Japanese corporations to engage with a wider sense of responsibility was coming not only from the domestic scene but also from overseas; for example due to the increased popularity for socially responsible investment (SRI).[1] Today, of course, most large corporations have established dedicated units that deal specifically with the promotion of CSR-related activities, including compliance, correspondence for the SRI index survey, CSR reporting and so forth; with compliance and environmental commitment remaining firmly on the agenda (see Fukukawa and Teramoto 2009). For some it would seem Japanese managers have been exposed to new, unfamiliar territory. Others, however, ask a more critical question about what values can be globally shared and pursued. Yet, in answering such a question, it is important to understand how concepts and practices are translated into different contexts and to what extent CSR should be seen to be either a singular or heterogeneous set of practices and beliefs.

The complexity and difficulty of bringing a largely Western-led concept into the Japanese context is marked by two important features specific to Japanese business. First, the manner of communication within high-context cultures such as Japan has been a long-standing point of interest for international business.[2] Second, and

---

1 Inevitably, with internationalisation, Japanese corporations have been more widely exposed to the idea of CSR, particularly in the Western context. New experiences in global markets and operations brought new opportunities to learn about the scope and nature of CSR agenda items and, subsequently, Japanese corporations began to satisfy CSR expectations in various new host countries, as well as importing the idea of CSR into their domestic operations (Lewin *et al.* 1995: 83-84).

2 According to Hall (1987), however, Japan is characterised as a high-context culture where 'close relationships are critical to effective communication because a message cannot be understood without its social context, which conveys important information such as the sender's values, personal background and corporate position' (cited in Lohtia *et al.* 2005: 1010). The characteristics of communication in high-context cultures immediately raise a challenge when adapting to more formal means of CSR reporting. Within high-context culture, words can seemingly carry less emphatic meaning. In addition, exercises in reporting and auditing can be seen to go entirely against the Japanese virtue of the 'quiet

perhaps rather more fundamentally, there is important philosophical discourse and cultural history of business–society relations. Japanese companies have long been associated with the formation of community, forming the basis of society to which an individual employee belongs. Thus, in Japan—in contrast to an Anglo-American model of community—*both* individuals and companies are members of society and hence responsible to it (Tange 2001: 102). For example, 'national champions' of business have tended to maintain close and supportive relations with their suppliers (known as *Keiretsu* or 'affiliates') which makes for relative stability in employment patterns and business relations with particular communities. Dore (1993) characterises business–society relations in Japan as being *solidaristic*; more akin, for example, to the German model than to the Anglo-American model. Dore, then, contrasts the Anglo-American 'property view' with the Japanese 'employee community view'. Thus, it is argued, in Japan, the individual devotes themselves to contributing to the wealth of society as a whole. While in the Anglo-American context the individual works to serve their own wellbeing which is located within the society. The difference is between a solidaristic and individualistic formation of society. In the Japanese context, while the welfare of individuals is taken to be extremely important (with businesses themselves providing much of the social framework within which they live), emphasis is placed upon the holistic relationship *between* individuals. The problem with such an emphasis is that it can miss out on some of the detail that is often expected of CSR reporting, as practised and imposed by the West.

Japanese values: a genealogy

In one study of CSR in Japan, Fukukawa and Teramoto (2009) found growing acknowledgement among Japanese managers of the importance of rebuilding trust by letting the public/society know more about a company and what it does. Given advancements in information technology and the pervasiveness of media reporting, one manager notes that even if a company does not say anything about its practice, the company is still open to debate and speculation. Another manager comments specifically on the notion of 'responsibility', which typically is translated as '*sekinin*', but suggests it is more appropriate to translate it as '*(sōgo) taiō*', meaning 'a (mutual) response to work together'.

In the years following the so-called *CSR gannen*, a shift can be witnessed from traditional, implicit forms of communication to the more explicit 'walk the talk' [*yūgen hujikko*] style of reporting associated with Western CSR. This period for

---

man of action' [*hūgen jikkō*]. Similarly, there is hesitancy among Japanese businesses to be seen to 'walk the talk' [*yūgen jikkō*]. There is still a strong belief in 'good karma' [*intokuyōhō*], whereby if you keep to good practices without needing to draw attention to the fact, the returns are more rewarding. There is, then, a perceived problem that CSR reporting itself can be taken as an unnecessary or even vulgar marketing tool.

the Japanese economy is clearly characterised as a moment in which progress is sought due to various *internal* drivers (due to various corporate scandals, and the 'lost decade' on from the bursting of the economic bubble). Yet solutions are drawn from *external* sources (cf. Nakamura 2011), in this case models of CSR drawn from a Western-led discourse, with philosophical and ideological underpinnings rooted in Anglo-American and European principles of liberal democratic rights, justice and societal structures. This can seem a very contemporary set of occurrences, in line with the forces of globalisation. However, if we take *CSR gannen* as simply one of a series of 'events' in Japanese business history, with progress prompting change and renewal, we can reveal a richer philosophical underpinning. The following brief history of Japanese business ethics foregrounds three instances of transition or transposition:

1. The incorporation of Buddhism (from the 6th century CE), which led to the reception of multiple ethical principles

2. The Edo era (1603–1868), during which time the country famously closed its borders, arguably allowing for a period of consolidation (and differentiation)

3. The Meiji restoration (1868–1912), when the country was forced to open again to outside trade

Through each of these periods we might suggest the sentiment of *taiō* (a response to work together), which is reminiscent of the language used today by Keidanren in its statement 'Toward a More Resilient Society' (Keidanren 2012) and which underlines Japan's particular 'Asian values' with respect to business–society relations.

Adaptation and co-existence

Robertson's (1992: 90) term of 'virtual uniqueness' to describe Japan's particularity in accepting or rejecting external elements can be viewed in several ways. We could suggest that a stringent process of selectivity acts as a filter, ensuring that what is distinctive about Japanese culture remains the dominant force. In other words Japan remains virtually (i.e. almost) unique. We might equally consider selection to be a creative process, whereby new elements are not only accepted but are combined or adapted in ways that leads to the creation of new qualities or significance. Through inventiveness, then, existing elements take on new or virtually unique properties. The Japanese have a term, '*eetokodori*', meaning 'taking only good parts' (see Sakaiya 2006: 40-45), which goes some way to describe this idea of generating unique characteristics through adaptation and refinement. Alternatively, the word 'virtual' could be read in terms of 'simulation', as something not in actual existence. As such, 'it might seem that Japan has drawn eclectically from a variety of traditions without any inherent sense of intellectual direction' (Kasulis 2000: 416). On closer inspection, however, the view generally taken is that, 'Japanese thinkers have seldom adopted any foreign philosophy without simultaneously adapting it' (Kasulis 2000: 416). Thus, however one considers Robertson's observation of 'virtual uniqueness', the underlying propensity is for adaptation and co-existence, which traces back to the country's early history; and specifically its mixed religious tradition.

Various religious beliefs have come to co-exist in Japan, most notably a combination of Buddhism, Shinto and Confucius teachings. Shinto is the Indigenous religious tradition and, in many senses, 'is the underlying value orientation of the Japanese people, forming the basis of the divergent and yet uniquely Japanese sensitivities, religious beliefs, and attitudes' (Bowker 1997: 892). The origins of Shinto are unrecorded, 'it has no founder, no official sacred scriptures, and no fixed system of doctrine' (Bowker 1997: 892). With no specific articulation of doctrine and ethics, Shinto has perhaps been uniquely open to the infusion of other religious beliefs. Yet, importantly, grounded in the notion of ancestral spirits, known as *kami*, Shinto provides a deep-level belief in community and exchange:

> ... it is a religion of participation in traditional rites and festivals in the shrine setting and, by extension, in the household. ... Important in worship at the shrine are rituals which bring about purification from defilements and which foster an integration of human life with the life-bearing power of the kami ... Shinto stresses the importance of gratefulness for the blessings of the kami and the benefits of the ancestors. Humans, like nature, are children of the kami and thus inherently good when defilements are removed and the original purity is restored. Humans received their sacred life from the kami and from the ancestors, together with all the blessings life involves. Their purpose in life is to contribute to the vital development of existence as it is entrusted to them and to realize the will of the kami and the ancestors as this pertains to the family, the community, and the nation. Shinto is thus a 'this-worldly' religion, in the sense that it is interested in tangible benefits which will promote life in this human world (Bowker 1997: 892-93).

Nevertheless, attempts to identify Japan's selectivity with its Shinto roots encounters two problems. First, Shinto is not recorded in any formal ways, so historically it appears less dominant. The Shotoku Constitution, for example, is the earliest political document of Japan and draws on borrowed religious doctrines. The document 'reflects the influences of Confucianism, Buddhism, Daoism and Legalism in its various provisions; it is strongly marked by Chinese thought rather than being influenced by Shinto' (Craig 2000: 827). Second, 'Shinto itself has also been profoundly shaped by foreign influences. The selection process has shaped Shinto as much as Shinto has shaped it' (Kasulis 2000: 416). During the 6th century, Prince Shotoku Taishi was a supporter of the introduction of Buddhism. Japanese agriculture at this time was evolving rapidly, with the land improved by water utilisation and deep ploughing. Such technological development lay behind Japan's shift from city-states to regional-states, and was bound up with the importing of Chinese know-how, ideologies and religions. Japan's unique ability to allow multiple religions (ideologies) to co-exist can in part be traced back to Shotoku Taishi's promotion of Buddhism, which was a necessary part of access to new technologies from China and Korea. In effect, the importing of the new religion was part and parcel of maintaining access to the new technology. In this way, Shotoku Taishi successfully brought Buddhism into the mainstream Indigenous (social/political) environment (Sakaiya 2006: 24-48). Again, this is an example of the notion of *eetokodori* (taking only good parts). Indeed, co-existence was encouraged with Buddhist temples being built next to Shinto shrines.

The confluence of Shinto, Buddhism and Confucius can be understood as bringing into dialogue the concerns of both the individual (in society) and society as a collective gathering. Shinto is a form of worship for the purpose of protecting a community (the collective) such as tribes and villages against bad luck. By contrast, Buddhism and Confucius relate more readily to the status of the individual (hence many Japanese hold Buddhist funerals). Thus, Buddhism and Confucius address the importance of morality and wellbeing, while Shinto is based on the value of community and the (environmental) natural forces in which the community lives together. The introduction of Buddhist and Confucius teachings brought a new moral and political dimension to a formerly collective, agricultural economy; yet this mapped onto rather than effaced the significance of Shintoism, which continued to provide a unique articulation of the individual, society and resources. In modern terms, we might suggest that Shinto's 'sense of world', which pertains to cosmological and 'spirited' forces, offers a greatly expanded notion of 'stakeholders'; it is concerned not simply with what suits an individual or even the community, but with what concerns the purpose (and spirit) of the object and/or land in and of itself. There is an echo in the contemporary context of the same process of inscription of one philosophy or ideology onto another. Adopting the discourse (or ideology) of CSR was necessary in a global economy in order to maintain certain 'technologies' of corporate governance and business ethics. Today, however, we might question the degree to which different viewpoints can co-exist in the way Shinto came to exist within Buddhism and Confucius. The discourse of CSR, for example, is far less flexible in the way it meets with different practices around the world.

Edo era

The Edo era (1603–1868) is famously the period during which the country was closed to the outside world. With respect to business ethics two schools of thought took root, one of which came from a commercial background, the *Ohmi* merchants; the other a more systematic, academic approach associated with the writings of Ishida Baigan. Teramoto (2006) reflects on the *Ohmi* merchants of the mid-Edo era (1700s) and their principle of '*sanpō yoshi*', which translates as 'good on all sides', specifically of a three-way relationship between the buyer, the seller and society.

Ohmi merchants were known for their business acumen, but also for the practice of their own unique managerial creed of *sanpō yoshi*. One merchant, Nakamura Jihei Sōgan (1684–1757), offers a lucid account of this creed in a letter to his grandchild: 'even when you huckster to another country, you do not only think about yourself but also care about every person in the country, and do not act out of your own interest. If one does so, one's heart becomes peaceful and it is good for one's health. It is important not to forget about gods and Buddha' (cited in Teramoto 2006: 128-29). As part of the creed, it was not that using money was one thing and earning money another, but that these transactions were of an inseparable relationship. In order to use personal fortune in a 'clean way' it was necessary to have a clean method of earning it. The same principle, according to Teramoto, is at stake in contemporary CSR practices (Teramoto 2006: 128-29). Of course, today, as Japanese businesses seek to come to terms with CSR as a concept and a set of practices, it is evident they are dealing not just with their own internal, local and historically informed interests, but with an entirely globalised phenomenon.

Concurrent but separate to the ideas of the *Ohmi* merchants, Ishida Baigan (1685–1744) espoused a moral education, referred to as '*Sekimon Shingaku*' ('Heart Learning'), which he sought to popularise among the lower classes. In the city of Kyoto, he taught ethical living to townspeople [*chonin*], including craftsmen [*shokunin*] and merchants [*shonin*]. *Chonin* were recognised as the lower classes in the Edo caste system (warriors ranked at the top, followed by farmers, craftsmen and merchants). *Sekimon Shingagu* addressed two aspects of merchant ethics: frugality [*kenyaku*]; and a combination of honesty [*shojiki*] and diligence/hard work [*kinben*]. *Kenyaku* refers to a mindfulness for the value of things and of avoiding wastage, as well as selfless action without personal greed. Honesty and diligence relate to hard work within business, as well as fairness. 'Baigan felt that a reasonable profit for merchants was legitimate, and equivalent to the stipend that samurai received, but he felt the basic calling of the merchant was to render service to society, not to maximize profit at the expense of all other considerations' (Bellah 2000).

In *Tokugawa Religion: The Values of Pre-Industrial Japan*, Bellah (1957) makes a comparison between the ideas of Baigan and Weber's Protestant ethic. As Nosco (1994: 441) explains, Bellah's analysis of this period marks 'the first attempt in English to describe the spiritual vitality of the *chonin* in general and urban merchants in particular, with specific attention to those values that provided meaning to the quotidian'. The argument put forward is that the tendency of the Tokugawa period to privilege the values of diligence or hard work [*kinben*] and frugality [*kenyaku*] contributed to the economic rationalism so favourable to Japan's modernisation, in the same way that an 'inner-wordly asceticism' in Protestantism contributed in fundamental ways to the modern economic development of Europe (Nosco 1994: 441). Of crucial importance for Baigan 'was a good form of life to which the economy contributes, but which the economy does not dominate'; thus, drawing on teachings from Confucianism, Buddhism and Shinto, 'what Baigan was most concerned with would seem to [be] a sense of larger meaning and an understanding that it is through our connectedness with others that we are fulfilled' (Bellah 2000). The obvious dilemma, however, lay between an industrious diligence [*kinben*] on the one hand, and honourable poverty [*seihin*] on the other (Sakaiya 2006: 229). Within Japanese Zen practice, which equally had its place at this time, the emphasis is upon honourable poverty. In Zen, sitting still for three years like a *daruma* doll (Buddhist talisman) is considered respectable (i.e. the propensity is not to engage in hard work *in the world* of productive activities). Zen might be appropriate for an individual, but it does not easily sustain a community. Thus, echoing the Protestant ethic, in which productivity is a virtue, Baigan proposed an ethic of hard work. It is worth noting that an assumption 'of those days which influenced [the dissertation] *Tokugawa Religion* was that the key issue was economic development, that if economy were sufficiently advanced everything else would take care of itself' (Bellah 2000).

During the middle Edo era, when Baigan is teaching hard work [*kinben*] *and* honourable poverty [*seihin*] for the *chonin* class, technological advances and resources were limited. Hence, the teachings manifested in part with a specific concern for an 'attention to detail'—putting maximum effort/labour into minimum resources. Baigan was in fact 'one of many who were opening up new possibilities of social and cultural life in the midst of the Tokugawa Period' (Bellah 2000). More specifically, Baigan, among others, represented an important difference between the country being closed and a general spirit of openness to ideas and technologies:

> ... in the midst of the period of the closed country (*sakoku*) there was a remarkable spirit of open country (*kaikoku*). What was important was not the source of the ideas—whether they came from India or China or the West—but how they could help in thinking through problems of the day—scientific, economic, social or spiritual. We might almost say that although Baigan lived under the repressive and closed Tokugawa regime, he was surrounded by the spirit of *kaikokushugi* (openness) (Bellah 2000).

To this day, such openness is often observed as a distinctive trait of Japanese industry (and again relates to a propensity to adapt and modify rather than simply adopt). Of course, while the spirit of 'attention to detail' remains, the higher costs of production are reflected in Japanese products, which puts a strain on competiveness—especially in a global market (Sakaiya 2006: 231-32). Today, globalisation is most often claimed as the key driver for Japanese MNEs adopting a new 'managerial creed'. Yet, this view needs to be tempered through consideration of the Edo era. Despite the country being closed to the rest of world, this period reveals specific philosophical and ethical principles that raise questions about viewing Japan as simply a latecomer.

Meiji restoration

The Meiji restoration (1868–1912) follows from the time the country is forced to open again to outside trade. The country undergoes dramatic transformation in all spheres of life and class hierarchy is de-emphasised (visually, for example, the samurai class, who had previously held power, no longer distinguished themselves by the carrying of a sword; and merchants, craftspeople and farmers were no longer categorised into separate classes). These changes were symbolic of key political and economic changes, not least the move towards capitalism. Of note, the industrialist Shibusawa Eiichi (1840–1931) is one key figure associated with the introduction of Western capitalism to Japan after the Meiji restoration.

Shibusawa is attributed with introducing important economic and administrative reforms, including use of double entry accounting, joint stock corporations and modern note-issuing banks (Odagiri *et al.* 1996: 72-73); indeed he founded the first modern bank, The First National Bank (Dai Ichi Kokuritsu Ginkō), now called Mizuho Bank, which today remains one of the major high-street banks in Japan. Shibusawa's progressive influence extended beyond the financial sector. He was involved in the foundation of hospitals, schools and universities (including the first women's university), and various charitable organisations including the Japan Red Cross (Odagiri *et al.* 1996: 72-73). However, despite the explicit influence of the West (with visits to much of Europe etc), Shibusawa maintained direct links with the philosophies of the Edo era. In his book *Rongo to Soroban* (written in 1916), the principles of *sanpō yoshi* and *Sekimon Shingaku* remain pronounced. The title of the book translates as 'The Analects of Confucius and the Abacus' (the latter standing for economics). In modern terms, *Rongo to Soroban* can be interpreted as a teaching of sustainability, whereby morality (based on the Analects) and economy (Abacus) should be 'two wheels of one cart' (Shibusawa 2010).

Shibusawa's philosophy lies at the root of Kōnosuke Matsushita's philosophy—the founder of Matsushita Electric Industrial Co Ltd in 1918 (known today as the Panasonic Corporation). However, despite a sense of progress linking both Shibusawa and Matsushita, an important difference of style emerges. Matsushita's is more obviously considered a successor of Iwasaki, an entrepreneur contemporary with Shibusawa. Between these two figures notable of the Meiji restoration is a growing differentiation of business ethics:

> Shibusawa's idea was to incorporate and get along with everyone. He believed that a specific company excelling in producing things cheaply would make the rest suffer. Thus, someone who is accommodating should become a leader and make an effort in coordinating within the company. There remain two types of managers after World War Two—Shibusawa's type and Iwasaki's type. Iwasaki's idea of how one can contribute to a society was to excel in one's ability in growing a company. Matsushita's ideas are considered to be in line with that of Iwasaki (Sakaiya 2006: 298-99).

At stake is a difference between two schools of thought; what Abe (1997: 299-300) refers to as 'managerial capitalism' (typical of the USA, and evident in Iwasaki's business philosophy and practice) and 'group-enterprise capitalism'. The former relates to the rise of professional managers and the separation between managers and owners of a company. Following World War II, Japan moves increasingly to this form of business practice, but it is relatively late in comparison to the West, and has its own distinctive evolution (Abe 1997).

The opening of the country, so defining of the Meiji period again reveals a tension between individual and society, as well as between productivity and ethics. The revered novelist Sōseki Natsume reflects on these concerns, and in a way that is inextricably bound to the opening of the country. Like Shibusawa, Natsume gains direct experience of the West, in his case with a visit to England. In a frequently quoted speech, 'My Individualism', which he delivered in 1914 to the students of the Gakushūin (an elite academy of the upper classes), he broaches the concept of individualism, which was of growing interest. His thoughts (drawn through literary analysis) express clear sympathies with that of the political economist Adam Smith; with both interested in the confluence of economy and morality (Natsume 1995: 36-37). We could argue—with access to new ideas and the affordance of a new level of expression granted from the opening up of the country—Natsume's writings are merely derivative of existing work. It is certainly the case that he similarly recognises rights and responsibilities as being inseparably bound together—and indeed evokes a Kantian view when he states: 'when we talk about perfecting our individuality, we must take account of that of others by considering and respecting it' (Natsume 2004: 48).

Yet, equally, as a scholar of English literature (and as a novelist himself), Natsume exhibits a very different style of engagement. As an essayist (and public speaker) he is deliberately provocative, and his line of thought is punctuated with numerous digressions. Where Adam Smith offers a rational account of the importance of a strong moral compass and of long-range thinking, Soseki Natsume weaves a more impressionistic account, and draws on darker themes in writing about issues of confidence and identity. In 'My Individualism' he appears to 'bring back' from England a clear notion of duty (as part of a philosophy of freedom and individualism), yet he retains ambivalence towards the country:

> To tell the truth, I do not like England very much, but in spite of this, I must allow it one thing, reluctantly: probably, in no other part of the world, are the people both as free and as policed. Japan, for example, cannot claim to compare with it. But the English are not only free: from childhood, society inculcates in them a love of freedom and, at the same time, a respect for the freedom of others. For this reason, their notion of freedom is accompanied implicitly by the idea of duty. Nelson's famous words: 'England expects that every man will do his duty', are not limited in their significance to the context of the period. They reflect a firmly established conviction that has developed in strict association with the idea of freedom: duty and freedom are two sides of the same coin (Natsume 2004: 48-49).

We hardly need concern ourselves with the accuracy of these observations, rather as a form of inverse 'orientatalism' we learn more about Natsume himself and his own context. For Natsume, 'the problem was less that of Western ideas than of the Meiji incarnation of modernity that dissolved earlier links of self and society while denying the individual any meaningful independence from the nation-state' (de Bary *et al.* 2001: 1162-63). The close of 'My Individualism' leads out to a delicate balance between patriotism and individualism. He maintains wariness on both sides. Nationhood he equates with a 'low level of morality', while 'if we take the perspective of individualism, then the importance of morality increases considerably' (Natsume 2004: 57). Natsume is attuned to a 'modern' problem of the Self—as bearing a split subjectivity. On the one hand the individual is freed from authority, tyranny and dogma, yet that same freedom raises questions about how to live together. As recently as the year 2000, the Japanese government was wrestling with these same issues. A commissioned report focused on the 'empowerment of the individual', alert to the idea that the '21st century will be the era of individuals. Individuals have become more important through globalization, the Internet, networking' (cited in Bellah 2000). At the same time, of course, the 'radical individualism' of countries such as America is being questioned (cf. Bellah *et al.* 1985; Putnam 2000). As Bellah (2000) puts it: '... while too much individualism is bad for Americans, Japanese don't have enough of it', though equally he points out, 'individualism is not something you can just turn on until you get the right amount and then turn it off again. Unless it is located in a strong ethical context and a sense of community obligation ... it undermines all forms of social connectedness and cultural meaning'. Thus, Bellah contends, 'for the Japanese to become more individualistic in a healthy way would require thinking carefully about the ethical and social context' (Bellah 2000).

Running through the key historical moments outlined here is a distinctively Japanese articulation of the Self (and society). Inevitably, there is a strong inflexion through Buddhist teachings. As Stambaugh (1999: xi) explains: 'One of the few utterances traceable to the Buddha himself involves the statement that all things are without self', which leads to the idea that ultimately we "suffer" because there is no such thing as a permanently enduring self. In fact, one of the lasting insights of the Buddha is that there is no enduring self in anyone or anything at all'. Natsume does not reflect any overt religious teachings, yet it would be hard to view his writings without considering the religious and philosophical context of Japan, which is typically very much part of the 'everyday' culture. The religious context of Japan is indeed central to the various accounts noted in this chapter, and to a proper understanding of so-called 'Asian values' in the Japanese context. As Bellah (2000) notes, 'there is a relationship between religious teachings and economic development', so that 'it is a mistake to view religion as simply the means for economic growth'. What is distinctive about the religious context of Japan is its openness to difference and co-existence. The result can often appear as ambivalence. Such ambivalence underlies Natsume's argument for an individualism 'grounded in the self that depended on neither Western referents nor the Japanese nation' (de Bary *et al.* 2001: 1169). And it is this same sort of ambivalence that today has arguably been the problem for how Japanese companies are 'seen' to have adapted/adopted CSR.

Conclusion

There is an obvious dilemma in placing, in such short succession, a series of rich historical moments. In expounding on historical method, Foucault is clear in saying: '[G]enealogy does not pretend to go back in time to restore an unbroken continuity'. Indeed, quite the opposite:

> ... to follow the complex course of descent is to maintain passing events in their proper dispersion; it is to identify the accidents, the minute deviations—or conversely, the complete reversals—the errors, the false appraisals, and the faulty calculations that gave birth to those things that continue to exist and have value for us; it is to discover that truth or being does not lie at the root of what we know and we are, but the exteriority of accidents (Foucault 1984: 81).

If we adopt a metaphor of water as it charts a course through the environment over many years, there are specific factors (such as impermeable rock) that will lead water to flow in particular ways. Yet, there are always other less determinable factors. As Foucault notes: 'heritage is [not] an acquisition, a possession that grows and solidifies; rather, it is an unstable assemblage of faults, fissures, and heterogeneous layers that threaten the fragile inheritor from within or from underneath' (Foucault 1984: 82). This chapter has sought to bring into play a confluence of differing factors past and present. There are key elements to consider (those impermeable rocks) such as Japan's religious and philosophical traditions and its relationship (and closure) to the rest of the world. But as we pick over the 'rocks' we do not find merely an unfolding path towards progress, but rather a series of undulating tensions regarding the individual and society and the ethics of commerce.

In reflecting back on the question posed in *The Barbarian and the Geisha*—'What is progress?'—and ask what progress is today, it can again mean many things. Following the financial crisis of 2008 and subsequent economic uncertainty, there has been an appetite for the recalibration of what we mean by 'progress' within and through capitalism. As Kidd and Ritcher (2010: 153) have pointed out in the context of CSR in Asia, just as 'trust is important where laws are poorly drafted and contracts are not easily enforced by law', so Asian firms should not necessarily 'rush to copy a "Western model" but try to use their own traditional elements'. Importantly, then, they note how it is not sufficient 'to say those in Asia "ought to be faster" or those in the West "ought to be slower" as these are too simplistic and serve only to make headlines that disguise the realities that people do try to accommodate one another'. Potentially, what is all too easily lost is the means of 'trusting to trust', a process that takes time and care to mature (Kidd and Ritcher 2010: 156-57). Historically, Japan has been, and largely remains, an insular and solidaristic society. Superficially, this has meant Japan appears a latecomer with regard to global agendas, such as CSR. As noted, it is only since 2003 that any formal and explicit attention has been given to the concept. Yet the longer view of history reveals the values of Japanese business–society are such that many of the interests and concerns we associate with contemporary business ethics have long been embedded. Japan can be seen to adapt business ethics to suit the needs of *both* the local and global context in equal measure, though arguably, along the way, the rhetoric of Japanese business ethics has gradually lessened its emphasis on a religious and philosophical tradition that goes back over centuries.

References

Abe, E. (1997) 'The Development of Modern Business in Japan', *Business History Review* 77.2: 299-308.

Bellah, R.N. (1957) *Tokugawa Religion: The Values of Pre-industrial Japan* (New York: The Free Press).

Bellah, R.N. (2000) 'Symposium on the 270th Anniversary of the Founding of Shingaku, Shingaku and 21st Century Japan', an address given in Kyoto, Japan (15 October 2000; www.robertbellah.com/articles_4.htm, accessed on 4 March 2013).

Bellah, R.N., R. Madsen, W.M. Sullivan, A. Swindler and S.M. Tipton (1985) *Habits of the Heart: Individualism and Commitment in American Life* (Berkeley, CA: University of California Press).

Bowker, J. (1997) *The Oxford Dictionary of World Religions* (Oxford, UK: Oxford University Press).

Burgin, V. (1996) *Different Spaces: Place and Memory in Visual Culture* (Berkeley and Los Angeles, CA: University of California Press).

Craig, E. (2000) *Concise Routledge Encyclopedia of Philosophy* (Oxford, UK: Routledge).

de Bary, T., C. Gluck and A. Tiedemann (eds.) (2001) *Sources of Japanese Tradition: Volume 2, 1600 to 2000* (New York: Columbia University Press).

Dore, R. (1993) 'What Makes Japan Different?' in C. Crouch and D. Marquand (eds.), *Ethics and Markets: Cooperation and Competition Within Capitalist Economies* (London: Political Quarterly).

Foucault, F. (1984) 'Nietzsche, Genealogy, History', in P. Rabinow (ed.), *The Foucault Reader* (New York: Pantheon Books): 76-100.

Fukukawa, K., and J. Moon (2004) 'A Japanese Model of Corporate Social Responsibility? A Study of Website Reporting', *Journal of Corporate Citizenship* 16: 45-59.

Fukukawa, K., and Y. Teramoto (2009) 'Understanding Japanese CSR: The Reflection of Managers in the Field of Global Operations', *Journal of Business Ethics* 85: 133-46.

Fukuyama, F. (1989) 'The End of History?' *The National Interest* 16 (Summer): 3-18.

Goodpaster, K.E. (2007) *Conscience and Corporate Culture* (Oxford, UK: Blackwell Publishing).

Hall, E.T. (1987) *Hidden Differences: Doing Business with the Japanese* (New York: Anchor Press/Doubleday).

Kasulis, T.P. (2000) 'Japanese Philosophy', in E. Craig (ed.), *Concise Routledge Encyclopedia of Philosophy* (London: Routledge): 415-16.

Keidanren (2012) 'Toward a More Resilient Society' (5 March 2012; www.keidanren.or.jp/en/policy/2012/013.html, accessed 2 July 2012).

Kidd, J., and F-J. Ritcher (2010) 'CSR: Virtuous Circle. But Which Circle? And Whose "Virtue"?', in K. Fukukawa (ed.), *Corporate Social Responsibility in Asia* (Oxford, UK: Routledge).

Lambourne, L. (2005) *Japonisme: Cultural Crossings Between Japan and the West* (London: Phaidon Press).

Lewin, A.Y., T. Sakano, C.U. Stephens and B. Victor (1995) 'Corporate Citizenship in Japan: Survey Results from Japanese Firms', *Journal of Business Ethics* 14: 83-101.

Lohtia, R., D.C. Bello, T. Yamada and D.I. Gilliland (2005) 'The Role of Commitment in Foreign–Japanese Relationships: Mediating Performance for Foreign Sellers in Japan', *Journal of Business Research* 58: 1009-18.

Nakamura, M. (2011) 'Adoption and Policy Implications of Japan's New Corporate Governance Practices After the Reform', *Asia Pacific Journal of Management* 28: 187-213.

Natsume, S. (1995) 'Eikoku Shijin no Tenchisansen ni taisuru Kannen' [The Notion of English Poets about Nature], in *Sōseki Zenshū Vol. 13: Eibungaku Kenkyū* [*Sōseki Collected Works Vol. 13: Studies on English Literature*] (Tokyo: Iwanami Shoten): 21-60.

Natsume, S. (2004) *My Individualism and the Philosophical Foundations of Literature* [translated by S.I. Tsunematsu] (Boston, MA: Tuttle Publishing).

Nosco, P. (1994) 'Confucian Values and Popular Zen: Sekimon Shingaku in Eighteenth-Century Japan by Janine Anderson Sawada' [Book Review] *Japanese Journal of Religious Studies* 21.4: 441-42.

Odagiri, H., A. Goto and R.R. Nelson (1996) *Technology and Industrial Development in Japan* (Oxford, UK: Oxford University Press).

Putnam, R.D. (2000) *Bowling Alone: The Collapse and Revival of American Community* (New York: Simon & Schuster).

Robertson, R. (1992) *Globalisation: Social Theory and Global Culture* (London: Sage Publications).

Sakaiya, T. (2006) *Nihon wo Tsukutta Juninin* [*Twelve People Who Made Japan*] (Tokyo: PHP Bunko).

Shibusawa, K. (2010) 'Rongo to Soroban ni Manabu: Kigyō no Jizokukanōsei wo Mezasu Shinozawa Eiichi no Shisō to Kōdō' ['Learning from Confucius and Abacus: Eiichi Shinozawa's Ideology and Action in Pursuing Corporate Sustainability'], an address given at the 2nd Business Ethics Symposium, Japan Society for Business Ethics Study, in Tokyo, Japan, 26 January 2010.

Stambaugh, J. (1999) *The Formless Self* (New York: State University of New York Press).

Tange, H. (2001) *Kigyo Keiei no Syakaisei Kenkyu* [*A Study of the Social Nature of Corporate Management*] (Tokyo: Chuo Keiza sha).

Teramoto, Y. (2006) 'Seifu no Shisō [Thought of Honest Fortune]: Shizai no Tsukaimichi [The Way of Using Personal Fortune]—Nihon no Jissenshatachi [Japanese Practitioners], Edo Jidai Hen [Edo Period Canto]', *Nikkei Venture*, November: 128-31.

Tsalikis, J., and B. Seaton (2008) 'The International Business Ethics Index: Japan', *Journal of Business Ethics* 80: 379-85.

Yamagami, T., and K. Kokubu (1991) 'A Note on Corporate Social Disclosure in Japan', *Accounting Auditing and Accountability Journal* 4.4: 32-39.

Žižek, S. (2011a) *Living in the End of Times* (New York and London: Verso).

Žižek, S. (2011b) 'Capitalism with Asian Values', interview with Tom Ackerman, *Al Jazeera* (www.aljazeera.com/programmes/talktojazeera/2011/10/2011102813360731764.html, accessed 2 July 2012).

Kyoko Fukukawa specialises in research in CSR and ethical decision-making in consumption and business practices. She edited a book entitled *Corporate Social Responsibility in Asia* (2010). She was a Japanese Studies Fellow of the Japan Foundation in 2006 and conducted research on multinational companies to examine CSR practices in Japan. She is currently serving as an editorial board member of the *Asian Journal of Business Ethics*.

Sunil Manghani is Reader in Critical and Cultural Theory at Winchester School of Art, University of Southampton. UK. He teaches and writes on various aspects of critical theory, visual arts and image studies. He is author of *Image Studies: Theory and Practice* (2013) and *Image Critique and the Fall of the Berlin Wall* (2008), and editor of *Images: A Reader* (2006) and *Images: Critical and Primary Sources* (2013).

5

Occupation or action
Are they more or less than the sum of their parts?

Sara Parkin
Forum for the Future, London, UK

> If you do not expect the unexpected you will not find it: for it is hard to be
> searched out and difficult to compass (Heraclitus).

The sense that all is not right with our world is nothing new. Human history is laced with anxieties about our relationships with each other; anxieties that manifest themselves mostly in tribal-type conflicts—over land or other resources, kingdoms, cultures, ideologies. The machinations are only partly the consequence of a clinical desire for power; more often their root cause is a visceral fear of losing control—the inevitable consequence of being without power.

It was fear of losing control that held the Soviet bloc together until, that is, 1989 and the November 'velvet' revolutions. By the time Mikhail Gorbachev visited East Berlin for the 40th anniversary of the state in October of that year, citizens had already considered a key question: Is it government policy that we should live like this (without freedom, short of food, decent housing and basic household goods such as light bulbs or toilet paper) or is the state powerless to stop it? The answer—that the state had lost control of the economy—was widely understood; so when Gorbachev stepped into the crowds to whisper repeatedly, 'If you want democracy, take it now', his message was clear—he would not order Soviet tanks to crush any popular uprising. Fear of violence was removed. People lit candles and took to the streets.[1]

In South Africa, a similar combination of a popular movement (the African National Congress [ANC] led by Nelson Mandela) and a leadership (The National Party led by F.W. de Klerk) brokered a transition from white to black rule. In Eastern Europe and in South Africa, however, the economic regime promoted by Washington succeeded in constraining options for new economic systems in both places.

This chapter considers whether the current financial crisis will speed a transition to what Thomas Kuhn (2012) would recognise as a new paradigm, something that happens when real-life experience and observations conflict with the predictions of the current paradigm (business-as-usual). A consequent period of questioning anomalies and experimenting with new ideas eventually results in a 'new normal'. Although Kuhn was talking about the scientific process, there are obvious parallels in the inability of today's dominant economic paradigm (whether crafted by capitalist or socialist ideologies) to offer a 'solution' to the deepening global financial, social and ecological crises. This chapter will ask if the Occupy movement is sufficient stimulus to complete the transition to a 'new normal', and will consider whether lessons from 1989 on how to sustain political change once it is underway have been learnt by the 'green' movement.

I open with a scene-setting—why is a transition necessary and to where do we want to transit? As the political fall-out spreads from the crisis in the financial sector and the distorted/corrupt relationships between it, politicians, media and other large corporate interests into what (without apparent irony) is called the 'real' economy, how far can the parallels between 2012 and 1989 be drawn? What happened then, and what needs to happen now? Some key intervention points are explored by way of illustration.

Finally, what means do we have at our disposal to pursue the necessary transition we have outlined? What strategies and tools do we need? How can the green movement bring its ideas into power, and how can we be sure they are transformed into practical actions that, in themselves, sustain the transition into the long term?

Why is a transition necessary?

How much is too much?

The transition we are necessarily talking about means no less than an irreversible shift to a new way of living on Earth. So great are our absolute numbers and our

---

1 During the 1980s, as co-secretary of the European Greens (a co-ordination of green parties, europeangreens.eu), I travelled a lot in eastern European countries in support of the dissident/green movements and was in East Berlin before and shortly after the Wall came down.

impact on the Earth's natural systems, it has even been proposed that this era of geological time be re-named the Anthropocene.[2]

Table 5.1 illustrates some key trends in the impact of people on the Earth—demand for land, water, food, energy—in the last 40 years. Population growth, the great multiplier, has wiped out many gains, for example in reducing hunger. Although the *proportion* of people who are hungry may have fallen (a Millennium Development Goal) the *absolute* number has not. As always with global averages, the figures hide huge differences between and within countries.

Table 5.1: **Some key trends over the last 40 years**

Source: Table collated by Sara Parkin from sources given in left hand column

	1972 1st Earth Summit	1992 2nd Earth Summit	2012 4th Earth Summit
Population (UN Population Information Network)	3.7 billion	5.3 billion	7 billion
Water scarcity (People without access; World Bank)	Not comparable	Not comparable	1.4 billion (2008)
Hungry people (FAO)	878 million (26%)	848 million (16%)	850 million (13%)
Arable land (Hectares per person; Food and Agriculture Organisation [FAO])	0.31	0.26	0.21
Electricity demand (kWh per person/per year; World Bank)	1300	2100	2800
CO_2 emissions (Metric tonnes per person/ per year; World Bank)	4.18	4.17	4.8
Forest cover (Global hectares, 6.2 billion before advent of farming; FAO)	4.9 billion	4.2 billion	3.7 billion (30% all land)
Global economy (World Bank)	GDP US$2 trillion DOW 1000	GDP US$22 trillion DOW 3301	GDP US$63 trillion DOW 13,250

Note: Shaded cells are per capita figures, the rest are global.

2   The term 'Anthropocene' was coined by Nobel Prize winning scientist Paul Crutzen and, in 2011, was used by the Geographical Society of America in the title for their annual meeting. It is under consideration for formal adoption in the Geological Time Scales. See www.economist.com/node/18741749, accessed 16 March 2013.

The one apparent good news story is the growth of the human economy over the same period. Until the crisis in the banking system started in 2007, it was assumed that there could be no other economic logic than one driven by ever more production and consumption of goods and services—even though, in order to thrive, this regime clearly damaged the environment and fostered social injustice and inequality. Nevertheless, it was this logic that won the battle of ideas in the former Soviet Union and in South Africa now. The evidence that this economic regime and its misplaced belief in free markets as the perfect regulator is practically, as well as theoretically and morally, bankrupt offers an opportunity to put forward a different logic, a new paradigm, for managing our economic relationships. It is on this territory that the necessary transition will succeed or fail.

Whole life systems: the transition's natural territory?

The purpose of life, is life itself (Hutton 2004 [1795])[3]

Attempts are being made to overcome the multiple disconnects between Earth systems and those of our own species. The Millennium Ecosystem Assessment,[4] Rockstrom and colleagues' (2009) nine boundary conditions for human impact and the Organisation for Economic Co-operation and Development's (OECD) The Economics of Ecosystems and Biodiversity (TEEB) project[5] all focus on the 'services' provided by the environment to human wellbeing. All, however, are partial in what they recognise as an 'Earth system' so fall well short of formulating a new logic within which we can make sense of what to do next.[6]

Earth systems are not really divisible—it is how they operate together that sustains life. Fertile circulating oceans, fresh water, diverse biological mass, fertile soil, atmospheric stratification, climate stability, chemical processing and the fundamental interactions (including electromagnetics and nuclear) are unimaginably more than a sum of their parts, although you wouldn't know it from the structure of academic departments.

The same conceptual mistake arises when it comes to what Tim Jackson (2006) calls the functions that make us healthy, flourishing individuals and communities. Academia and policy circles rarely, if ever, consider as indivisible the physical, psychological, social, reproductive and spiritual functions that make up our humanity. Certainly, conventional economics is incapable of seeing people in this fullest sense, using theories that relegate them to cogs in the cycle of production and consumption of goods and services. The full flourishing of people, and that of the Earth's systems, is not and never has been the point of economics.

3 James Hutton was a friend and contemporary of Adam Smith, and is considered the father of the Earth sciences.
4 www.unep.org/maweb/en/index.aspx, accessed 16 March 2013.
5 www.teebweb.org, accessed 16 March 2013.
6 For the wider story see, for example, Vitosek *et al.* (1997) or www.wwf.org.uk/what_we_do/about_us/living_planet_report_2012, accessed 16 March 2013.

The challenge, therefore, is how can we, as an amazing species, get smart about strategies for flourishing, not just now but for millennia to come. It is only by going back to basics that a clear view of what 'good' would look like becomes possible— that is, a planet back in control of *all* its systems, and a species—us—mediating our full flourishing in a way that keeps it that way. It is only from this position, rather than by rehashing elderly economic theories, that the transitional path becomes clear. All the great economists—Adam Smith, John Stuart Mill, Karl Marx, John Maynard Keynes, Joseph Schumpeter—acknowledged that whatever 'regime of capital' they promoted, it had its limits (Heilbronner 1985: 143-44). So why try to resuscitate what they knew was time-limited anyway?

From here to sustainability

Being ready to succeed

> Always do the right thing. This will gratify some and astonish the rest
> (Mark Twain, 1835-1910).[7]

At the start of 1990, on the east side of the Berlin Wall, I photographed two bits of graffiti symbolic of the choices facing the people of the former communist states. One, in rough red paint, said 'fresh food=fresh people'. But it was the world view behind the other that won the day. In sharp capitals it read: 'SAATCHI & SAATCHI', the logo of a global advertising company. In the absence of a countervailing set of ideas, never mind a plan, the European Bank for Reconstruction and Development was (in its own words) 'inaugurated less than two years after the fall of the Berlin Wall … to support the development of market economies in the region following the widespread collapse of communist regimes'. This was the first time that a multilateral bank had a political objective in its articles (promoting a North American style economy), and the 'shock therapy' that followed caused immense damage in Russia and many former soviet countries, including a rise of criminal behaviour and severe deprivation for many. Yet, no one in Eastern Europe (or the West for that matter) was articulating an attractive vision of what could happen if the reconstruction and development plan invested *directly* in refreshing the lives of people, in their communities.[8] The ANC did have a vision—a Freedom Charter—but lost the battle over the best economic plan for implementing it.

When the Occupy movement started on Wall Street, stimulating similar manifestations in London and around the world, it was as if a global community of people echoed the 1989 dissident movements: 'Hold on! Is it government's intention that the financial system makes 1% of the population fabulously wealthy while incomes of 99% stagnate or decline, too often from already low levels?' Evidence of not just

---

7 www.working-minds.com/MTquotes.htm, accessed 19 March 2013.
8 Even Die Grünen, the West German Green Party campaigned for the first all-Germany elections on climate change and lost all their seats in parliament.

venality but criminality in the financial sector has been joined by revelations of how much governments are powerless to stop it, not least because they have been complicit in much of it.

The anger of a substantial and growing fraction of the 99% is beginning to turn to fear too, as communities—indeed, whole countries—understand that their governments and financial institutions have not the foggiest idea what to do next. The leaders are not in control. Occupy is the cosy exciting manifestation of this fear, as is the impression of a huge number of people connected by social media, united in their concern for their own future and that of their children. But other things are happening too that resemble what happened after 1989. The necessary transition will not be without competition for selling its new logic into the expanding political void. European and North American politics is now infested with a growing number of extremist political parties and groups that prey on uncertainty and fear by offering simple, extreme, populist solutions. Golden Dawn, which won 7% of the vote and 18 seats in national elections in Greece, and the French National Front with two seats for nearly 14% of the vote in France are two 2012 examples. Rising support for the ever more extreme views of the US Republican Party is another. There are more (see, for example, Bartlett *et al.* 2011).

So success for the necessary transition means not only an attractive vision and the outline of a plan (like the ANC's), but also a plausible economic model to go with it, plus a pretty hard-nosed strategy for getting both into power. The biggest learning of the past 40 years is that it is not enough to have scientific evidence on your side, nor is it sufficient to be right about your ideas for the future. It is about *how* to complete Kuhn's paradigm shift. There may be a lot of questioning and experimenting around new ways of running economies and countries, but there will be fierce competition about which set of ideas win, with the old ideas not ready to give up yet.

However hard it is, the necessary transition will have to keep in mind the interconnected whole—all life on Earth, including us—with mutual flourishing the ultimate goal. It is only by using conceptual models based on that outcome that nearer-time policy can be kept coherent yet adaptable enough to build confidence in voters, and others, that the new normal is a sustainability-oriented one, and is something of which they want to be part.

Key intervention points

> The crisis is in implementation (Kofi Annan, Johannesburg, 2002).
> The key challenge is implementation (Ban Ki Moon, Rio de Janeiro, 2012).

It is said that we have more or less all the technologies and policies needed for the necessary transition, but the lesson from not only 1989 but also the history of the environmental movement is that having an attractive narrative—for people in power as well as for citizens—is what gets results. A top lesson from the last 40 years is that making this an environmental story has not worked. Sustainability is about what we, the human species, do next; so the story has to speak to the hopes and fears of people directly.

The transition will be a complex, muddled process—less blueprint, more learning as we go. Here are just four different ways of framing any narrative about sustainability. They are followed by five policy areas as examples of where applying the new ways of thinking about policy can help the transition to a 'new normal'—a new logic for sustainability that has the wellbeing of people at its heart.

Four transitional fundamentals

Resilience

Resilience, in our communities and between them, is a keystone attribute of a sustainable society. Simply put, resilience is the capacity of ecological and social systems (and individuals) to absorb shocks and still be able to function (Folke *et al.* 2010). For example, a community dependent on one cash crop (such as pineapples or making coir doormats), or one industry (such as mining), is vulnerable should that one activity fail. At a personal level, some people are better able to withstand multiple set-backs through psychological robustness, which is usually enhanced by belonging to strong social networks. On a different scale, we know climate-regulating systems are not resilient if the chemical balance of the atmosphere, on land and in the sea is altered.

Resilience is not a static concept looking back to past stability, but a dynamic forward-looking one. In fact, policy and strategies aimed at 'restoring' stability or equilibrium ignore the reality that both natural and social systems are always in flux, eternally adapting. More sensible are strategies that create robust and resilient systems, recognising that, for social as well as biological systems, these are the product of a myriad of evolving relationships, all of which require nurturing in order to grow in strength (Leach *et al.* 2010). Moreover, a transitional proposition based on growing good relationships has an attractiveness that competitive individualism does not.

Real capital growth

The word 'capital' means 'head', so wealth originally calculated as head of livestock and 'interest' as the offspring of the herd meant something real (De Soto 2000). Today, the word 'capital' on its own is synonymous with 'money'. That total global debt is estimated to be over US$158 trillion, with government debt at US$50 trillion, and rising,[9] using GDP or dollars to measure things such as carbon intensity

---

9 See McKinsey Institute (August 2011) *Mapping Global Capital Markets 2011*: 3, www.mc kinsey.com/insights/global_capital_markets/mapping_global_capital_markets_2011, accessed 18 March 2013. For global government debt totals see *The Economist* Debt Clock on www.economist.com/content/global_debt_clock, accessed 18 March 2013.

or human wellbeing becomes meaningless. Finance has lost its ability to value anything in a useful way. For this reason, recent publications such as *The Inclusive Wealth Report 2012* (UNU-IHDP and UNEP 2012) incorporate natural, social and human capital to create comprehensive measures of *real* wealth.

Thinking of growing stocks of natural, human and social capital, instead of sacrificing all three to the pursuit of growing financial capital is not new (see, for example, Seregeldin and Steer 1994; Ekins *et al.* 1992). But never has the time been more propitious for elaborating economic, social and political programmes for doing just that. Unfortunately, most 'green' economy proposals are still arguing from *inside* the conventional economic logic of growth of 'green' jobs and consumption, stopping short of identifying strategies for replacing them with growth of natural, human and social capital.[10] The way 'conventional capitalism' operates is illustrated in Figure 5.1. It shows physical capital has its tightest relationship with people as labour and consumers, with success measured in the resultant growth in production of goods and services. Human wellbeing—flourishing—is not the immediate objective of this process, and the state has to intervene to compensate for its failures. Finance, instead of oiling the wheels of the process has become a 'usurping' capital, with its own growth as a primary purpose. This compounds the errors within the system. Nature is fuel for the furnace of this sort of economic regime. As a whole Earth system, and as the source of all wellbeing, it is nowhere.

Figure 5.1: **Conventional capitalism**
Source: Parkin 2013

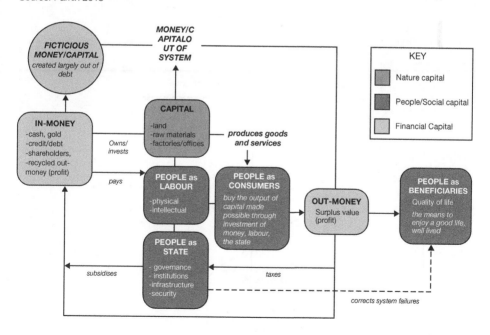

---

10 See, for example, www.unep.org/greeneconomy, accessed 16 March 2013.

Figure 5.2 offers a different view of how the economy might operate. The goal is resilience. By broadening the idea of capital to mean all natural, human and social capital, plus that represented in existing infrastructure and buildings, it is only a short step to seeing how the flow of different types of benefits is possible if all human activity was simultaneously concentrated on repairing, maintaining and enhancing all those capital stocks.

This new regime for capital restores the intimacy between capital and human wellbeing. The economy is featured as a subset of social capital and, like democracy, adds directly to human flourishing and is subject to continually improving processes. In Figure 5.2, people as beneficiaries of a happy relationship with capital are seen as a 'pull-out' of human and social capital (as is finance). Perversities are removed, the circle becomes virtuous and a new logic for the human economy is created. Growth in this economic model is of the four capital stocks (and the concomitant flow of benefit to people), not of money, which is returned to a facilitating role.

Figure 5.2: **A new regime for capital**

Source: Parkin 2013

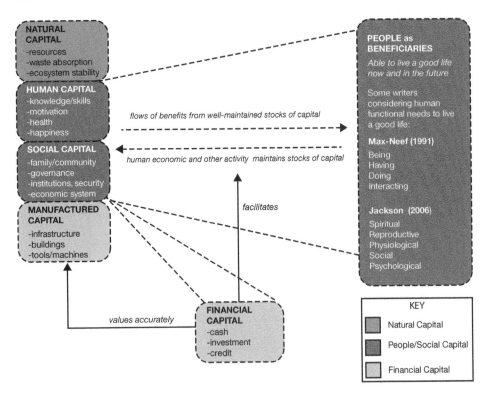

Psychology and sociology of change

Unpack the sentiments behind the 'happiness' or 'life satisfaction' research and you find that most of all we want to feel good about ourselves, our relationships and the place where we live (see, for example, Layard 2005). Anthropologists studying our evolutionary journey identify some profound human needs: co-operation; avoidance or regulation of conflict; commitment to kin and wider group(s); as well as social and personal meaningfulness. Sociologist Tim Jackson (2006), for example, expresses human motivation through satisfying five aspects of human functioning—physical, psychological, social, reproductive and spiritual. Such human sentiments and motivations are all artfully deployed by brand managers and advertising agencies to encourage us to buy into certain lifestyles and patterns of consumption, but are less deftly used, if at all, by non-governmental organisations (NGOs) or governments to rally support for more sustainable ways of living.

So when Occupy or pressure groups call for extreme and/or rapid change they should not be surprised when people are reluctant. Unless in desperate circumstances we like things to stay much as they are—habits, even bad ones, die hard (O'Toole 1995; Shove 2003). When change is feared, the problem is worse. It is a long road from there to acceptance and active participation.[11]

Which is why abstract and nihilistic slogans, such as Occupy's 'Communiqué from an Absent Future'[12] will not work without a practical agenda attached that worries less about the negative and the unknowable and more about the enjoyable and do-able. The necessary transition will learn the best of the tricks of the ad agencies and use language and processes that build confidence in people that this is a change they want to buy into—psychologically as well as practically.

Living in truth

Former oft-jailed dissident and later first President of Czechoslovakia, the late Vaclav Havel, insisted on living in truth—that is, living as if citizens in his country enjoyed freedom of expression, movement and association. His lived integrity made the transition out of communism in his country one of the smoothest. It should not be too hard for us to imagine living now as if sustainability was normal—part of the mainstream. The power of thinking and, wherever possible, behaving and living 'in truth' is mostly unrealised. Imagine if the arguing stopped about where environmental boundaries lay—how far we could go in taking down forests or how many more greenhouse gases we could emit before catastrophic temperature rises. And, instead, the public debates, political energy and research funds focused on how quickly we could shrink our impact on nature, assuming the smaller it is the better.

11 See Figure 8.10 in Parkin (2010: 216).

12 See www.radicalphilosophy.com/news/faint-signal for a good article about how the Communiqué's call spread from a student occupation in California, and the relevance of nihilistic, anti-statist politics to 21st century activism. The Communiqué is at wewanteverything.wordpress.com/2009/09/24/communique-from-an-absent-future, accessed 5 April 2013.

Not the old hair-shirt arguments that pitch environmental health above human comfort, but a positive story about how good a life could be *for people* in such a world. It is easier than you think to decide and act 'as if' we were already living in a world where the economy depicted in Figure 5.2 was a reality. Doing so would help others design near-time policies and actions that will help get us there. This is not to say the necessary transition will be roses all the way, it won't, but living and working with a positive agenda makes it a much more attractive proposition.

With these four transition fundamentals in mind—resilience as a quality of good relationships; a broad interpretation of capital as a foundation for a new economic logic; psychological literacy when it comes to proposing change; and using the technique of acting and deciding 'as if' we were living in a sustainable society as a way of inspiring others to join in—I turn to five different policies to illustrate what I mean. How does a resilience–broad-capital–people-sensitive–living-in-truth way of looking at each stimulate new thinking—and at least turn up new questions to explore, if not yet full answers? (An essential step in Kuhn's paradigm-shifting process.)

Policy in transition: new ways of thinking

Ecological demographic transition

It is anticipated that most of the Millennium Development Goals will be missed.[13] As Table 5.1 illustrates, the absolute number of hungry people has barely changed since 1972; all the effort on this statistic, and others, such as access to safe water supplies, undone by growth in the number of people. Since the first Earth Summit in 1972, the population of the world has almost doubled to 7 billion. New UN projections suggest a further 3 billion by the end of the century.[14] In July 2012, a brave speech by Melinda Gates, a Roman Catholic, sought to put family planning and contraception back to the forefront of the development agenda.[15] The initiative brings hope to the nearly half a million women in poor countries who say they want contraceptives but cannot get them, and is linked to other Bill and Melinda Gates Foundation programmes to help ensure the children they do have reach a healthy adulthood. What is less well known is that 40% of pregnancies are unplanned in rich countries, the same proportion as in poor ones, but with these children born into a lifestyle that has a hugely greater impact on the environment. The UN offers high, medium and low figures in its population projections. At the moment we are on trend to go above the medium one (10 billion by 2100) but could, with a conscious effort (and absolutely no coercion), hit the lower one of just over 6 billion. There

13 www.un.org/millenniumgoals, accessed 16 March 2013.
14 www.un.org/esa/population, accessed 16 March 2013.
15 www.londonfamilyplanningsummit.co.uk, accessed 16 March 2013.

is, on average, only 0.5 children per woman difference between the two projections. With that target in mind, nothing would convince poor countries more that rich countries are genuine in their commitment to sustainable development than if they ran serious family planning initiatives at home as well as abroad.[16] Applying country-specific figures, a population of 6 billion would bring greenhouse gas emission rates down to under 30 billion tonnes/year (instead of nearly 50 billion tonnes/year on the medium population projection). For rich and poor countries alike this would constitute a demographic transition towards a stable population (loss equals gain) at a lower total, with massive collateral benefits not only for women and the chances for their children to thrive, but also for the environment and older generations. We all would benefit from more innovative, low impact ways of organising our lives—work, leisure, learning—as countries transition through their 'age bulge'.

Extreme community energy

The fear factor in disconnecting our dependence on fossil fuels is not fully comprehended by climate change or renewable energy campaigners. The transition will necessarily include a move to a system that provides the *services* of energy—heat, cooling, power, light—in a secure, low-carbon way. Again necessarily, the mix of energy *sources* will vary from location to location, but ultra-efficiency will be common to everywhere. This will mean distributed generation and a highly sophisticated interconnected grid. Why is this logic so difficult to get over to governments? Doesn't it play to an economy with jobs and consumption as a motor; there are huge numbers of jobs in such a transition.

That is to miss the point. Governments fear renewable energy, efficiency, distributed generation and interconnected grids, because they are very dependent on the tax intake from big energy companies which together form a massively well-funded voice in government's ear. So dependent it is worth providing a subsidy.

The necessary transition will have to address that fear (which is similar for 'big' food and 'big' finance) and explain how the transition would work for the state without blackouts and chaos. It will also have to show how the current multiple local initiatives happening all over the world may be taken to scale—some in size, some through multiplication—and get serious about promoting associated low energy dependent development models that will combine social and environmental outcomes for local communities.[17]

---

16 Many environmental groups won't tackle population issues, some saying poor people have comparatively little impact, so dropping consumption in rich countries is *more* important. They are wrong. In effect, they are saying it is alright to have lots of babies as long as you stay poor. See www.populationmatters.org, accessed 16 March 2013.

17 See, for example, www.forumforthefuture.org/project/community-energy-coalition/ overview, accessed 16 March 2013.

Really, truly, deeply Fair Trade

During the recession, sales of organic food dropped substantially, but those of Fair Trade goods did not. One of the reasons for this is that people resonate more with goods that offer social justice along with environmental benefits. Any necessary transition will have to take thinking about Fair Trade a lot further; it will mean increasing global interconnections, not reducing them as some campaigners imply when urging us to 'buy local'. The sort of resilience implicit in sustainable development means local—where I am—diversity of home-grown goods and services, and similarly resilient localities with which I trade at a distance. Just what is the ratio of trade—local, regional, national, continental, international—that would work best to sustain resilient communities all over the globe? Obviously it would be different from place to place, but just trying to work it out would, in itself, drive the necessary transition. Moreover, it would build on an existing momentum of interest in personal ethical purchasing and corporate supply chains.

Working as little as is possible

Some time ago I visited a German-sponsored project in a favela near Rio de Janeiro. It took foul water from the hillside and cleansed it through snail breeding ponds (for pig food) and a horticultural system before returning it safely to the river. It was noon and the two Brazilian workmen were sitting in the shade of the only tree. My companion opined that the country was unlikely to develop as long as its citizens preferred gossiping in the shade and holding fiestas to working. It was a revelatory moment for me. How come we have designed an economic system that uses ever-increasing human productivity per unit of GDP as a globally important performance indicator? Shouldn't the indicator be how much human benefit we can get for as little work, and with as few resources used, as possible? Gossiping and partying are two central components of social capital building. Shouldn't we be maximising opportunities to do both? Are there other ways to share the joys and pains of work and mix it all with learning and leisure?

Radical and just localism

'Democratic accountability evaporates when we think globally ... culture, identity and politics are going local ... states must act locally in a globalised world'. These words from Sir Jeremy Greenstock, former UK ambassador to the UN, are part of his argument that global security can only be realised if it stands on a multitude of locally resilient communities (Greenstock 2008). National security is only as good as how secure people feel in their localities, he argues—not just safe from terrorists, war and crime, but from extreme weather events and shortage of food. It is in the local communities that terrorists will not be harboured and greenhouse gases not emitted. So why don't we trust localities? Why don't we build their capacity or equip them? This is not to argue that the necessary transition will happen automatically from the bottom up. Greenstock points out that strong institutions for democracy and justice will be needed to avoid a descent into tribalism. The necessary transition will require a shift from *laissez-faire* and partial democracy to active and continual improvement of systems that will be a quintessential element of high performing social capital.[18]

A good framework for thinking about how radical localism might be organised was proposed by the late Elinor Ostrom, winner of the 2009 Nobel Prize for Economics (although she was not an economist). Her life's work was the rigorous examination of the complexity of effective governance systems for common-pool resources. She identified key success factors that have something to say to every scale of human organisation, from local fisheries to global banks (Ostrom 1990):

- Clear boundaries and memberships
- Congruent (locally appropriate) rules
- Collective choice arenas (places and processes for decision-making)
- Monitoring systems
- Graduated sanctions to punish rule breaking
- Conflict resolution mechanisms
- Recognised rights to organise
- 'Nested' units or enterprises (each obeys the rules set higher up)

Ostrom's final success factor echoes the principle of subsidiarity, which roughly translated means that the people who decide something should be contiguous with those who pay for and live with the consequences of that decision. Although not foolproof, it is much the best way to ensure that decisions are good or, at least, continually improving in an iterative fashion. Any resilient system will not be static, it will be continually striving to add quality.

These are just a few examples of how new thinking can influence key policy areas. In each case, as with the preceding suggested transition fundamentals, the trick will be to take current problems and find a necessary transition/sustainability-oriented solution to them and champion it wherever possible.

The necessary but ever missing ingredient: leadership

Which brings me to a final point for this section. The missing factor in all the failures to embark on the necessary transition over the last 40 years is that of properly competent leadership. All interventions will depend on the quality of leadership available.

18 See www.freedomhouse.org for the latest state of national institutions for political rights and civil liberties. Missing is a reflection on the global message sent by the dysfunction of so-called 'mature' democratic systems such as in the USA and UK.

My take on 'living-in-truth' is the idea of 'positive deviance'—'doing the right thing for sustainability despite being surrounded by the wrong institutional structures, the wrong processes and stubbornly unco-operative people'. As institutional change (including laws) tends to follow rather than precede social change, positive deviance (just getting on and doing it) is the only leadership strategy that will meet the challenges of the 21st century (Parkin 2010). As a 2008 report from the US National Intelligence Council (NIC) from which the following quote is taken argues, individual and collective leadership have been (for bad as well as good) the biggest game changers of the last century. The report told the incoming President (Obama) that the hallmarks of tomorrow's world will be scarcity—of land, water, oil, food and 'air-space' for greenhouse gases—thus putting key sustainability concerns at the heart of geopolitics:

> Lessons from the last century, however, suggest that: leaders and their ideas matter; economic volatility introduces a major risk factor; geopolitical rivalries trigger discontinuities more than does technological change … leadership matters, no trend is immutable, and … timely and well-informed intervention can decrease the likelihood and severity of negative developments and increase the likelihood of positive ones (NIC 2008: 5).

Means at our disposal

To critique the quality of today's leaders generally would require more space than is possible here, but it is worth asking how the leadership of today's green movement stacks up.

When the candles were lit in East Germany in October 1989, Joschka Fischer, then a leader of the German Green Party and a veteran of 1960s' student movements, said that, for a moment, he heard the rustle of angels' wings. The Occupy movement brought with it the same surge of identity and agency, magnified by social media, not just to old and young revolutionaries, but to middle-class matrons who brought food to the camps. Over-excited journalists wrote 'the first draft of history' linking what was happening in London, New York and Madrid with Cairo and Tunis to 1989, 1968 and 1914—or was it more 1848? (See, for example, Mason 2012.)

But it didn't last. Within a very few months the Occupy movement had fizzled out. By the time the Rio+20 Earth Summit took place in June 2012, its legacy remains its mobilising global shout against grotesque inequality—but no plan for action. Small single-issue campaigns survive, ranging from the Move Your Money campaign to Pussy Riot's demand for freedom of expression in Russia. All of which makes it worthwhile reflecting on just how the necessary transition is to come about, and who might be the main actors.

Part of that reflection has to encompass a hard look at why, in the 40 years since the first Earth Summit in 1972, none of the big trends taking humanity in an *un*sustainable direction have been slowed, never mind reversed. In brief, and from the perspective of both governments and their citizens, the reasons may be summarised as follows:

- *Demand-side*: citizen (why civil society is resistant/weakly active)

  - Problems are framed as environmental ... and often presented as competition between environmental and human welfare. People are too often cast as wrong-doers instead of beneficiaries.

  - Ignorance ... about basic biology, physics and human psychology and about the systemic nature of problems and solutions inhibits confidence in taking right actions

- *Supply-side:* governments (why governments fail to provide frameworks that support citizen behaviour change)

  - Failure of leadership ... which is widely sustainability illiterate and untrained in working with systems, complexity and uncertainty. Consequently, it can be paralysed by fear of losing control

  - Capture of governance systems ... which themselves are trapped in wrong institutional structures and processes (for the private as well as the public realm), and distorted by wrong/corrupt use of power (as well as parasitical economic theories)

In *Blessed Unrest*, Paul Hawken (2007) gives an optimistic view of a huge ecosystem of environmental and social groups laying the ground for radical change—the advance guard of the necessary transition—but it is hard to see where and how the movement is influencing the power structures that are marching in the opposite direction on anything like the scale needed. Indeed, the sense of failure caused by the mismatch between their personal values and the response of society has led some long-term environmental activists to retreat into moaning about the inevitability of doom.[19] Not only is this a failure to comprehend the long haul of a paradigm change, it is also an abdication of responsibility to the new generation of citizens and campaigners who are sustainability literate, who do get the idea that this is a *big* social project, and who do see the necessary transition as a mission that may not be easy but is definitely possible.

The new generation will, however, have to learn carefully the lessons of past generations of 'green' campaigners and, critically, the strategy and tactics of those who led the revolution that brought the ideas of economic liberalism into power. Believers in the perfectability of markets, such as Freidrich von Hayek and Milton Friedman, did not take to the streets but planned a long game from just after World War II until their zenith in the 1980s when Ronald Reagan and Margaret Thatcher took their ideas to the peaks of global power. They openly styled themselves as 'freedom fighters' using guerrilla warfare tactics.[20]

19 See, for example, the Dark Mountain Project, www.dark-mountain.net, accessed 16 March 2013.
20 For the story from a UK perspective see Cockett (1994).

What green campaigners got wrong over the last 40 odd years is to imagine (as many still do) that, because we are on the side of the angels, victory is certain to be ours. It is not that we don't fight hard. We do. But in hundreds of full-frontal and disorganised charges, rather than in a sophisticated and co-ordinated campaign. Occupy was just another charge, without consequence to the overall battle, and over dispiritingly soon.

I apologise for the military allusions in this section, but strategy is a military word and, without aping the worst, there is much to be learnt from the masters of the arts of war. From the 1970s' women's movement I also learnt that the principle of non-patriarchal hierarchies (much favoured by the green movement) led to anarchy with multiple loci of power clustered around strong personalities. The battles between them took over external-facing campaigns, which is one reason the women's movement did not manage to become more than the sum of its parts. In a now famous 1970s' paper called *The Tyranny of Structurelessness*, Jo Freeman (1972: 9) pointed out that lack of organisation 'generates much motion but few results'.[21] More recently, UK *Guardian* columnist Zoe Williams has warned the new generation of women's rights campaigners that they should not go too far in the other direction and try to be like a synchronised swimming team. A much better model is a football team; made up of players of different styles and skills but working to a game plan and all with the same objective—to get the ball in the back of the net.[22] And just because male models of leadership are in bad shape right now, doesn't mean that the better examples of team leadership are not possible.

Translating the learning from military strategy and the women's movement, what strategies should the necessary transition/sustainability movement adopt if the goal is to get our ideas into power within, say, the next 40 years?

Green divisions

Without taking the football analogy too much further, the movement may be classified into four distinct divisions:

1. Single issue campaigners	3. 'Moles'
The pressure groups and campaigning specialists in different policy areas	Those in current institutions and other political parties influencing 'from within'
2. Practitioners and policy wonks	**4. Green political parties**
Those providing exemplars, practical policies, intellectual underpinning, innovation	Those who turn the demands, exemplars and new ideas into a choice for the democratic process

Source: Parkin 1987

21 Incorporating the activists in the Arab Spring is beyond the remit of this chapter, but there are parallels.
22 www.guardian.co.uk/commentisfree/2012/mar/07/feminists-international-womens-day, accessed 16 July 2012.

An immediate observation is that within each of the first three divisions there are multiple subdivisions covering environmental and social policy areas but rarely do they meet.[23] In addition, although green parties make themselves unnecessarily vulnerable, with poor thinking through of policy proposals they have done the most to develop thinking across all policy areas. Per Gahrton, former MP for Sweden's Green Party, analysed green party programmes from nearly 50 countries and found 'no Green ideology, but a common thinking' (Gahrton 2008: 109).

Frustratingly, each 'division' operates in its own particular arena, with, none particularly active in what Kuhn (2012) identified as the critical stage before the 'new normal' takes over. That is, in the case of sustainability, the consolidation of ideas into new models - particularly economic ones that have as their purpose the growth (and therefore the resilience) of human, social and environmental capital. There are, of course, some honourable exceptions, such as Paul Ekins, Tim Jackson and the New Economics Foundation in the UK, but it remains the case that while the economy can become greener, without that shift in how capital growth is defined, it can never be green.

Strategy and tactics

In 1947, a group of liberal economists (neocons) founded The Mont Pelerin Society, so creating a global network of like-minded people and organisations through which to conduct their intellectual warfare systematically and, eventually, to great effect.[24] They ensured their ideas colonised air and print media, influenced posts (including Alan Greenspan, chairman of the US Federal Reserve 1987–2006), shaped key policies such as the 'Washington consensus' (the economic rules that governed countries receiving loans from the USA or the International Monetary Fund), and laid an ideological groundwork through network-sponsored think-tanks in eastern Europe (Cockett 1994: 331).

The nearest the putative necessary transition movement has in scope to this scale of influencing strategy is the Global Greens, a network of green parties with members from over 90 countries,[25] some of whom have think-tanks and/or foundations.[26] Otherwise it is only the biggest campaigning organisations—Friends of the Earth, Greenpeace, WWF, Amnesty International, Save the Children—that have

---

23 On two occasions in the UK over 30 organisations campaigning across environment, social and development issues collaborated on two books, published under the name of the Real World Coalition *The Politics of the Real World* before the 1997 general election, and *From Here to Sustainability* prior to the 2001 election. On neither occasion did a sustained follow-through occur, despite much attention at the time (Real World Coalition 1997, 2001).

24 www.montpelerin.org, accessed 16 March 2013.

25 www.globalgreens.org, accessed 16 March 2013.

26 Heinrich Böll Stiftung and Green European Foundation (2010) *The Green Directory: A Who's Who in Europe ... Green Political Foundations Revisited*, available from www.boell.eu or www.gef.eu.

international networks. Some campaigns are co-ordinated globally but, by and large, any coming-together is more for consolation in a hostile world. Nowhere is there a Mont Pelerin equivalent hard-nosed strategy dedicated to getting sustainability-oriented ideas into power. The green movement tends to be strident, demanding of others, and a bit fast and loose with the evidence. Not to mention weak in understanding what it is that makes people, and governments, tick in their psychological as well as their political souls. One modern example of stupendous subversion from which we can draw is that of the late Wangari Maathai. Her Kenyan Green Belt movement, on the surface, was about women who planted trees in Africa.[27] But along with the infinitely fundable, non-politically challenging tree-planting, women passed from one village to another information about growing their own capacity and power, family planning, child care, nutrition, tactics for handling male village elders, and the rewards to be had from persistent, consistent effort.

To succeed, the necessary transition will have to do over the next 20 years, what the economic liberals did over 40 and adopt more sophisticated strategies for achieving their goal. The occupation will have to be of the intellectual high ground, collating and generating ideas that make sense to both politicians and citizens. The action will have to be pilots and evaluations of initiatives in and between communities, and a sharing of what works to build confidence and take actions to scale.

But first, a collective and honest reflection on where the movement stands in history needs to be made. According to a UK government negotiator at the Copenhagen climate talks in 2009, the unco-ordinated clamour of NGOs led to politicians realising the movement was not as powerful as the sum of its parts, so could be ignored—a view that carried over to the Rio+20 summit in June 2012. That cannot be how we want history to remember us, surely?

In this chapter, I have tried to reaffirm why the necessary transition is so important, and to argue that unless we prepare to succeed we will indeed be bypassed by history. On its own, the financial crisis will not trigger an automatic transition to a sustainability-oriented paradigm. Nor, I fear, will social or environmental breakdown. As I have argued, leadership will be what makes the difference. And, as we know, leadership can be for bad as well as good. So a great deal will depend on how quickly we, as a movement, can offer a positive and coherent response to the questions about what happens next, and whether we can organise around strategies that have the best chance of getting our ideas into power. All in a way that gives people the confidence to come with us.

And I have to end by saying I do not know what will galvanise us to become more than the sum of our parts, except perhaps a revelation that our time has come and it deserves the best of us all sooner rather than later.

> Practical wisdom is a reasoned and true state of capacity to act with regard
> to the human good (Aristotle).

27 www.greenbeltmovement.org, accessed 16 March 2013.

References

Bartlett, J., J. Birdwell and M. Littler (2011) *The Rise of Populism in Europe Can Be Traced Through On-line Behaviour* (London: Demos).

Cockett, R. (1994) *Thinking the Unthinkable: Think-tanks and the Economic Counter Revolution 1931–1983* (London: Harper Collins).

De Soto, H. (2000) *The Mystery of Capital: Why Capitalism Triumphs in the West But Fails Everywhere Else* (New York: Basic Books).

Ekins, P., M. Hillman and R.Hutchison 1992) *Wealth Beyond Measure: An Atlas of New Economics* (London: Gaia Books).

Folke, C., S.R. Carpenter, B. Walker, M. Scheffer, T. Chapin and J. Rockström (2010) 'Resilience Thinking: Integrating Resilience, Adaptability and Transformability', *Ecology and Society* 15.4: 20 (www.ecologyandsociety.org/vol15/iss4/art20, accessed 4 April 2013).

Freeman, J. (1972) 'The Tyranny of Structurelessness', *Berkeley Journal of Sociology* 17: 151-65 (www.jofreeman.com/joreen/tyranny.htm, accessed 4 April 2013).

Gahrton, P. (2008) *Is There a Need for a Green Ideology?* (Lund, Sweden: Cogito).

Greenstock, J. (2008) 'States must act locally in a globalised world', *Financial Times*, 15 May 2008.

Hawkin, P. (2007) *Blessed Unrest: How the World's Largest Movement Came Into Being and How it is Changing the World* (New York: Viking Press).

Heilbronner, R.L. (1985) *The Nature and Logic of Capitalism* (New York: W.W. Norton).

Hutton, J. (2004[1795]) *Theory of the Earth* (Whitefish, MT: Kessinger Publishing).

Jackson, T. (2006) 'Consuming Paradise? Towards a Socio-cultural Psychology of Sustainable Consumption', in T. Jackson (ed.), *The Earthscan Reader in Sustainable Consumption* (London: Earthscan).

Kuhn, T. (2012) *The Structure of Scientific Revolutions: 50th Anniversary Edition* (Chicago, IL: University of Chicago Press).

Layard, R. (2005) *Happiness: Lessons from a New Science* (London: Penguin).

Leach, M., I. Schoones and A. Stirling (2010) *Dynamic Sustainabilities: Technology, Environment, Social Justice* (London: Earthscan).

Mason, P. (2012) *Why it's Kicking Off Everywhere: The New Global Revolutions* (London and New York: Verso).

Max-Neef, M. (1991) *Human Scale Development* (London and New York: The Apex Press; www.max-neef.cl/download/Max-neef_Human_Scale_development.pdf, accessed 5 April 2013).

NIC (US National Intelligence Council) (2008) *Global Trends 2025: A Transforming World* (Washington, DC: NIC).

Ostrom, E. (1990) *Governing the Commons: The Evolution of Institutions for Collective Action* (Cambridge, UK: Cambridge University Press).

O'Toole, J. (1995) *Leading Change: The Argument for Values-based Leadership* (San Francisco, CA: Jossey-Bass).

Parkin, S. (1987) 'Green Strategy', paper presented at *Green Thinking for Global Linking*, 3rd European Green Co-ordination Congress, Stockholm, Sweden, August 1987.

Parkin, S. (2010) *The Positive Deviant: Sustainability Leadership in a Perverse World* (London: Earthscan).

Parkin, S. (2013) 'Leadership for Sustainability: The Search for Tipping Points', in T. O'Riordan and T. Lenton (eds.), *Addressing Tipping Points* (Oxford, UK: Oxford University Press).

Real World Coalition (1997) *The Politics of the Real World* (London: Earthscan).

Real World Coalition (2001) *From Here to Sustainability* (London: Earthscan).

Rockström, J., W. Steffen, K. Noone, Å. Persson, F.S. Chapin III, E.F. Lambin, T.M. Lenton, M. Scheffer, C. Folke, H.J. Schellnhuber, B. Nykvist, C.A. de Wit, T. Hughes, S. van der Leeuw, H. Rodhe, S. Sörlin, P.K. Snyder, R. Costanza, U. Svedin, M. Falkenmark, L. Karlberg, R.W. Corell, V.J. Fabry, J. Hansen, B.H. Walker, D. Liverman, K. Richardson, P. Crutzen and J.A. Foley (2009) 'A Safe Operating Space for Nature', *Nature* 461: 472-75.

Seregeldin, I., and A. Steer (1994) 'Epilogue: Expanding the Capital Stock', in I. Seregeldin, A. Steer and M. Cernea (eds.), *Making Development Sustainable: From Concept to Action* (Washington, DC: World Bank, Environmentally Sustainable Development Occasional Paper Series No 2).

Shove, E. (2003) *Comfort, Cleanliness, Convenience: The Social Organisation of Normality* (London: Berg).

UNU-IHDP and UNEP (United Nations University-International Human Dimensions Programme on Global Environmental Change and United Nations Environment Programme) (2012) *Inclusive Wealth Report 2012: Measuring Progress Towards Sustainability* (Cambridge, UK: Cambridge University Press; www.ihdp.unu.edu/article/iwr).

Vitosek, P., H.A. Mooney, J. Lubchenco and J.M. Melillo (1997) 'Human Domination of Earth's Ecosystems', *Science* 277: 494-99.

Sara Parkin is Founder Director of Forum for the Future and Chair of the Richard Sandbrook Trust. She is adviser or patron to a number of organisations and was a former co-secretary of the European Greens. She was awarded an OBE in 2001 for services to sustainability and education, and leadership education remains her principal campaigning interest.

6

The pillars of peace
Identifying the elements that allow human potential to flourish

Steve Killelea
Institute for Economics and Peace, Sydney, Australia and New York, USA

Introduction

During the last 20 years humanity has entered into a new epoch in its history. This has been brought about by a convergence of many factors—finite environmental barriers are now being reached, and on multiple fronts. World population recently hit 7 billion and in many places it is already straining capacity. Technology is fuelling change at an ever increasing pace, which in many ways underpins the growth of globalisation. The world is connected in ways that were unimaginable even 20 years ago. Wars are no longer economically viable (Geys 2010; Glick and Taylor 2010) and change is occurring so fast that nations are struggling to keep up with both the legal and social ramifications of these changes.

Global challenges call for global solutions and these solutions require co-operation on a scale unprecedented in human history. Peace is an essential prerequisite because without peace we will never be able to achieve the levels of co-operation, trust, inclusiveness and social equity necessary to solve these challenges, let alone empower the international institutions necessary to address them. Peace lies at the centre of being able to manage the transition, simply because peace creates the optimum environment in which the other activities that contribute to human growth can take place. In this sense, peace is a facilitator making it easier for workers to produce, businesses to sell, entrepreneurs and scientists to innovate, and governments to regulate.

But if peace is an essential prerequisite for solving our sustainability challenges and improving our economic and social wellbeing, then having a good understanding of peace is essential. This poses the question: How well do we understand peace? Fifty years ago peace studies were virtually non-existent. Today, there are thriving peace and conflict centres in numerous universities around the world. But most of these are focused on the study of conflict rather than on the understanding of peace. A parallel can be drawn here with medical science. The study of pathology has led to numerous breakthroughs in our understanding of how to treat and cure disease. However, there is more than that to health. It was only when medical science turned its focus on the study of healthy human beings that we understood what we need to do to stay healthy—the right physical exercise, a good mental disposition and a healthy diet. This could only be learnt by studying what was working. In the same way, the study of conflict is fundamentally different from the study of peace.

Over the last century we have moved from having departments of war to departments of defence and we are now seeing the emergence of organisations that are lobbying for the creation of departments of peace within governments. While these changes are beneficial in improving our understanding of peace, peace is not yet seen as germane to the major academic disciplines, nor is there a methodological approach to the cross-disciplinary study of peace. There are no courses on the literature of peace in any of the literature departments of the major universities, yet there are profound works on peace. Similarly, there is no university chair of peace economics in any major economics faculties, yet most business people believe that their markets grow in peace and that their costs decrease with increasing peacefulness.

The simplest way of approaching the definition of peace is in terms of harmony achieved by the absence of war, conflict or violent crime. Applied to states, this would suggest that the measurement of internal states of peace is as important as those external factors involving other states or neighbours. This is what Johan Galtung (1985) defined as 'negative peace'—the absence of violence. The concept of negative peace is immediately intuitive and empirically measurable, and can be used as a starting point to elaborate its counterpart concept, 'positive peace'. Having established what constitutes an absence of violence, is it possible through statistical analysis to identify which structures, institutions and social attitudes create and maintain peace?

Measuring peace

Measurement is the key to understanding any human endeavour, and peace is no different. If we do not measure peace, then how can we know whether our actions are either helping or hindering us in the achievement of a more peaceful world? Only by measuring and understanding the patterns of peace can we move to a better understanding of how it can be improved.

The Global Peace Index (GPI) was developed in 2007 by the Institute for Economics and Peace (IEP) as one of the first rigorous attempts to measure the relative levels of the peacefulness of nations. By aggregating and generating a comprehensive and reliable data set which measures direct violence, the GPI adds to the current stock of harmonised cross-country data. Since 2007 it has informed policy-makers, academics and civil society organisations about the objective state of direct violence in countries, covering over 99% of the world's population. The purpose of this research is to better understand the cultural, economic and political conditions associated with peaceful environments.

Up until now, the GPI has focused on measuring 'negative peace', which was described by Johan Galtung (1985: 13-14) as the 'absence of violence' and the 'absence of the fear of violence'.[1] Hence, the GPI utilises 23 indicators of safety and security in society, militarisation, and ongoing domestic and international conflict to determine the multi-dimensional nature of negative peace in 158 countries.[2] This means that nations with a high ranking in the GPI are considered more peaceful because they are relatively safer and more secure than countries lower in the rankings.

In contrast to negative peace, Galtung (1985) described a second dimension called positive peace. Broadly understood, positive peace is derived from preventative solutions which are optimistic and facilitate a more integrated society. According to Galtung (2012), this results in 'co-operation for mutual benefit, and where individuals and society are in harmony'. From this conceptual basis, IEP defines positive peace to be the set of attitudes, institutions and structures which when strengthened, lead to a more peaceful society' (IEP 2011: 4).

This resulted in the development of the 'pillars of peace'—an eight-part taxonomy which categorises the data sets that are statistically significant with the GPI. Conceptually, this emphasises the importance of a holistic set of institutions which work together to systematically shape the environments that lead to peace. It is important to understand that this framework is not deriving causality between any of the attributes of the pillars of peace; rather, they work as an inter-dependent set of factors where causality and strength of a relation will change depending on the individual set of a country's specific political, economic and cultural circumstances.

---

1 The definition of violence is adapted from the World Health Organisation (WHO): '[T]he intentional use of physical force or power, threatened or actual, against oneself, another person, or against a group or community, that either results in or has a high likelihood of resulting in injury, death, psychological harm, destruction of property, maldevelopment, or deprivation' (WHO 2002: 4).

2 For a full list of GPI indicators see Global Peace Index 2012, www.visionofhumanity.org/wp-content/uploads/2012/06/2012-Global-Peace-Index-Report.pdf, accessed 1 October 2012.

Utilising the eight-part pillars of peace taxonomy, the IEP has developed a Positive Peace Index (PPI) with 21 indicators covering 108 countries. In order to derive these indicators, the IEP compared over 300 cross-country data sets with the GPI to conceptualise eight factors strongly correlated with peaceful countries as measured by the GPI. Under each of the eight domains of the index there are between two and three indicators which have weightings determined by the relative strength of the indicator's correlation to the GPI score. Further detail on this is provided in the methodology section below.

Why a Positive Peace Index?

In contrast to negative peace, positive peace can inform our understanding of the appropriate attitudes, institutions and structures which, when strengthened, lead to a nation's capacity to harmoniously and non-violently resolve conflict. The approach in this work stands in contrast to the extensive quantitative conflict literature which is predominately focused on understanding the causes for outbreak of war as a key dependent variable (Human Security Report Project 2011: 36). The output of the PPI can be used for comparative studies which will further inform the understanding of the key economic, political and cultural factors that can improve peace and resilience of all societies, not just fragile states.

By seeking to identify institutions that help a society move away from violence, it is hoped a more holistic picture of the key factors which drive peace can be identified. While focus on 'trigger' factors or individual case studies are insightful they cannot reveal global or regional trends, or help in identifying longer term causes of conflict. As the 2009/2010 *Human Security Report* identifies, there is still a '... remarkable lack of consensus in the research findings on the causes of war and peace ... also the inability of conflict models to predict the outbreak of conflicts.'(Human Security Report Project 2011: 35). To date, there are only a small number of robust findings that have widespread consensus in the research community, and according to Hegre and Sambanis (2006) only three key findings have broad agreement on the causes of civil war:

- The lower a country's average income, the higher the risk of war

- War is more likely if a country has already experienced a war; the more recent the war the more likely the risk

- The risk of war increases as a country's size increases

While there is some dispute about the number of robust findings (Human Security Report Project 2011: 37-38) it is clear there are conflicting empirical conclusions as to the causes of conflict. In contrast, by measuring positive peace it is possible to determine another way to better understand how to reduce violence and, more importantly, how to build resilience within societies so they are less likely to fall into conflict. It is hoped this research can influence debate on how international institutions can facilitate a more holistic and positive approach to peace and state building.

The composite index approach of the PPI was chosen because positive peace is a latent and multi-dimensional concept that is represented in different social, political and economic forms. Defining positive peace as 'the set of attitudes, institutions and structures which, when strengthened, lead to a more peaceful society' (IEP 2011: 4) it is clearly an unobservable variable that cannot be represented or embodied in any single factor.

What is peace?

While there are many nuanced definitions of peace, this article uses two concepts, both of which have a rich history in peace studies. These two types of peace are commonly referred to as 'positive' and 'negative' peace, as defined by Johan Galtung (1985). Negative peace is the absence of violence or fear of violence, an intuitive definition that most people will agree with. This was used in defining the measures for the GPI which include indicators that measure both the internal peacefulness of nations as well their external peace in relation to other states. This body of work by IEP is the only known quantitative approach to defining positive peace, and as such occupies a unique position in peace studies. This work provides a foundation for researchers to deepen their understanding of the empirical relationships between peace, social development and other development variables.

The empirical link between negative peace and the factors in the PPI appear to hold in both developing and developed contexts. Both negative and positive peace can be seen as the producer and product of forms of trust and cohesion that are a pre-requisite for well-functioning and prosperous societies. Countries higher in positive peace also tend to have many other fundamentally positive social and economic outcomes. For instance, IEP finds high peace countries have:

- Higher per capita incomes
- More equitable distribution of resources
- Better health and education outcomes
- Improved trust between citizens
- Greater social cohesion

By moving countries away from direct violence and towards positive peace, this demonstrates that it is also possible to reap a significant social and economic dividend as a primary by-product of creating peace.

Methodology

The PPI is similar to the GPI in that it is a composite index attempting to measure a multi-dimensional concept. The PPI is the first known attempt to build an empirically-derived index aiming to measure the latent variable of positive peace from the definition of 'the set of attitudes, institutions and structures which, when strengthened, lead to a more peaceful society' (IEP 2011: 4).

The starting point for developing the PPI was to correlate the GPI against over 300 cross-country harmonised data sets measuring a variety of economic, governance, social, attitudinal and political factors. This aggregation of data attempted to cover every known quantitative and qualitative data set measuring factors at the nation-state level. Each data set that was significantly correlated was then organised under eight distinct headings or factors, previously referred to as the pillars of peace.[3] These structures were derived by empirical inspection and were taken from the large body of qualitative and quantitative literature highlighting the importance of these factors.

Under each of the eight domains, the data sources most closely correlated with the GPI were then aggregated for each country. This resulted in the PPI having the following key features:

- Twenty-one indicators under eight domains (Table 6.1)
- One hundred and eight countries covered
- Time series covering only 2010

The eight domains of the PPI are:

- Well-functioning government
- Sound business environment
- Equitable distribution of resources
- Acceptance of the rights of others
- Free flow of information
- Good relations with neighbours
- High levels of education
- Low levels of corruption

---

3 Significance (or significance threshold) is the qualitative level at which IEP considers that a relationship between two variables is meaningful. Statistical significance (significance level) indicates something that passes the appropriate statistical test (for correlation, the t-test which distinguishes the correlation from zero). All correlations presented, other than societal attitudes, have a determined level of significance > 0.5 or < --0.5. The threshold for a meaningful correlation from global surveys was considered more appropriate at > 0.4 or < –0.4.

Table 6.1: **Domains and indicators of the PPI**

Source: IEP 2012: 72

Positive peace domain	Indicator	Data source	Weight	% of total index
Well-functioning Government	Government effectiveness	World Bank, World Governance Indicators	0.73	5.64
	Rule of law	World Bank, World Governance Indicators	0.77	5.94
	Political culture	Economist Intelligence Unit (EIU) Democracy Index	0.66	5.13
Sound business environment	Global Competitiveness Report	World Economic Forum, Global Competitiveness Index	0.60	4.63
	Index of Economic Freedom–Business Freedom	Heritage Foundation, Index of Economic Freedom	0.57	4.39
	GDP per capita (PPP)	World Bank, World Governance Indicators	0.58	4.51
Equitable distribution of resources	Inequality Adjusted Human Development Index (IHDI)*	United Nations Development Programme	0.53	4.14
	Life expectancy	World Bank, World Development Indicators	0.51	3.94
	Infant mortality	World Bank, World Development Indicators	0.51	3.94
Acceptance of the rights of others	CIRI Empowerment Index	CIRI Human Rights Dataset	0.74	5.76
	Gender Gap Index	World Economic Forum	0.53	4.07
	Inter-group cohesion	Indices for Social Development, International Institute of Social Studies	0.80	6.19
Good relations with neighbours	Interpersonal safety and trust	Indices for Social Development, International Institute of Social Studies	0.50	3.90
	Extent of regional integration	Economist Intelligence Unit	0.64	4.99
Free flow of information	Press Freedom Index	Freedom House	0.60	4.65
	World Press Freedom Index	Reporters Without Borders	0.56	4.34
	Internet usage	International Telecommunications Union and United Nations	0.62	4.82

Positive peace domain	Indicator	Data source	Weight	% of total index
High levels of education	Mean years of schooling	UNESCO, Institute of Statistics	0.53	4.13
	Secondary school enrolment rate	World Bank, World Development Indicators	0.48	3.69
Low levels of corruption	Control of corruption	World Bank, World Governance Indicators	0.73	5.69
	Corruptions Perception Index	Transparency International	0.71	5.52

Note: * Some data points for the IHDI are missing, so the standard HDI measure has been supplemented for countries missing the IHDI. These countries are: Afghanistan; Malaysia; Japan; Botswana; Papua New Guinea; New Zealand; Libya; Iran; Bahrain; Qatar; Myanmar; Kuwait; Equatorial Guinea; Algeria; and Saudi Arabia.

Indicator weightings

All indicators are scored between one and five, with one being the most 'positively peaceful' and five the least. This means countries that score closer to one are likely to have *relatively* more institutional capacity and resilience in comparison to nations that score closer to five.

The weightings are between 0.5 and 0.8 and have been derived by the strength of the indicator's statistical correlation to the 2011 GPI score. The stronger the correlation to the GPI the higher the weighting in the PPI. The lowest weighting is given to the 'secondary school enrolment' indicator, which is weighted at 0.48 and accounts for 3.69% of the index. This is in comparison to the most heavily weighted factor of 'inter-group cohesion', which is weighted at 0.80 and accounts for 6.2% of the PPI.

Results

Table 6.2 shows the rankings and scores of the 108 countries in the PPI. Due to the small difference in scores between some nations the results are best understood in groups of ten, as in the top ten, 11 to 20 and so on.

Key observations from the results are:

- The top five are all Nordic nations which all score highly in the GPI

- There are only two countries that are not high income in the top 30—Chile and Lithuania; both are upper middle income nations

- The bottom ten nations are dominated by seven Sub-Saharan African nations; the remaining three are from the Asia Pacific region

- North America and Western Europe are the most positively peaceful regions, on average (Fig. 6.1)

- Sub-Saharan Africa is the least positively peaceful region, on average (Fig. 6.1)

- Positive peace is close to equal in Central and Eastern Europe, the Asia Pacific region, Latin America, and the Middle East and North Africa

- Singapore is the only hybrid regime in the top 20

- France is the only flawed democracy in the top 20

Table 6.2: **PPI results**

Source: IEP 2012: 80-81

Rank	Country	Score	Rank	Country	Score
1	Sweden	1.170	22	Slovenia	1.839
2	Norway	1.174	23	Czech Republic	1.913
3	Finland	1.240	24	Portugal	1.931
4	Denmark	1.267	25	Cyprus	2.003
5	Iceland	1.328	26	South Korea	2.009
6	Netherlands	1.381	27	Chile	2.058
7	Switzerland	1.382	28	Hungary	2.088
8	Canada	1.383	29	Lithuania	2.139
9	New Zealand	1.412	30	Slovakia	2.141
10	Ireland	1.472	31	Italy	2.157
11	Germany	1.491	32	Qatar	2.181
12	Australia	1.507	33	Poland	2.185
13	Belgium	1.520	34	Latvia	2.187
14	United Kingdom	1.521	35	Uruguay	2.200
15	Austria	1.522	36	Greece	2.216
16	United States of America	1.545	37	United Arab Emirates	2.242
17	Japan	1.634	38	Costa Rica	2.296
18	France	1.707	39	Israel	2.353
19	Singapore	1.747	40	Croatia	2.421
20	Spain	1.829	41	Bulgaria	2.516
21	Estonia	1.838	42	Kuwait	2.547

Rank	Country	Score	Rank	Country	Score
43	Botswana	2.561	76	Egypt	3.112
44	Jamaica	2.585	77	Ecuador	3.114
45	Trinidad and Tobago	2.589	78	China	3.114
46	Bahrain	2.592	79	Philippines	3.117
47	Malaysia	2.595	80	Paraguay	3.118
48	Argentina	2.630	81	Russia	3.128
49	Macedonia	2.677	82	Sri Lanka	3.147
50	Albania	2.684	83	Indonesia	3.150
51	South Africa	2.698	84	Bolivia	3.208
52	Panama	2.700	85	Honduras	3.210
53	Namibia	2.783	86	Guatemala	3.223
54	Brazil	2.784	87	India	3.297
55	Mexico	2.785	88	Senegal	3.338
56	Georgia	2.828	89	Venezuela	3.346
57	Peru	2.829	90	Malawi	3.374
58	El Salvador	2.858	91	Tanzania	3.385
59	Dominican Republic	2.885	92	Zambia	3.395
60	Colombia	2.889	93	Syria	3.400
61	Turkey	2.910	94	Madagascar	3.400
62	Tunisia	2.915	95	Iran	3.427
63	Saudi Arabia	2.924	96	Kenya	3.459
64	Guyana	2.939	97	Mozambique	3.485
65	Mongolia	2.942	98	Mali	3.495
66	Thailand	2.982	99	Bangladesh	3.526
67	Jordan	2.997	100	Cambodia	3.528
68	Moldova	2.998	101	Uganda	3.542
69	Ukraine	3.001	102	Burkina Faso	3.589
70	Kazakhstan	3.019	103	Cameroon	3.760
71	Ghana	3.021	104	Ethiopia	3.761
72	Armenia	3.027	105	Pakistan	3.808
73	Nicaragua	3.102	106	Nigeria	3.845
74	Morocco	3.104	107	Cote d' Ivoire	3.881
75	Azerbaijan	3.108	108	Zimbabwe	4.016

Figure 6.1: **Positive peace averages by region (the lower the score the more positive peace)**

Source: IEP 2012: 80-81

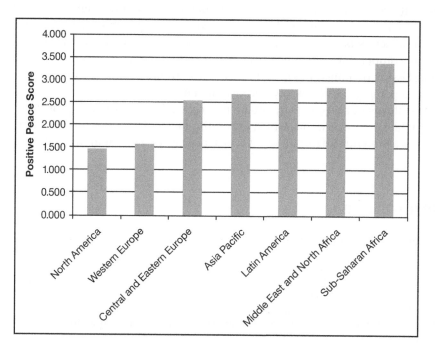

Conclusion

The results of the PPI enable one to conceptualise a nation's multi-dimensional institutional capacity and resilience to deal with external shocks and avoid conflict. Perhaps unsurprisingly, the nations at the top of the PPI tend to be high on the GPI, in the high income category, and full democracies as defined by the EIU Democracy Index. On average, North America and Western Europe are the most positively peaceful regions, with Sub-Saharan Africa clearly well behind on positive peace (Fig. 6.1). Interestingly, the average positive peace score is close to equal in Central and Eastern Europe, the Asia Pacific region, Latin America, and the Middle East and North Africa (Fig. 6.1). This suggests these diverse regions on average face similar challenges in terms of building resilience and institutional capacity.

The lower ranked nations in the PPI tend to be lower income nations with hybrid or authoritarian regimes. Despite the fact that hybrid regimes are on average slightly less peaceful than authoritarian regimes in the GPI, they tend to have the same average PPI score. Evidently, the countries facing governance or economic constraints will have ongoing challenges in boosting their levels of positive peace. Additionally, with the available trend data showing purported declines in inter-group cohesion, slight increases in corruption and declines in press freedom, there may be future challenges to boosting positive peace.

For humanity to grow and prosper in a world facing finite resource constraints, global threats and the potential of economic devastation through warfare, there needs to be a new paradigm for international affairs. Much of the interaction of nation-states is based on competition and win/lose outcomes. Although some level of competition is healthy the current inability the reach agreement on many critical issues demonstrates the failures of the current system. A focus on peace can create a paradigm shift simply because the attitudes, institutions and structures that create peace also create by-products such resilience, economic prosperity and international co-operation, which are at the heart of a viable future. Therefore, peace is a prerequisite for the survival of society as we know it in the 21st century.

References

Galtung, J. (1985) 'Twenty-Five Years of Peace Research: Ten Challenges and Some Responses', *Journal of Peace Research* 22.2: 141-58.

Galtung, J. (2012) 'An Interview with John Galtung', Insight on Conflict (12 March 2012; www.insightonconflict.org/2012/03/interview-johan-galtung, accessed 29 March 2013).

Geys, B. (2010) 'Wars, Presidents, and Popularity: The Political Cost(s) of War Re-examined', *Public Opinion Quarterly* 74.2: 357-74.

Glick, R., and A.M. Taylor (2010) 'Collateral Damage: Trade Disruption and the Economic Impact of War', *The Review of Economics and Statistics* 92.1: 102-27.

Hegre, H., and N. Sambanis (2006) 'Sensitivity Analysis of Empirical Results on Civil War Onset', *Journal of Conflict Resolution* 50.4: 508-35.

Human Security Report Project (2011) *Human Security Report 2009/2010: The Causes of Peace and the Shrinking Costs of War* (New York: Oxford University Press).

IEP (Institute of Economics and Peace) (2011) *Pillars of Peace: Finding the Attitudes, Institutions and Structures Most Closely Associated with Peace* (Sydney, Australia: IEP).

IEP (Institute of Economics and Peace) (2012) *Global Peace Index 2012* (Sydney, Australia: IEP).

WHO (World Health Organisation) (2002) *World Report on Violence and Health: Summary* (Geneva, Switzerland: WHO).

Steve Killelea is an accomplished entrepreneur and philanthropist. He is the Founder and Executive Chair of the Institute for Economics and Peace, an independent research institute dedicated to better understanding the social and economic factors that develop a more peaceful society. Steve serves on a number of advisory boards including the International Crisis Group, the Alliance for Peacebuilding and the Club de Madrid, and is an International Trustee of the World Council of Religions for Peace.

7

The wicked problem of developing a new social contract for the necessary transition

Sandra Waddock

Boston College, Carroll School of Management, Chestnut Hill, Massachusetts, USA

> The conclusions ... are inescapable: during the last few decades, humans have emerged as a new force of nature. We are modifying physical, chemical, and biological systems in new ways, at faster rates, and over larger spatial scales than ever recorded on Earth. Humans have unwittingly embarked upon a grand experiment with our planet. The outcome of this experiment is unknown, but has profound implications for all of life on Earth (Lubchenco 1998: 491).

There is plenty of evidence to suggest that the world is in trouble and that the social contract that exists between business and society, and, indeed, between people and their societies (and governments), not to mention with planet Earth itself, is badly broken. Hurricane Sandy's devastating impact on New York and New Jersey in the USA in the autumn of 2012 is only one of many examples of climate-change related shifts that are focusing attention on this issue. We know that in this difficult context many progressive and leading companies are trying mightily to become more sustainable—and also that few, if any of them, actually are so today. Indeed, John Ehrenfeld (2008) has made the important point that becoming less unsustainable, which is where virtually all companies working this arena currently are, is quite different from becoming sustainable, which implies a wholly different mind-set and approach to business, one in which profits at all costs may no longer be the sole objective (Jensen 2002).

In their efforts to understand and cope with both societal and ecological sustainability issues (not to mention business issues), many companies have joined initiatives such as the World Business Council for Sustainable Development (WBCSD), the UN Global Compact and the Principles for Responsible Investment (for financial firms), among numerous others. Today, as a result of a growing infrastructure on corporate responsibility (Waddock 2008), some companies use monitoring and certification approaches to guide their internal management systems and decision-making (e.g. SA 8000, AA 1000, ISO 9000, ISO 14000 and, in the future, ISO 26000). Still others report on their sustainability, responsibility and innovation activities through multiple bottom-line reports using the Global Reporting Initiative (GRI) guidelines. KPMG described this approach in 2011 as having become de facto, albeit voluntary, law, with 95% of the world's largest 250 companies now undertaking such reporting.[1]

Whatever their corporate social responsibility/corporate responsibility (CSR/ CR) efforts may be, and however far some leading companies have moved (and some indeed have), there is still far too much greenwashing and too little reality to sustainability initiatives. Too many CR initiatives are still done only to enhance reputation rather than being truly integrated into company practices. Not to mention that too many companies are well behind on the learning curve around CR and sustainability in the first place. Further, even among companies that develop terrific CSR/CR initiatives, there is still an inability or unwillingness on the parts of many to deal with the problematic ecological and societal impacts of their business model, which is of course where the biggest impacts are. Despite efforts such as the WBCSD's Vision 2050 (WBCSD 2010), which tries to map out what it calls a platform for dialogue on sustainability and a vision of a sustainable future that is quite radical in its approach, there is still an emphasis on continuing business-as-usual.

If there is not downright resistance to significant change at least on the part of some progressive businesses, there is certainly in many instances an inability to see a different way forward (Schor 2010). Much of today's business expertise, in fact, lends itself to keeping the system as it is intact (business-as-usual thinking) through tactics of stalling, power and leverage, political action committees and campaign contributions, particularly in the USA, though such behaviour is also evident elsewhere. We see many companies that, on the one hand, talk a pretty good game around issues of sustainability and, on the other, use their (growing) political clout to forestall any real changes that might actually limit business behaviours with negative ecological or social impacts. As one respondent to a SustainAbility survey on the relationship between public affairs and corporate responsibility

---

1 KPMG International Survey of Corporate Responsibility Reporting 2011, www.kpmg .com/PT/pt/IssuesAndInsights/Documents/corporate-responsibility2011.pdf, accessed 17 January 2012.

stated: 'Companies will always lobby for what is in their interests. What we have to be careful of is where lobbying is not in the interest of the market as a whole' (Beloe *et al.* 2007: 1). We could add, in the interests of society and the natural environment to the good of the market.

In part, what has happened is that the social contract that has existed between business and society, as well as between people and government/society, and the planet during the past century—and particularly since the early 1980s—is no longer working. The idea that the sole purpose of business is to maximise profits for share-holders—which really took hold of the business mindset during the early 1980s, and seemed on the surface to work reasonably well—has been shattered. Among events that showed the cracks in the system were the numerous corporate scandals of the early 2000s (led, of course, by Enron) and the bursting of the 'dot.com' bub-ble, followed by the 2007–2008 global financial crisis, accompanied by growing rec-ognition of the stark realities of climate change (to wit, Hurricane Sandy, increasing wild weather patterns, droughts and floods) and other sustainability issues, some of which threaten human civilization itself (Brown *et al.* 2009; Lovelock 2006, 2010; McKibben 2010; Gilding 2011).

To these stark realities we could add growing global inequity between rich and poor, and a population-related set of resource crises around issues of food produc-tion and supply, energy, safety and security, water and healthcare. Combine these factors with virtually instantaneous global connectivity through social media and other forms of electronic communication, and you get increased public awareness of various issues as well as new ways of organising to protest what is going on. In other words, you get the Arab Spring and the Occupy movement, both of which emerged in 2011, and you get the ongoing protests against austerity measures being imposed in numerous southern European nations to deal with those countries' debt crises. The digital world has created transparency for companies, whether they desire it or not, and an inability for them to hide their actions and impacts as they once were, at least reasonably better, able to do. Combined, these and related fac-tors mean that the presumed social contract between people(s) and their societies and with nature itself is fundamentally shifting in ways that cannot be predicted.

The idea of social contract

In *Of the Social Contract*, Jean-Jacques Rousseau states: '… the social order is a sacred right which is the basis of all other rights. Nevertheless, this right does not come from nature, and must therefore be founded on conventions' (Rous-seau 1947[1762]: 6). The key point made by Rousseau, who also played important roles in early thinking on the social contract) was that the relationships that exist between people (societies) and their governments are humanly-constructed rather than deriving from nature, and that these relationships constitute a kind of agree-ment between people and their governments about what is and is not appropriate.

The idea of a social contract, which as Keeley (1995) points out is metaphorical rather than literal, originally applied to the relationship between people and government (Rousseau 1947[1762]). Today the term is used to describe multiple different types of relationships. For example, there are discussions about the social contract between individual citizens and their governments, which is, of course, the traditional view, but also between human institutions and society at large, between labour and management, and between employees and employers. And, increasingly, we see talk about the social contract among humanity, its institutions (particularly business enterprises), and the very Earth itself, especially when the planet is conceived as Gaia—a living system (Lovelock 1979, 1988, 2006, 2010; Waddock 2011).

In the past, humanity and its business creations were generally able to essentially assume that the Earth would supply plentiful resources to support human civilization. But as humanity has spread like a virus on the planet, quadrupling in numbers during the 1900s and, in 2011, surpassing 7 billion with projections of stabilising around 9 billion by 2050, it has been using up resources faster than they can be renewed. Indeed, the WWF's Living Planet Index estimates that, by 2007, humanity's demands on renewable resources had put us into ecological overshoot by 50%, meaning that each year humanity uses 1.5 times the amount of renewable resources that can actually be regenerated by the planet, using up existing stock that can no longer be replaced just like drawing from a bank account until the money is fully exhausted (WWF 2011). The impact is one of depleting virtually all renewable stocks such as forests, fisheries, water supplies and agricultural land in ways that could well lead to what Diamond (2005) has called collapse on a global or at least regional scale.

In their integrated social contract theory, Donaldson and Dunfee (1994, 1999) argue that what they call 'ties that bind'—the underlying social contract—when legitimate, arise from specific cultural and geographical contexts, and can exist at multiple levels, including national, industry or even company levels. These ties that bind have moral standing that arises from some level of agreement from the communities that formed them and, as these norms shift, so do the opportunities and challenges with which business must contend. Since the early 1980s, we have been living through an era in which the social contract for business with society appeared to involve following the dictates of neoclassical economics to maximise shareholder wealth. Since the 2000s opened, we have experienced a wave of scandals, led by Enron and followed by the 2008 global financial crisis, fuelled by rampant speculation in financial markets, mortgage fraud and unfettered greed at many levels (Davis 2009), accompanied by wild weather patterns that increasingly suggest the reality of climate change. The world, as noted above, continues to experience numerous protests against the current system. In this context, it has become increasingly clear that the narrow conception of business's purpose to maximise shareholder wealth is no longer viable as the sum of business's social contract, despite many believers in business-as-usual still clinging to it.

Today, it is humanity's relationship with the planet itself, through businesses and other types of institutions, that is creating problems—and the need for a dramatically new and different form of social contract. In a paper written for *Science* just before the transition to the 2000s about the need for a new social contract between scientists and society, Lubchenco presented indisputable scientific evidence of humanity's impact on the planet, and emphatically noted:

> The conclusions from this overview are inescapable: during the last few decades, humans have emerged as a new force of nature. We are modifying physical, chemical, and biological systems in new ways, at faster rates, and over larger spatial scales than ever recorded on Earth. Humans have unwittingly embarked upon a grand experiment with our planet. The outcome of this experiment is unknown, but has profound implications for all of life on Earth (Lubchenco 1998: 491).

Further, as Lubchenco noted in the *Science* paper, so dramatic are not only the biological and ecological changes on Earth, but also the social and cultural ones (e.g. derived from growing inequity, globality in all respects, and digital communication capabilities, to mention a few), that the past does not readily predict the future. Although Lubchenco was speaking explicitly about the role of science, she could have been talking about economic, social, cultural and political systems as well, when she concluded,

> The world at the close of the 20th century is a fundamentally different world from the one in which current scientific [or other] enterprise has developed. The challenges for society are formidable and will require substantial information, knowledge, wisdom, and energy from the scientific community. Business as usual will not suffice (Lubchenco 1998: 491).

Rethinking the social contract[2]

Minimally, in the sustainability context described above, it is clear that the social contract going forwards needs to change away from a consumption-oriented, growth-at-any-cost, more-is-always-better orientation towards a model that is more realistic given the planetary constraints humanity is facing. And the social contract itself is broken, with a clear need for greater social equity, and more ways for people to support themselves in meaningful ways that add value to life-giving

2 The point of view of these comments is progressive (versus conservative), i.e. based on the belief that climate change is real and needs to be addressed, that sustainability issues present the risk of significant harm to humanity, and that democracy, social justice and equity for all will be to the benefit of humanity at large and the ability of the planet to support human civilization in the future.

and generative aspects of society, community and nature; that is, to wellbeing, not just financial wealth. It is also clear that the digital technologies and the connectivity they provide, especially with respect to emerging forms of social media—the so-called Web 2.0 technologies—have created desire for (and realisation of) greater 'voice' and input on the part of many people. Some of these can be seen in the uprisings associated with the Arab Spring in 2011, about which writer Salman Rushdie has stated, 'The Arab spring is a demand for desires and rights that are common to all human beings'.[3] These protests, also termed the Arab Awakening, generally represent efforts to foster more democratic regimes and, in many cases, upend sometimes long-existing repressive regimes.

Problems with the social contract, then, generally relate to broad issues of economic welfare and wealth distribution, climate change and sustainability, and democracy and voice. Further, protests against current regimes that were spawned in 2011 were not limited to Arab nations where repression, lack of economic opportunity and democratic deficiencies were the norm. The demands found expression in a huge variety of places around the world, including Athens, which was confronted with political and economic rioting; Russia, where political protests followed questionable election results; Madrid, Barcelona and London, which experienced protests because of lack of economic opportunity; Chile where protests were about labour and social spending; and India, where efforts focused on anti-corruption (Andersen 2011; Rachman 2011).

By the end of 2011, the European Union's currency, the euro, was in trouble because of potential defaults by the governments of Greece, Portugal, and Ireland, with several other eurozone nations not far behind. Writing in August 2011, Gideon Rachman of the *Financial Times* noted that the rage about rising inequality, threats to middle-class living, and anger against the business and social elite had not yet hit the USA. Then, in September 2011, the Occupy Wall Street movement exploded in the USA, with many of the same issues at its core. Indeed, *Time* magazine named 'the protester' as its 'person of the year' in 2011 as a result of all of the issues and demands being raised in the wide array of demonstrations around the world (Andersen 2011). Public unwillingness to stand for the current social contract became even more apparent in the autumn of 2012 when co-ordinated protests against austerity measures emerged in the southern European countries of Spain, Portugal and Italy.

All of these protests, it can be argued, signal problems with the existing social contract. In designating 'the protester' as person of the year, *Time* noted that the protesters around the world, despite many differences, shared a number of characteristics—they are mostly young, middle-class, mostly educated, and are finding it hard to make their way in today's economic and social system (Andersen 2011). I would argue that, despite their differences, these protesters share a common sense that the existing social contract is badly broken and needs a radical shift. Even

---

3 Quoted in *The Observer*, 26 June 2011, www.guardian.co.uk/theobserver/2011/jun/26/salman-rushdie-luka-fatwa-tim-adams, accessed 16 March 2013.

before the Occupy movement began, the *Financial Times* had called 2011 'the year of global indignation' (Rachman 2011) and, despite its diminishment in 2012, the Occupy movement only highlighted the shifting public mindset even in the highly developed USA where the conversation shifted to include language about the 99% (lower- and middle-class) and the 1% (wealthy) in an ongoing way.

Many demonstrations have not necessarily been organised around explicit demands or common themes (and many in the public media have complained that protesters really do not know what they are protesting). There is, however, clearly an undertone in all of them of protest against the current economic system, against lack of employment and economic opportunities, against 'elites' who seem disconnected from the realities of everyday people, against lack of social mobility, and against a system that seems slanted in favour of the already rich—at the expense of the poor and the natural environment. Or as *Time's* Kurt Andersen puts it: 'All over the world, the protesters of 2011 share a belief that their countries' political systems and economies have grown dysfunctional and corrupt—sham democracies rigged to favour the rich and powerful and prevent significant change' (Andersen 2011). The sustainability and climate change crises, which pose potentially even graver threats to humanity, are an undercurrent in many protests as well.

The varied and numerous 'demands' of the Occupy movement shed an interesting perspective on some of the details about exactly where the current social contract, at least in the USA, is broken and help to highlight the underlying rationale for many of the protests elsewhere as well. There are numerous articulations of the Occupy movement's 'demands' in various places on the Internet but no consolidated set of demands that are fully agreed. Still, there is consistency with the desires of other protesters around the world. Among the changes articulated by the movement in the USA are: eliminate corporate personhood; repeal the *Patriot Act 2001*; make the Federal Reserve Bank a public institution; restructure campaign finance legislation (including banning corporate donations); make healthcare affordable and available to all; end the 'war on drugs'; reform education; repeal capital punishment; end gender discrimination and institute equal pay for equal work; create an Office of the Citizen; force the USA to comply with international human rights law; put the rights of victims first in courts; prosecute crimes committed by financial institutions; create environmental responsibility reform; and repeal martial law in the USA.[4]

In a related gesture, *YES!* magazine issued a 'community bill of rights for occupied communities' that articulates a number of directions that communities could go in the USA to satisfy some occupier demands, most of which are already embedded in law in some places. The community bill of rights argues that 'recognition that political power is inherent in the people', not in corporations (from which some legal powers would be removed) if it were adopted. Specific potential local regulations could include: the right to a locally-based economy; the right to affordable and safe

---

4 Occupy Wall Street demands, coupmedia.org/occupywallstreet/occupy-wall-street-official-demands-2009, accessed 16 March 2013.

housing; the right to affordable preventive healthcare; protective rights for nature; the right to water; a sustainable food system and affordable and renewable energy; the right to constitutional protections in the workplace; and the right to determine the future of neighbourhoods. Other elements include: rights to a free, open and accessible Internet; a citizen-managed and accountable police force; clean and fair elections free from corporate interference; clean government; and marriage equality. The bill, if fully adopted, would also prohibit corporate personhood and privileges, ban electioneering and lobbying by corporations, and protect people's right to self-government (Reifman and Linzey 2012).

In one of the few mainstream press articles early in the Occupy movement's history that actually understood what was going on, the *Washington Post* reported: 'To the participants in Occupy Wall Street, business and political leaders have lost their footing. They have detoured the country away from the basic tenets of our government: life, liberty, equality and the pursuit of happiness' (Love 2011). In a similarly motivated but earlier initiative, the New American Foundation held a conference in 2010 that highlighted some of the following problems with the current social contract, at least as it exists in the USA. Among the issues cited, which apply to the USA but are equally problematic in other parts of the world, are: growing inequity (i.e. a growing rich–poor gap); wage stagnation; increased household, and national, indebtedness; loss or migration of good paying jobs to low wage countries (a downward spiral that some call a race to the bottom); a growing need for high-skilled employees, but high unemployment rates for lower-skilled individuals; and growth in poverty rates.[5] Add in the sustainability and climate change issues now documented to be affecting human civilization and forecast to be worse in the future (IPCC 2007; Gilding 2011), and you get a very similar array of issues suggesting where the social contract is broken.

Protests in Europe raise strikingly similar issues, as the *New York Times* reported, with protesters 'reflect[ing] widespread unhappiness with high unemployment, slowing growth, and worsening economic problems in Europe' (Minder 2012). The *New York Times* article called the co-ordinated protests 'historic', noting that numerous different entities, including 'railroad workers in Belgium, airline workers, autoworkers, and teachers in Spain; civil servants in Italy, and transit workers in Spain' were involved in the actions.

The key questions, of course, are: What to do about all of these issues and inequities? What changes will be needed and how, on our divided and fractured Earth, will they begin to happen?

---

5 See Megan Current, 'A Social Contract for the Next Generation', 27 October 2010, www.firstfocus.net/news/reading-list/a-social-contract-for-the-next-generation, accessed 23 January 2012; and Lauren Damme, 'Overview: The Great Recession Exposes Weaknesses in the American Social Contract', newamerica.net/sites/newamerica.net/files/policydocs/NSC%201.pdf, accessed 23 January 2012.

Changing the social contract of business in society: finding common ground

Einstein famously stated, 'We can't solve problems by using the same kind of thinking we used when we created them'.[6] What this epigraph means in practice is that, to deal with the enormous (wicked) problems that we face, we must rise up at least a level of abstraction and find out where there is common ground on which people of differing opinions can actually agree. That is not always easy to do, of course. But if common ground can be found—first on the reality that the planet has problems and, second, on the notion that we all want our grandchildren to be able to survive reasonably successfully—that might be a starting point. Tapping into the aspirations of people of all creeds and colours for a better life might be the first step towards the kinds of open-ended and democratically-based processes that allow for voice and participation (e.g. open space, mind mapping, future search).

Simply coming to an agreed-upon definition of the systems problems that humanity is facing, their causes and what should be done about them (i.e. to change the social contract), then itself becomes a wicked problem, especially given the conflictual ways in which sustainability and climate change issues have evolved. However much denial some might wish to be in about the condition of the world and what is needed—not just to survive or even 'sustain' in the future—but actually to thrive, it seems we need to face serious new realities. Below I will briefly review some of my own ideas about what might be done to reshape the future social contract, as well as the one we have made with nature. These are the premises that underpin my discussion below. In the world where we actually live today, climate change is already upon us and adaptation is now what is needed (McKibben 2010). In this world, something also needs to be done to narrow the currently widening gap between rich and poor, and ensure that there is what the International Labour Organisation calls decent work for the millions and millions of people who are unemployed or under-employed. We also need to find ways to provide sufficient food, energy, housing and work for the world's population in a way that stops trashing the planet.

These issues are but a few of the ones that have been raised about the existing (largely tacit) social contract, and all of them can be classed as wicked problems. Underlying the current social contract of business in society are a number of core assumptions that will need to shift to bring business, and humanity, into alignment with planetary and social realities and, not incidentally, make the world a more liveable place for many more people. By definition, wicked problems (which include most social and ecological problems) are boundary-spanning, poorly formulated, hard to understand, and have many different stakeholders with different perspectives on the nature of the problem, the potential resolutions and the best

---

6 See, for example, articles.businessinsider.com/2012-04-19/strategy/31366385_1_business-lessons-success-business, accessed 27 March 2013.

path forward (Churchman 1967; Rittel and Webber 1973; Grint 2005; Batie 2008). Obviously, as with any wicked problem, any number of perspectives might be brought to bear and issues raised. We are facing a quandary to the extent that problems of the system that companies, and the rest of us, face fall into the category of wicked problems.

The first assumption—and perhaps one of the most problematic since it drives so much else—is the assumption that growth is always necessary and good for the economy, for societies and, in particular, for business. Yet it is increasingly apparent that growth is itself the problem of growth—because we cannot continue to 'grow' material consumption of planetary resources in a world with over 7 billion people where we are using up resources at what is clearly an unsustainable rate. Two other core assumptions are related—first, that wealth is the amount of financial resources one has (i.e. purchasing power) and, second, that having more of this material wealth is always better.

The assumptions about wealth are directly linked to related assumptions—that more consumption of 'stuff', material and other goods and services, is better than less consumption; and that such a materialistic orientation will result in happiness. Two related factors are particularly relevant in the current business environment. One is that accumulation of power and the ability to exploit other people and resources (e.g. by externalising costs) is always good and a source of status. Finally, also in the business realm (though applying in many others as well), is the notion that competition is at the core of doing business and, generally, of human existence.

From growth to thrivability

Businesses and whole economies are constrained by the ever-present 'need' for growth rather than, say, an orientation towards wellbeing, health and 'enough' (some might call it 'sufficiency' and economic sociologist Juliet Schor [2010] calls it 'plenitude' in a book by that name). Such a reorientation is based on a sense that people seeking meaning, connection and a capacity to contribute to create meaningful lives, might well foster a more credible orientation towards sustainability. A group at the Business as an Agent of World Benefit in 2008 called this notion 'thrivability', indicating a movement beyond sustenance implied in the term sustainability.

The very idea of growth is fundamental to capitalism as we know it, because it rests on the notion that credit and interest rates will always be present (Binswanger 2009) and thus that growth is inevitable. The concept of limits to growth, however, was very publicly promulgated by the Club of Rome (Meadows *et al.* 1972) as long ago as the early 1970s, but widely discounted in the public press, despite most of its predictions actually coming true (Turner 2008). Today, we face even more constraints arising from the assumption that material and monetary growth is always needed and will always be possible. Governments, too, are constrained by the continued sense that economic growth, viewed through the lens of gross domestic product (GDP), is the best way to assess the state of the economy and the welfare of society. In some important respects, leaders need to have the courage and insight to redefine what is meant by success away from GDP/GNP (gross national product), measures known to be flawed since their inception (Costanza *et al.* 2009).

What if, instead of focusing on constant growth, we developed and used other measures? Some have tried this already, for example with the genuine progress indicator (GPI) and Happy Planet Index. Perhaps we can think beyond these measures. What if we try to redefine growth in terms of the way that people and systems 'grow'; that is, in terms of greater complexity—and with an orientation towards wellbeing rather than material goods and services? The critical challenges we face are posed by the need to deal considerably more effectively with the sustainability crisis, the need for true innovation—not just in products and services that foster more growth, which indeed is part of the problem—but in the ways we relate to each other, in how we think about the role of the economy and businesses in society, in creating new and innovative mindsets that allow us to think differently about the core purposes of businesses and how they serve us (not the other way around), and in fostering a more collaborative orientation that seeks the good of all. Human and other types of development, complexity theory informs us, grow towards greater complexity—but not always greater size (Prigogine *et al.* 1984; Nicolis and Prigogine 1989; Kauffman 1995; Capra 1997; Gleick 1997; Kegan 2002).

Another form of alignment—aligning human interests and business purposes with the constraints of nature—will likely also become significantly more vital in the future. Blended value (i.e. blending social, ecological and material/financial value; Emerson 2003), multiple bottom-lines and shared value creation (Porter and Kramer 2006, 2011) are all likely to be part of more humanised (human scale, human values, principled) enterprise in the future. As stakeholders demand both business and social/ecological purposes from businesses to meet 21st century needs (see, for example, the Corporation 2020 website[7] for an outline of some of these demands), and as sustainability constraints impose demands that necessitate these orientations, it is possible that people can find common ground more readily (Gilding 2011).

Finally, in addition to everything else, there is a crisis of meaning in the workplace. This crisis has generated growing democratic aims linked to the connective potential of social media and transparency of information. As the power of these technologies grows, and more people become comfortable with them, many internal stakeholders—employees, customers, investors—are likely to demand that enterprise leaders demonstrate how their work is meaningful—and how it contributes to solving the problems of society and the natural environment as people become more aware of the issues facing the world. Skills in dealing with ambiguity and paradox or the tension of opposite positions, stakeholder engagement and meaning-making become important in this context.

---

7 www.corporation2020.org, accessed 16 March 2013.

From more money and 'stuff' to wellbeing

Another possibility is to place sustainability and responsibility to stakeholders and nature at the core of business enterprise scaled along human dimensions even when its reach is global. In such a model, success would be redefined as creating true economic stability, productive and meaningful work that is built on productive assets used to meet real (versus made-up and marketed through sophisticated channels) needs. In such an approach, financial services institutions would return to their original function of serving the business community's real needs for financing rather than building a global financial house of cards, such as currently exists. Rather than recruiting talented individuals with high-level reasoning and quantitative skills to be put to use in creating new financial instruments that add little (if any) value, these individuals would better put their talents towards the service of science and technology and the betterment of humanity. Such a transition involves revaluing education, revaluing science, engineering and mathematics as social goods, and rethinking how we, as societies, reward the kinds of talent we really want to foster. At least in the USA, it also involves revaluing primary and secondary education and the job of teaching.

Making this transition means that leaders will need to step forward consistently—into the business and political arenas—and argue for a future-preserving and enhancing orientation towards business. Some of this can focus on products that actually implement what some call 'servicisation'—improvement of existing services of goods and services. A servicisation approach is quite different from the constant replacement and a throw-away mentality that plans short-term obsolescence into products and services, with which we are now familiar. In this process, we will also need to rethink what wealth really means, and move away from materialism and ever-increasing consumption towards satisfying actual needs for products and services. Underlying this shift is recognition of what wealth really means to most people—wealth based on productive enterprise, connection, community, health, happiness and creativity. Further, who will step forward from the business community and articulate the problems that ever-increasing pace and complexity create for humans, and argue for slowing down to a pace that is more reasonable and, perhaps, both more sane and more liveable?

From power, exploitation and externalities to ... ?

Add to these considerations the need to internalise costs that are currently legally allowed to be externalised, an attitude towards nature that permits and even valorises exploitation, and similar attitudes towards the acquisition and use of power. All of these assumptions and attitudes create social and ecological costs that reside somewhere in the system, even if they are not captured by traditional measures such as GDP. Hence, these costs are paid for by society either via degraded environmental or social conditions or through taxes.

Globally, to conserve resources and enhance quality of life, we need to move towards a full-costing approach to production of goods and services. In full-costing, enterprises of all sorts would be asked to be fully responsible for all of the costs incurred during their productive activities. By making these costs known and publicised, which could happen through social media in a relatively short period of time, various social entrepreneurs might gain traction for internalisation of all relevant costs via full-cost or life-cycle accounting approaches, enhancement of an attitude that celebrates and even reveres what nature can and does provide, with an orientation towards preservation and enhancement rather than exploitation. Further, whether current leaders like it or not, the accessibility of social media has 'trained' many people, especially younger individuals, to expect voice, access and input into decisions that they are currently excluded from making. Continued business-as-usual under these new circumstances is unlikely even though strong efforts to preserve the status quo are likely.

At a more macro level, if the USA or other developed nations changed the way that they measure productivity and economic health away from the highly flawed GDP towards something more like the GPI (or even a gross national happiness indicator), significant shifts in orientation would readily happen. This shift, despite its fraughtness and the associated political difficulties, is important because, as accountants frequently say, what is measured is what gets done, and as organisational theorists note, what is rewarded and measured is where the focus of leaders and managers goes. Simply (!) by shifting what is being measured on a national and global scale, we could then go a long distance to making the necessary transition towards thrivability.

From competition to collaboration and synergy

One other key factor needs to accompany that shift, and that is a reorientation away from emphasising competition and a winner-takes-all mentality in business towards a more collaborative win-win mindset. Ironically, such an orientation is deeply embedded in biological and ecological systems. Collaboration, co-operation and, sometimes, competition are, in this view, at the core of what success will mean in the future. Collaboration will occur within enterprises of all sorts, across functional boundaries (which are increasingly permeable in any case), across organisations within industries to achieve new goals and standards (e.g. the Forest Stewardship Council or Marine Stewardship Council's work on preserving their domains) and, increasingly, across sectors. More such collaborative efforts are needed to articulate and effect a new definition of the common good in different contexts, using perspectives from representative stakeholders as input, and making decisions for the good of the whole.

Given resource constraints, an orientation towards efficiency will be insufficient, and a capacity to do more with less in an entrepreneurial spirit, no matter what size the enterprise is, will become more important. Combined with the courage and ability to manage across boundaries of all sorts, to engage productively with stakeholders with enormously different perspectives, and recognition of the need for human-ness, human scale, humanity in the best senses of those words, will create the baseline for future leaders.

Making the transition?

The sustainability crisis the world faces is so significant that over time radical changes will be needed in the business–society relationship and in humanity's own relationship to the planet. Such changes are never easy and they are unlikely to come without a fight from entrenched interests who stand to gain from continuing the current model; that is, from business-as-usual (Schor 2010). In the context of wicked problems such as changing the social contract, there are numerous points of view. People with a conservative or liberal bent, an ecological or religious orientation, a particular political persuasion, different cultural and ethnic backgrounds, and even economic vs. other educational backgrounds (and so on) are likely to look at the same problem and come to quite different conclusions. Dialogic, multistakeholder approaches, enhanced listening and engagement skills, and innovative ways of finding common ground are needed to cope with these differences and work towards generally (albeit, typically, not fully) agreed resolutions.

Difficult as it sounds, what future leaders will really need in the context and set of necessary changes described above is a capacity for wisdom. One definition of wisdom is the integration of moral imagination (the ability to see the moral and ethical nature of situations and decisions; Werhane 1999, 2002, 2008, 2010), systems understanding (the ability to think through systemic implications of actions and decisions; Senge 1990, 2006, 2008) and aesthetic sensibility (the ability to see and change when necessary the fundamental structural or design components of a decision or action) in the service of decisions and actions taken for the greater good (Waddock 2010). In short, we need, as I have argued elsewhere, to recognise that 'we are all stakeholders to Gaia', and that we can only push the limits of her capacity to sustain life as we know it so far before things are irrevocably changed and there is no turning back (Waddock 2011). That, I believe, is the challenge tomorrow's leaders face. And it is also the opportunity.

References

Andersen, K. (2011) 'The protester: *Time* person of the year 2011', *Time Magazine* (14 December 2011; (www.time.com/time/specials/packages/article/0,28804,2101745_2102132, 00.html, accessed 27 March 2013).

Batie, S.S. (2008) 'Wicked Problems and Applied Economics', *American Journal of Agricultural Economics* 90.5: 1176-91. DOI: 10.1111/j.1467-8276.2008.01202.x

Beloe, S., J. Harrison and O. Greenfield (2007) *Coming In From the Cold: Public Affairs and Corporate Responsibility* (London: WWF).

Binswanger, M. (2009) 'Is There a Growth Imperative in Capitalist Economies? A Circular Flow Perspective', *Journal of Post Keynesian Economics* 31.4: 707-27.

Brown, L.R., Plan B 3.0 and Earth Policy Institute (2009) *Plan B 4.0: Mobilizing to Save Civilization* (New York: W.W. Norton, 1st edn).

Capra, F. (1997) *The Web of Life: A New Scientific Understanding of Living Systems* (Norwell, MA: Anchor).

Churchman, C.W. (1967) 'Wicked Problems', *Management Science* 14.4: B141-42.

Costanza, R., M. Hart, S. Posner and J. Talberth (2009) *Beyond GDP: The Need for New Measures of Progress* (Boston, MA: The Frederick S. Pardee Center for the Study of the Longer-Range Future, Boston University, *The Pardee Papers* No. 4).

Davis, G.F. (2009) 'The Rise and Fall of Finance and the End of the Society of Organizations', *Academy of Management Perspectives* 23.3: 27-44. DOI: 10.5465/AMP.2009.43479262

Diamond, J.M. (2005) *Collapse: How Societies Choose to Fail or Succeed* (New York: Viking).

Donaldson, T., and T.W. Dunfee (1994) 'Toward a Unified Conception of Business Ethics: Integrative Social Contracts Theory', *Academy of Management Review* 19.2: 252-84. DOI: 10.5465/AMR.1994.9410210749

Donaldson, T., and T.W. Dunfee (1999) *Ties That Bind: A Social Contracts Approach to Business Ethics* (Boston, MA: Harvard Business Press).

Ehrenfeld, J. (2008) *Sustainability by Design: A Subversive Strategy for Transforming Our Consumer Culture* (New Haven, CT: Yale University Press).

Emerson, J. (2003) 'The Blended Value Proposition: Integrating Social and Financial Results', *California Management Review* 45.4: 35-51.

Gilding, P. (2011) *The Great Disruption: Why the Climate Crisis Will Bring on the End of Shopping and the Birth of a New World* (New York: Bloomsbury).

Gleick, J. (1997) *Chaos: Making a New Science* (New York: Random House).

Grint, K. (2005) 'Problems, Problems, Problems: The Social Construction of "Leadership"', *Human Relations* 58.11: 1467-94. DOI: 10.1177/0018726705061314

IPCC (Intergovernmental Panel on Climate Change) (2007) *Working Group 1 Fourth Assessment Report. Climate Change 2007: The Physical Science Basis* (Bern, Switzerland: IPCC).

Jensen, M.C. (2002) 'Value Maximization, Stakeholder Theory, and the Corporate Objective Function', *Business Ethics Quarterly* 12.2: 235-56.

Kauffman, S.A. (1995) *At Home in the Universe: The Search for Laws of Self-organization and Complexity* (New York: Oxford University Press).

Keeley, M. (1995) 'Continuing the Social Contract Tradition', *Business Ethics Quarterly* 5.2: 241-55.

Kegan, R. (2002) *In Over Our Heads: The Mental Demands of Modern Life* (Cambridge, MA: Harvard University Press).

Love, A. (2011) 'What Occupy Wall Street demands of our leaders', *Washington Post* (11 October 2011; articles.washingtonpost.com/2011-10-11/national/35280329_1_protestors-movement-wall-street, accessed 27 March 2013).

Lovelock, J. (1979) *Gaia: A New Look at Life on Earth* (New York: Oxford University Press).

Lovelock, J. (1988) *The Ages of Gaia: A Biography of Our Living Earth* (New York: Norton, 1st edn).

Lovelock, J. (2006) *The Revenge of Gaia: Earth's Climate in Crisis and the Fate of Humanity* (New York: Basic Books).

Lovelock, J. (2010) *The Vanishing Face of Gaia: A Final Warning* (New York: Basic Books).

Lubchenco, J. (1998) 'Entering the Century of the Environment: A New Social Contract for Science', *Science* 279.5350: 491-97.

McKibben, B. (2010) *Eaarth: Making a Life on a Tough New Planet* (New York: Times Books, 1st edn).

Meadows, D.H., D.L. Meadows, J. Randers and W.W. Behrens (1972) *The Limits to Growth* (New York: Universe Books).

Minder, R. (2012) 'Workers across Europe synchronize protests', *The New York Times* (14 November 2012; www.nytimes.com/2012/11/15/world/europe/workers-in-southern-europe-synchronize-anti-austerity-strikes.html?_r=0, accessed 15 November 2012).

Nicolis, G., and I. Prigogine (1989) *Exploring Complexity: An Introduction* (New York: W.H. Freeman).

Porter, M.E., and M.R. Kramer (2006) 'The Link Between Competitive Advantage and Corporate Social Responsibility', *Harvard Business Review* 84.12: 78-92.

Porter, M.E., and M.R. Kramer (2011) 'The Big Idea: Creating Shared Value', *Harvard Business Review* 89.1-2: 62-77.

Prigogine, I., I. Stengers and A. Toffler (1984) *Order Out of Chaos* (New York: Bantam Books).

Rachman, G. (2011) 'The year of global indignation', *Financial Times*, 29 August 2011.

Reifman, J., and T. Linzey (2012) 'A bill of rights for occupied communities', *YES!*, 3 January 2012.

Rittel, H.W.J., and M.M. Webber (1973) 'Dilemmas in a General Theory of Planning', *Policy Sciences* 4.2: 155-69.

Rousseau, J.J. (1947[1762]) *Of the Social Contract, or Principles of the Political Right* (Chichester, UK: Wiley).

Schor, J. (2010) *Plenitude: The New Economics of True Wealth* (New York: Penguin Press).

Senge, P.M. (1990) *The Fifth Discipline: The Art and Practice of the Learning Organization* (New York: Doubleday, 1st edn).

Senge, P.M. (2006) *The Fifth Discipline: The Art and Practice of the Learning Organization* (New York: Doubleday/Currency, 2nd edn).

Senge, P.M. (2008) *The Necessary Revolution: How Individuals and Organizations Are Working Together to Create a Sustainable World* (New York: Doubleday).

Turner, G.M. (2008) 'A Comparison of the Limits to Growth With 30 Years of Reality', *Global Environmental Change* 18.3: 397-411.

Waddock, S. (2008) 'Building a New Institutional Infrastructure for Corporate Responsibility', *Academy of Management Perspectives* 22.3: 87-108.

Waddock, S. (2010) 'Finding Wisdom Within: The Role of Seeing and Reflective Practice in Developing Moral Imagination, Aesthetic Sensibility, and Systems Understanding', *Journal of Business Ethics Education* 7.1: 177-96.

Waddock, S. (2011) 'We Are All Stakeholders of Gaia: A Normative Perspective on Stakeholder Thinking', *Organization and Environment* 24.2: 192-212. DOI: 10.1177/1086026611413933

WBCSD (World Business Council for Sustainable Development) (2010) *2050—The New Agenda for Business* (Geneva, Switzerland: WBCSD).

Werhane, P.H. (1999) *Moral Imagination and Management Decision-making* (New York: Oxford University Press).

Werhane, P.H. (2002) 'Moral Imagination and Systems Thinking', *Journal of Business Ethics* 38.1: 33-42.

Werhane, P.H. (2008) 'Mental Models, Moral Imagination and Systems Thinking in the Age of Globalization', *Journal of Business Ethics* 78.3: 463-74.

Werhane, P.H. (2010) 'The Centrality of "Seeing As" and a Question About "Truth": A Response to Sandra Waddock', *Journal of Business Ethics Education* 7.1: 197-200.

WWF (2011) *Living Planet Report 2010: Biodiversity, Biocapacity and Development* (Gland, Switzerland: WWF).

Sandra Waddock is Galligan Chair of Strategy, Carroll School Scholar of Corporate Responsibility, and Professor of Management at Boston College's Carroll School of Management. Sandra has published ten books and more than 100 papers on topics related to corporate responsibility, system change and collaboration. She received the 2011 Bradford Outstanding Educator Award from the Organizational Behavior Teaching Society, and the 2005 Faculty Pioneer Award for External Impact by Aspen Institute.

8

Together: the power of collaboration

Caroline Digby
Eden Project, Cornwall, UK

For the last two decades we have been increasingly warned of impending doom if we fail to respond to the challenges of resource depletion, energy and food security, burgeoning populations and growing inequality. Everywhere are signs of our world as wasteful, disconnected, short-sighted and destructive. Yet even people who are listening struggle to know how to respond at an appropriate scale.

New business models, governance structures, planning systems, enabling legislation and unexpected collaborations are beginning to deliver a glimpse of what the future could look like if these ideas were embraced by the mainstream. At Eden we are very keen on collaboration—the art of working together, often with people we don't know. This chapter will draw on our recent experience to explore why collaboration is a common theme underpinning success.

The Big Lunch: the spirit of collaboration

The Big Lunch is a very simple idea from the Eden Project—to get as many people as possible to have lunch with their neighbours on one day a year, sowing the seeds for stronger communities by coming together and using food and an event to make that happen. The word 'community' comes from *communio* meaning 'together in gift', which is at the heart of this idea, stemming from the belief that we, as a society, are better equipped to tackle the challenges we face when we face them together.

The ambition is for The Big Lunch to become a permanent date in the annual calendar, an event owned by the people; similar to North American Thanksgiving, but for neighbours. Since the initiative began in 2009 it has gained momentum each year. In 2012 The Big Jubilee Lunch formed part of the official Diamond Jubilee events programme, and no fewer than 8.5 million people participated; more than one in ten of the UK population. Lunches also took place in 70 countries internationally—across the Commonwealth and beyond—showing that the desire and need to strengthen communities is universal.

The great thing about The Big Lunch is that no one really owns it; it has to be owned by the people. But it needs investment. From its inception, the success of The Big Lunch has relied heavily on collaboration. Eden's partners include the government, in the shape of the Department for Communities and Local Government, the Big Lottery, EDF Energy, MasterCard, Asda and Kingsmill; a most unusual relationship between public and private enterprise brokered by an educational charity.

But collaboration can be as simple as two neighbours, who have got to know each other over a Big Lunch, sharing a lawnmower or keeping an eye on each other's houses; or something deeper where people, groups, organisations and local councils work together to tackle social problems, reduce isolation and improve the local environment.

While the shared aim of putting on an event is a worthwhile end in itself, it is the interaction between residents, the talking and the planning that takes place in the build-up to the day—and, indeed, the lasting effects once the trestle tables are put away—that really matter. And the beauty is that people are not aware of what is happening—something seemingly simple, fun and light-hearted often goes on to have a profound effect. The crucial question that remained after the 2009 lunches was whether the positive impact would last. People said they were planning on staying in touch with the neighbours they had met and doing things with them in the future. But did they actually do so? Findings from this year show that, overwhelmingly, they did. Nearly nine out of ten participants have kept in touch with their neighbours. Different faiths, ages and backgrounds have been brought together. Areas of significant deprivation, with high levels of unemployment, crime and anti-social behaviour, have improved as a result of people getting to know each other, highlighting problems such as vandalism, fly-tipping and dog fouling, and working together to find practical solutions to address them. Hidden talents have been uncovered to the benefit of neighbours, leading to formal and informal skill-sharing schemes.

A copper roof: sourcing collaboration

An integral part of our mission at Eden is to push the boundaries on sustainable practice in all areas of business, creating opportunities that go beyond expectations and demonstrating just what might be possible through collaboration with a wide range of partners. Having built our Project from scratch we are well versed in the field of sustainable construction, and we have challenged the norm in all sorts of areas such as energy efficiency, accessibility, water use, waste management and materials selection. One of our proudest achievements thus far is to move the discussion on sourcing metals and minerals to a new level.

Metals and minerals are fundamental to construction—from wiring to window frames, from internal beams to insulation—and yet, to date, there has been very little focus on how these building materials are sourced. Information on their provenance and their subsequent chain of custody is seldom available and, perhaps crucially, few are asking the questions.

Metals and minerals have an important role to play in sustainable construction. Through careful selection, the environmental (and social) footprint of a building can be reduced considerably by way of reduced energy consumption, improved efficiency and recycling potential. By ensuring that the materials are sourced, processed, fabricated and produced with environmental and socially responsible rigour, the entire supply chain can also add to the overall beneficial impact of construction of a building. To stimulate debate in this area, we ran an ambitious experiment—and convinced others to join us. It was an atypical effort, but it happened because those involved recognised that a debate is needed over materials supplied to the construction industry, as part of the move towards more sustainable construction practices.

In 2005, the copper roof of the Core, Eden's education building, was sourced from a single responsibly managed mine—Kennecott Utah Copper Company's Bingham Canyon mine in the USA (owned by Rio Tinto, see Chapter 13)—and carefully tracked through the production process. It was believed to be the first time that anyone was able to say that the metal in a building could be directly traced back to a single source.

A key barrier to metals and minerals stewardship is the lack of traceability. Supply chains vary enormously in complexity depending on the commodities in question. The route from ore to end product often involves numerous transformations and dilutions, and can be further complicated when metals and minerals from other supply chains become incorporated. The end product may consist of a range of raw materials sourced from many different mines around the world, which may have been through a diverse range of different processes making traceability virtually impossible.

The construction sector has relatively simple supply chains that use large amounts of some metals and minerals, making stewardship schemes potentially very effective. As shown with the Core's roof at Eden, market forces can bring about change. The 'informed client' (i.e. Eden) drove the sustainability agenda throughout the construction process by demanding that tracking and monitoring systems were in place. Therefore, for this approach to be taken up more widely, there is an imperative for a better understanding of such issues by the clients (as well as the other key interest groups). Also, clearly defined and universally agreed standards are needed for sustainability in construction to become the norm, with a major rethink in building regulations and planning requirements pushing the agenda for material selection and building design—rather than just cost.

As a result of the work on our roof, the Eden Project was awarded a grant by the European Social Fund (with matched funding from Eden and Rio Tinto) to raise awareness of issues surrounding metals and minerals supply chains and to take the debate wider. Over the next six years, working with key individuals in the metals and buildings industries, the Minerals Supply Chain Stewardship project sought to develop recommendations for a more integrated approach and look at the potential role of metal stewardship in green building.

There are a growing number of initiatives that examine how buildings should be designed and operated more sustainably but few, to date, have looked at the role metals and minerals can play. Many companies in the metals and minerals in buildings supply chain are developing sustainability initiatives that lead to improvements within their own sector. What is commonly lacking, though, is a dialogue with others further up and downstream.

Eden took a first step in addressing this disconnect by bringing together, in an open forum, individuals from all stages of the metals and building value chain (mining and processing, fabrication, building design, construction, operation, and renovation and demolition) to learn from each other. More focused workshops followed, leading to the responsible sourcing of metals in buildings being addressed in green building schemes and establishing the groundwork for a sector-specific responsible sourcing scheme for aluminium.

We at Eden were in a unique position to be a catalyst in this debate. We were able to offer an independent platform for the very diverse range of organisations involved in the metals and minerals in buildings supply chains and we were fast building a reputation for pushing the boundaries in this important arena. The responsible sourcing of metals and minerals in construction is now addressed in green building schemes in the UK, and a pilot responsible aluminium scheme is emerging internationally.

Sustainable construction: building collaboration

But it wasn't just about the roof. Sir Robert McAlpine's impressive website tells a story of corporate social responsibility, exemplary projects and a catalogue of achievements and successes in sustainable construction. The company's commitment to sustainability and its proud record of achievement have been influenced significantly by its close working ties with Eden, a relationship that has grown during the years since it was commissioned to build the Project in a disused clay pit in Cornwall. The relationship has changed from a straightforward client–supplier model to something much more collaborative as the two organisations have recognised the strengths of partnership and have pushed the boundaries of what is possible within sustainable construction.

After building the original Eden site with its iconic biomes, McAlpine was commissioned to build the Core, the education centre that would be built on uncompromisingly sustainable principles (see above). As there was little existing practice to draw on, key principles had to be agreed and a set of targets embedded within the project to ensure that sustainability underpinned every aspect of the design and build. These 'challenging but achievable' targets were not drawn from BREEAM,[1] the industry framework, but were arrived at by negotiation between Eden's sustainable construction manager and McAlpine's project manager.

At the time, in 2004, these targets and the method of working were way ahead of current practice, particularly in their key areas of focus—skills and training; supply chain management, and site waste management. Specific targets were set for aspects of landscape, energy, inclusive design, waste and water, with a clear understanding that all of these would have implications for the cost of the project and that these should be identified and managed.

Eden's view of the Core project was that embedding principles of sustainability into the design and build would encourage behaviour change. Eden's 'seeing is believing' approach had to be rigorously applied and there could be no compromise. McAlpine's project manager, despite coming from a more conventional construction background, readily embraced this approach and understood that if corners were cut or compromises made, the construction team on site would lose faith in the project and it would fail. Their united stance and knack for clear communication contributed substantially to the success of the Core construction process. An external assessment partner, Professor Peter Guthrie of Cambridge University, provided triangulation and a neutral space for discussion and assurance. It also ensured the learning was captured and could be employed in future projects.

In a study of the project, Donna Ladkin of Exeter University's Business School identified their inclusive and low-key way of working as 'quiet leadership'. So what were the key ingredients that made the collaboration a success? From the outside the two companies make an unlikely alliance, and there was huge potential for a clash of cultures between a highly commercial company and a values-based organisation such as Eden. Eden's sustainable construction manager identified communication, and the ability to speak the right language, as critical; her personal knowledge of the construction industry meant she could frame the discussions appropriately with the McAlpine team and understand the deal breakers in terms of cost within the contract from their perspective. Conversely, the McAlpine team was led by a natural collaborator, inclusive in approach and extremely receptive to new ways of working.

The collaboration was so successful that when McAlpine bid for a contract to build a new retail development in St Austell, called White River Place, they seconded Eden's sustainable construction manager to the project. This request took

---

1 BREEAM is the world's foremost environmental assessment method and rating system for buildings, www.breeam.org.

the relationship a stage further, with McAlpine recognising the value that Eden could bring to this flagship project in Cornwall. It was also an overt commitment by the company to adopt sustainable construction principles as part of its commercial work.

White River Place was a very different proposition to the Core as it was commercially-focused, although part funded by regional government in the form of the South West Regional Development Agency. Sustainability was an ambition that had to be achieved in a tougher economic climate and without the underlying values and ethos of a project commissioned directly by Eden. The development was a mixed-use scheme of 14,400 m² of retail space, 69 homes, a cinema and a large car park. It had been long-awaited in St Austell, a run-down town in need of regeneration, and expectations were high that it could provide the upturn that was badly needed.

The team that had collaborated so successfully to build the Core at Eden had, in effect, been reconvened, which meant there was a shared knowledge and understanding of the ambitions for White River Place. In addition, though, there were large numbers of new teams on site and it was a considerable challenge to win over their hearts and minds. The leadership style remained broadly the same—consensus-building and inclusive—but there were many conflicting views and at times it became fractious.

The sustainability principles adopted were based on those that had worked well for the Core but also focused specifically on social sustainability; local employment and subcontracts that were within the reach of smaller firms. One of the biggest challenges for a large construction company is finding a way to employ small businesses. The solution was to phase the work around the site and then to parcel up work into reasonable-sized contracts that were accessible to local small and medium sized enterprises. Skills and training were made integral to all contracts, which encouraged an uplift in skills locally and an opportunity to benefit from training while on the job. The team took an ambitious stance and aimed for the levels typically associated with a national skills academy, rather than a standard apprenticeship approach. In addition, there was a major focus on schools and colleges, effectively capacity building for the future by engaging young people in the construction industry, offering them a window into the world of work and alerting them to career opportunities.

Local materials were used to good effect and lower-carbon products preferred wherever practicable; for example, ground granulated blast furnace slag (GGBFS) in place of cement. All the 120,000 bricks came from south Devon and the 370,000 blocks were made with secondary aggregate from the local clay works and delivered on reusable pallets. Eden worked closely with its partner organisation The Sensory Trust to help McAlpine incorporate inclusive design principles into White River Place. Blindfolding architects and leading them around the site, and hosting an open forum for many local people with disabilities, ensured a strong emphasis on accessibility and has made the development a showcase. When the development was complete it won numerous awards, including a BREEAM 'excellent' rating, and was nominated Regeneration Project of the Year at the Insider's 2010 South West Property Awards.

The legacy is evident in the projects McAlpine has built since the Core in 2004–2005 and White River Place in 2009. Becoming a leader and advocate for sustainable construction has provided the company with both commercial and reputational advantage, and it has employed the principles developed with Eden on many other projects, including London's Olympic Stadium.

Eden too has benefited in numerous ways from the collaboration. The practical and commercial expertise in sustainable construction that has been acquired can be shared locally, nationally and internationally, whether on a small- or large-scale. It has also opened up future possibilities for the development of sustainable construction skills locally, and the prospect of creating a centre of green skills and expertise within mid-Cornwall, marking it out as the 'green capital' of the south-west.

Conclusion

In all these cases, the Eden Project's role as broker has been fundamental to their success. Whether the parties involved are a multinational mining company, one of the UK's biggest building firm or the entire population of the UK, Eden has persuaded people to work together to achieve great things who might otherwise have had nothing at all to say to each other.

Caroline Digby is Sustainability Director at the Eden Project. She is responsible for Eden's sustainability and education outreach programmes, and for developing collaborations that help Eden deliver its charitable mission. Her team explores ideas and delivers projects and education programmes which focus on resilient communities, place-making and the green economy. She has overall responsibility for setting Eden's sustainability targets and monitoring progress towards achieving them.

9
Boundary objects, HRM tools and change for sustainability

Suzanne Benn
UTS Business School, University of Technology, Sydney, Australia

Cathy A. Rusinko
School of Business, Philadelphia University, Philadelphia, Pennsylvania, USA

Introduction

This chapter illustrates a novel approach to using boundary objects (BOs) as change agents. In particular, the chapter illustrates how tools from stages of the human resources management (HRM) process can be used as BOs in order to facilitate changes necessary to create and maintain more sustainable organisations. BOs, which are discussed in greater detail below, can translate, transfer and/or create knowledge across diverse boundaries or groups of stakeholders. In organisations, BOs can translate, transfer and/or create knowledge between and among functions, departments and other groups. This chapter illustrates how knowledge about sustainability can be translated, transferred and/or created between and among all organisational functions by using HRM tools as BOs. It builds on arguments made by other scholars (e.g. Jabbour and Santos 2008) that the HR function should be integrated with organisational sustainability by formulating HRM policies and practices that stimulate the social, economic and environmental strategies of the organisation. It also builds on earlier work analysing the role of BOs in generating and supporting organisational change (Oswick and Robertson 2009), and on the role of BOs in underpinning the formation of a community of practice around sustainability (Benn and Martin 2010).

HRM tools that can act as BOs include HRM practices and policies with respect to planning, recruiting, selection, orientation, training, evaluation and replacement. HR planning tools, and other HRM practices and policies that reflect an organisation's commitment to sustainability, can function as BOs to bridge the gap between traditional HR strategy and sustainability strategy in organisations. The chapter finds that the use of HRM tools as BOs needs to be integrated throughout the HRM process, and also needs to be carefully considered in terms of the capacity to impede or support an integrated approach to sustainability in organisations.

First, the challenges of implementing sustainability in organisations are explored as examples of boundary problems. Next, we provide a detailed definition and characteristics of BOs. We illustrate how organisations can use HRM tools as BOs in order to facilitate change and create and maintain sustainability—including environmental, social and economic/financial sustainability—across all organisational functions. Practical examples of how organisations are using HRM tools as BOs to pursue or enhance sustainability are also included. Lastly, critical perspectives and future research directions are discussed.

Sustainability challenges as boundary problems

At the business level, the Brundtland definition of sustainability can be interpreted as: 'meeting the needs of a firm's direct and indirect stakeholders (such as shareholders, employees, customers, suppliers, pressure groups, communities etc) without compromising its ability to meet the needs of future stakeholders as well' (Dyllick and Hockerts 2002: 131). Hart and Milstein (2003: 66) describe a sustainable company as one that 'produces concurrently economical, social and environmental benefits—known as the three pillars of sustainability'. Correspondingly, some researchers refer to these three pillars or dimensions of sustainability as 'the triple bottom-line' (e.g. Elkington 1997). Examples of environmental sustainability include efforts to conserve, reuse and regenerate resources in order to ensure that future generations have access to the natural resources they require. Examples of social sustainability include efforts to promote equity, diversity and social justice across and between communities and nations. Examples of economic/financial sustainability include efforts to promote long-term survival of the organisation and stakeholders, while reducing poverty and promoting fair trade. Organisational applications of these sustainability dimensions will be discussed in later sections.

While sustainability is a holistic concept, its implementation as such is highly challenging. There are temporal, spatial and, for the purpose of this chapter, knowledge-based boundary issues to consider. The three 'pillars' are each associated with specific sets of knowledge. Bringing about change that enables sustainability to be implemented in organisations requires integrating across multiple knowledge boundaries, and between and among many and diverse stakeholders with respect to the three dimensions or types of sustainability—environmental, social and economic/financial. It requires bringing together scientific or technical experts with managers and employees from across the organisation, and hence, a wide range of disciplinary and functional backgrounds and their knowledge bases. The development of successful sustainable products, for example, requires high-level marketing and raw material scale-up innovations, as well as product redesign according to sustainability principles and standards, which may have very specific technical requirements (Nidumolu *et al.* 2009). Advancing sustainability performance is a matter of addressing the systemic and holistic nature of sustainability knowledge, and of recognising, for instance, the interconnectedness and complexity of sources of environmental impact and their relationships to social and economic concerns of the organisation (Porter 2008).

Addressing this complexity and working towards implementing sustainability means collaborating with a range of other organisations that may have very different understandings of the importance or applicability of sustainability. For example, raising awareness and developing such knowledge may require corporations to form partnerships with long-time adversaries such as advocacy-based environmental organisations (Jamali and Keshishian 2009; Seitandi and Crane 2009). Employees may need to work with 'partners' from different professional, occupational or social backgrounds that represent organisations or organisational groups or teams with very different priorities and sources of power. Developing a shared understanding of what sustainability might mean between/among organisations and their supply chain partners, and/or other business alliances and networks, becomes difficult because of these multiple priorities and contextual understandings of sustainability (Selsky and Parker 2005). The challenges described above, all of which arise as a result of working across multiple and diverse boundaries, are known as boundary problems.

As illustrated above, boundary problems beset the theory and practice of corporate sustainability, and sustainability constraints can be conceived of as occurring at boundaries (Ny *et al.* 2006). Boundaries are constructed by value judgements; they are temporal, spatial and both intra- and inter-organisational. Boundary problems have the potential to interfere with the key principles that are widely acknowledged as underpinning the integration of sustainability into business practices. These principles include the creation, translation and integration—throughout the organisation—of shared understandings, meanings and knowledge around the relatively malleable concept of sustainability. Issues of group identity can impinge on developing an integrated sense of sustainability across an organisation. For example, Angus-Leppan *et al.* (2009) found different stakeholder groups within a major bank had very different interpretations of the bank's corporate social responsibility (CSR) and sustainability messages, and of their importance.

The resolution to boundary problems is not just a matter of working across different knowledge boundaries, since issues of sustainability are complex concepts, open to multiple interpretations by multiple stakeholders (Basu and Palazzo 2008; Angus-Leppan *et al.* 2010). Hence, the challenge of integrating sustainability involves developing meaning around sustainability that is holistic, that brings together understandings from the natural and technical sciences into management thinking, that can be shared across functional and disciplinary boundaries, and that considers all levels of systems thinking (Benn and Martin 2010). Essentially, firms need to establish a community of practice centred on sustainability-related knowledge across the organisation, and the competitiveness of the firm will depend on the extent to which differences in sustainability practice can be co-ordinated (Brown and Duguid 2001). Traditional approaches to either incremental or transformational change in the extant literature do not adequately recognise or address this key problem (Dunphy *et al*. 2007; Benn and Baker 2009). In this chapter, we argue that BOs in the form of HRM tools can meet this challenge, as is further discussed in sections below.

Characteristics of BOs

In the literature, the term used for objects that can travel across knowledge and meaning-related boundaries is 'boundary object'. Star and Griesemer (1989) first introduced the concept of BOs as a means by which co-operation and managing diversity could be facilitated across a heterogeneous group of scientists. They defined BOs as conceptual tools:

> … which both inhabit several intersecting worlds and satisfy the informational requirements of each of them. Boundary objects are objects which are both plastic enough to adapt to local needs and the constraints of the several parties employing them, yet robust enough to maintain a common identity across sites. They are weakly structured in common use, and become more strongly structured in individual use. These objects may be abstract or concrete. They have different meanings in different social worlds but their structure is common enough to more than one world to make them recognisable means of translation. The creation and management of boundary objects is key in developing and maintaining coherence across intersecting social worlds (Star and Griesemer 1989: 343).

BOs can be artefacts in the form of made things, such as tools or visual representations, or discourses, terms, concepts, processes or technologies (Star and Griesemer 1989; Wenger 1999). Reports, standardised forms and methods, protocols, models, repositories, maps of interdependencies such as Gantt charts, all help actors differentiate their knowledge domain, but also have the capacity to help them share or collaborate to solve problems and develop new knowledge (Star 1989). In the different domains, specialised knowledge can be built utilising the BO. Yet the BO is plastic enough for the separate domains to share some commonalities. In this way, BOs have a role in initiating and supporting change that involves actors from different social roles or disciplinary areas. Specifically, they have a role in sharing and transforming knowledge and changing practices across social, occupational and professional boundaries, such as across the different interests and knowledge backgrounds of members of a community of practice (Wenger 1999; Carlile 2002, 2004).

BOs enable discrepant arrays of knowledge and meaning to be shared and transformed across such boundaries because they act as 'empty vessels that are filled differently by whatever is the local beverage' (Sapsed and Salter 2004: 1519). We should point out that a BO is not the same as organisational culture, which may be represented through certain artefacts, but is an artefact that specifically provides a means of sharing and transforming knowledge across various types of boundaries.

This chapter builds on earlier work analysing the role of BOs in generating and supporting organisational change (Oswick and Robertson 2009). In particular, our contribution focuses on using BOs in the HR function, and throughout the HRM process, to span knowledge- and meaning-related boundaries that exist as organisations pursue or enhance a commitment to sustainability. As Soliman and Spooner (2000) point out, HRM is essentially a knowledge-management function and HR managers need to be able to manage knowledge transfers across multiple areas of the organisation.

BOs may be structural, symbolic or visionary, or have combinations of these properties. In organisations, records such as employee payroll records and a wide range of other records concerning outcomes, products and targets are examples of structural BOs. Structural BOs also include policies and practices such as planning and evaluating, and the corresponding tools used to plan and evaluate. Structural BOs have been most studied, with a particular research emphasis on the relative usefulness of different degrees of structure.

Symbolic BOs, such as metaphors, are also referred to in the literature and are useful in the context of developing shared meaning around ambiguous or complex terms (e.g. Thompson 2005). Koskinen (2005) found that metaphoric BOs can play an important role in knowledge co-ordination and sharing of innovation processes in an organisation. The visionary boundary object is a conceptual object that prompts emotive responses from a range of people and is regarded as so sacred that it is difficult to argue against (such as 'world's best practice'; Briers and Chua 2001; Benn and Martin 2010). As with other BOs, the visionary object must be able to be tailored into specific settings. It must have a 'hard' core and a 'soft' or 'plastic' periphery that allows for different interpretations to be constructed by different constituencies within their specialised knowledge bases.

Carlile (2004) has listed characteristics of BOs to include shared language, specification and transformation. That is, they can be understood by a range of actors, they are specific to a certain task and they generate change. Hence, BOs can address boundary problems by bridging learning boundaries that distinguish the different practices of different inter- and intra-organisational groups (Scarbrough *et al.* 2004).

Standardisation has always been regarded as a characteristic of BOs. Lutters and Ackerman (2007) found that loose routinisation, punctuated crystallisation and meta-negotiation streams are central properties of BOs. Essentially, these findings mean that BOs can be in a state of continual modification; they are relevant and utilised at particular points of time, but as an aspect of an ongoing process and set of interrelationships. Since BOs can be in a state of continual modification, they are appropriate tools to facilitate organisational change.

HR, BOs and sustainability

So how can the HR function of the organisation—which is often charged with the processes of change—facilitate more sustainable organisations, which includes addressing the corresponding issue of boundary problems across the organisation? In this section of the chapter, we examine how HRM policies and practices, acting as BOs (as we have described them above—structural, symbolic or visionary concepts), can help to unite and transform disparate organisational functions and stakeholders around a shared concept of sustainability; and thus, resolve boundary problems and create more sustainable organisations.

In the literature there is a fairly long history of contributions that view the HR function as a locus for organisational change. For example, Storey (1992) and Sherriton and Stern (1997) believed that HR can and should play a major role in implementing change. Caldwell (2001) held that HR managers should be at the forefront of organisational change initiatives. In 1997, Ulrich suggested compatibility between HRM and change-oriented HR roles.

HRM tools as BOs

HRM tools can play the role of BOs, as they (BOs) are defined above. As BOs, HRM tools can create and share meaning, knowledge and practices that can be integrated throughout the organisation. Specific HRM tools that can act as BOs include employee record and report keeping, policies and practices such as diversity policies, and other sources and examples of formalisation and standardisation. Additional HRM tools that can act as BOs include job planning and descriptions, criteria for recruiting, selection and evaluation, and training programmes. These HRM tools can bridge the gap between traditional HR strategy and sustainability strategy in organisations.

In both textbooks and the academic literature, HRM in organisations is often addressed as a series of stages or processes, including: HR auditing and strategic planning; job analysis/descriptions; recruiting; selection; orientation; evaluation and development; training; and replacement (e.g. Jabbour and Santos 2008; Ivancevich 2009). Correspondingly, each stage is characterised by specific tools, processes and/or practices. These tools, processes and practices can act as BOs to create a set of shared meanings and practices that are integrated between and among the many and diverse functions and members of the organisation.

For example, at the HR auditing and strategic planning stages, auditing and planning tools such as SWOT analysis and PERT charts are knowledge-management tools that can be used to analyse the current situation and future needs, and to develop a strategic plan for HR that can be accessed and built upon separately by different groups across the organisation. This strategic plan is then integrated throughout the organisation in the form of other HRM tools such as job descriptions and criteria for recruiting, selection, orientation, evaluation, training and replacement. Hence, these HRM tools play the role of BOs by creating and sharing meaning, knowledge and practices that are integrated throughout the organisation.

Likewise, tools at each of the HRM stages can be used as BOs to create and share meaning, knowledge and practices in order to create more sustainable organisations, as is illustrated in Figure 9.1. In the next section, we explore how BOs in the form of HRM practices and policies can facilitate the changes necessary for implementation of sustainability across the organisation.

Figure 9.1: **Using HRM tools as boundary objects to create more sustainable organisations**

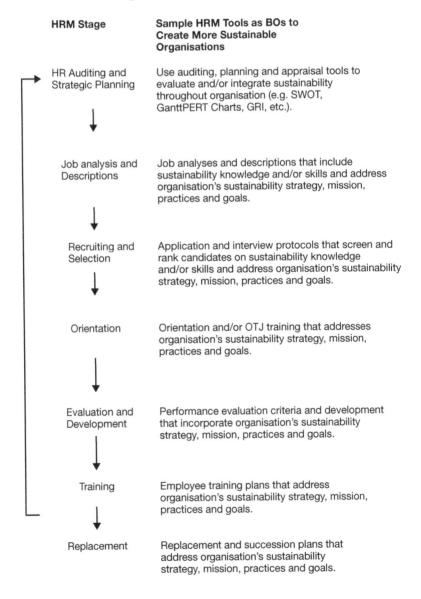

HRM Stage	**Sample HRM Tools as BOs to Create More Sustainable Organisations**
HR Auditing and Strategic Planning	Use auditing, planning and appraisal tools to evaluate and/or integrate sustainability throughout organisation (e.g. SWOT, GanttPERT Charts, GRI, etc.).
Job analysis and Descriptions	Job analyses and descriptions that include sustainability knowledge and/or skills and address organisation's sustainability strategy, mission, practices and goals.
Recruiting and Selection	Application and interview protocols that screen and rank candidates on sustainability knowledge and/or skills and address organisation's sustainability strategy, mission, practices and goals.
Orientation	Orientation and/or OTJ training that addresses organisation's sustainability strategy, mission, practices and goals.
Evaluation and Development	Performance evaluation criteria and development that incorporate organisation's sustainability strategy, mission, practices and goals.
Training	Employee training plans that address organisation's sustainability strategy, mission, practices and goals.
Replacement	Replacement and succession plans that address organisation's sustainability strategy, mission, practices and goals.

HRM tools, BOs and environmental sustainability

As discussed earlier, environmental sustainability includes efforts to reduce and reuse resources. Previous empirical work has indicated that HRM practices are critical factors in implementing environmental management schemes in organisations (Wee and Quazi 2005; Sammalisto and Brorson 2008) and in encouraging environmental innovations (Ramus 2002). The specific operations of HRM tools as BOs can explain these general findings.

At the HR auditing and strategic planning stages, tools such as SWOT analysis and/or Global Reporting Initiative (GRI) criteria for sustainability reporting can be used as BOs to analyse the organisation's current status with respect to environmentally sustainable practices (e.g. reusing resources and reducing consumption), and to develop plans for the future. Acting as BOs, these tools can span the diverse functions, such as the accounting, finance and engineering or environmental divisions, within the organisation, and co-ordinate different perspectives around sustainability planning and strategy.

BOs such as HR audit and strategic planning tools that focus on co-ordinating sustainability across the organisation can lay the groundwork for additional HRM tools to act as BOs in diffusing sustainability throughout the organisation. For example, job analyses and descriptions can act as BOs to co-ordinate sustainability across different organisational functions. In keeping with Star and Griesemer's (1989) definition (cited above) of BOs, the job analyses and descriptions must be both universal across multiple functions and malleable within specific functions. For example, a BO in the form of an organisation-wide policy to include responsibility for conserving resources in job analyses and descriptions can be subsequently custom-tailored for each individual job acting as a form of knowledge development within each function. Hence, BOs must be malleable and must function at multiple levels—including organisation and function/department levels—in order to create more sustainable organisations.

Likewise, recruiting and selection tools can act as BOs in the form of organisation-wide recruiting and selection protocols and criteria that demand candidates' knowledge of and/or experience with environmentally sustainable practices consistent with the organisation's environmental sustainability plans, mission and goals. However, each function or department can customise these BOs by developing specific definitions and measures for the type of knowledge and experience that is appropriate for their particular mission, within the context of the larger organisation.

Organisation-wide orientation and training programmes and tools can act as BOs to facilitate more sustainable organisations by including information on environmental sustainability that is consistent with the organisation's environmental sustainability plans, mission and goals. Each function or department can customise these BOs by developing supplementary training that is appropriate for their function within the context of the larger organisation.

Likewise, evaluation and promotion criteria can act as BOs to diffuse sustainability throughout the organisation by including employee contributions to the organisation's environmental sustainability plans, mission and goals. Individual functions and departments can custom-tailor these organisation-wide BOs to fit their mission in a way that is also consistent with the larger organisational mission.

The same goes for organisation-wide replacement and succession plans. Organisation-wide criteria that address environmental sustainability knowledge and expertise in replacement and succession can act as BOs to facilitate organisation-wide diffusion of environmental sustainability. Individual functions and departments can adapt these organisation-wide BOs to fit their specific missions, in a way that is consistent with the organisation level mission.

Hence, the tools and practices used in these stages in the HRM process, acting largely as structural BOs, can create, transfer, translate and/or integrate knowledge about how organisations can be more environmentally sustainable across organisational boundaries such as diverse knowledge bases and functions. The various protocols, records and plans may be interpreted differently according to the needs of the specific functions, stakeholder group or knowledge area within the organisation, but they act to align the different actors around some shared understanding or knowledge base concerning sustainability.

Of course, the HRM stages are not as linear as they are depicted in Figure 9.1. However, as is illustrated in Figure 9.1, the process is iterative, so that the cycle continues to loop back to HR auditing and strategic planning, which evaluates the present situation, and uses that information to plan for the future. Likewise, the arrows between HRM stages in Figure 9.1 illustrate how each successive stage facilitates the next stage and, correspondingly, how BOs at each stage can facilitate sustainability at current and successive stages.

HRM tools, BOs and social sustainability

As discussed earlier, social sustainability includes efforts to promote equity, diversity and social justice. Some researchers (e.g. Pfeffer 2010) observe that social sustainability is addressed less frequently in organisations than environmental and economic/financial sustainability and, when addressed, the focus is often external stakeholders rather than employees. HRM is uniquely positioned to facilitate social sustainability within organisations through its responsibility for recruiting, training, developing, evaluating and retaining employees. Therefore, with respect to HRM, a good example of a BO that can facilitate social sustainability throughout the organisation is a diversity policy. Jabbour and Santos' (2008) summary of the literature, including several empirical studies, finds that diversity management can add value to the organisation with respect to enhancing sustainability. We suggest the reason is because a diversity policy can promote equity and diversity by attracting and retaining a qualified set of employees from diverse backgrounds, and because it acts both as a visionary and as a structural boundary object.

A diversity policy begins as part of the HR strategic plan, which can be integrated throughout the organisation via BOs in later HRM stages. In effect, it can then act as a job classification scheme, accessible to a wide range of employees but with a hard core of meaning around a job description. For example, job descriptions, and recruiting and selection criteria, can act as BOs to facilitate attraction of a diverse employee population. Retention of a diverse employee population can be facilitated through BOs such as orientation, training and development programmes. In addition, diversity policies can facilitate attraction and retention of a diverse employee population through BOs such as organisation-wide zero tolerance policies, and policies prohibiting hostile, predatory or otherwise negative work environments.

Some researchers (e.g. Pfeffer 2010) argue that social sustainability in the workplace also includes issues such as organisation-wide transparency, ethical treatment of all employees and respect for all employees. Under these circumstances, BOs to facilitate social sustainability in organisations would include policies on transparency, ethics and mutual respect, which can be included as part of the HR strategic plan.

HRM tools, BOs and economic/financial sustainability

As discussed earlier, economic or financial sustainability includes efforts to promote long-term survival of the organisation and stakeholders, while reducing poverty and promoting fair trade. While we deal with each of the 'three pillars' of sustainability separately in this paper in order to highlight the potential role of specific HRM tools as structural boundary objects, we stress that a key function of BOs in an organisational or inter-organisational context can be to bring together the three separate elements of sustainability in a holistic approach. Previous work has explored the role of visionary BOs in performing this role (Benn and Martin 2010).

HRM tools that act as BOs can promote synergies between and among the three types of sustainability and how they are manifested in organisations. Boudreau and Ramstad (2005) have linked the HRM function to environmentally, socially and financially sustainable outcomes, arguing that strategic success for the organisation is dependent upon a long-term perspective that allows for an emphasis on human capital, as well as on environmental and financial responsibility. Our exploration of BOs supports this claim. For example, developing protocols around environmentally sustainable practices, such as reusing resources or reducing resource usage, can have the effect of decreasing costs, which is also economically/financially sustainable (e.g. Rusinko 2007).

BOs in the form of diversity policies, which promote social sustainability, also help to promote the long-term economic survival of the organisation, since they facilitate attracting and retaining the best and brightest employees from all backgrounds, which can foster speed and innovation (Shena *et al.* 2009). Similarly, BOs that facilitate environmental and/or social sustainability at HRM stages—including job descriptions, recruiting and selection criteria, orientation and training programmes, and evaluation and replacement plans—can also act as BOs to facilitate economic/financial sustainability, since environmental and/or social outcomes can also facilitate the long-run financial survival of the organisation.

HRM, BOs and sustainability: examples in practice

While the concept of using HRM tools as BOs to facilitate sustainability in organisations is new and under-researched in the literature, there are a few examples of organisations that are using the HR function as a major player in integrating sustainability into their strategic plans, and, although their initiatives are not stated as such, they may be interpreted as examples of using HRM tools as BOs in order to facilitate sustainability throughout their organisations. In effect, the HR functions of their organisations are providing an 'infrastructure' of BOs to bring about change, as suggested by Oswick and Robertson (2009. According to Lutters and Ackerman (2007), BOs in the form of HRM tools operate at specific points of time, but as an aspect of the ongoing HRM process, and are embedded in a historical set of interrelationships.

For example, Casler and colleagues' (2010) report on the Sierra Nevada Brewing Company (SNBC), which was founded in 1980 and has always valued environmental, social and economic/financial sustainability, found that SNBC aligns its HR practices with an emphasis on environmental sustainability. This approach to HR results in environmentally sustainable initiatives that also decrease costs and, therefore, positively impact economic/financial sustainability. One of the ways that SNBC addresses social sustainability is through a standardised employee benefits package that focuses on protocols for healthy employees. For instance, the company offers a comprehensive wellness programme, including on-site healthcare for employees and dependents, and massage therapy and on-site childcare. Interpreted variously across the organisation, these protocols and standards assist in building new knowledge around employee health and wellbeing. As these tools are dealing with more explicit knowledge about employee health, they are relatively strongly structured.

Likewise, SNBC has integrated sustainability into its HR strategic planning process, and into each of its HRM stages, with the end result of disseminating sustainability throughout the organisation. Hence, while it may not realise it or acknowledge it at this time, SNBC is an example of a company that is using HR tools as BOs in order to create and maintain a sustainable organisation. For example, SNBC created two positions with the title of sustainability co-ordinator. Their new employee orientation process, which includes the sustainability co-ordinators as instructors, emphasises the sustainability values that define the company—effectively providing a visionary BO with which the employees from across the organisation can identify and learn to apply in their own work context. With respect to selection and retention, SNBC values employee fit with sustainability values as equally important or more important than employee–job fit. SNBC encourages employee feedback and suggestions with respect to sustainability practices and policies. It focuses on hiring and promoting from within the company to maintain its culture of sustainability.

Wirtenberg *et al.* (2007) surveyed a convenience sample of firms from the Global 100 Most Sustainable Corporations in the World, and found that HR played a major role in integrating sustainability in those companies. The HR function helped to integrate sustainability into strategic planning, and also used traditional HRM tools, such as recruiting, training, development programmes and policies (including diversity policies), to integrate sustainability throughout these organisations and across various communities of practice. Therefore, the firms in this study can also be viewed as examples of organisations that are using HRM tools as BOs to create and maintain sustainable organisations.

In another example, Benn *et al.* (2011) describe the organisational change processes that underpin the sustainability successes of Fuji Xerox Australia Eco-Manufacturing Centre in Sydney. This centre now accounts for 80% of Fuji Xerox Australia's spare parts requirements—these parts would otherwise have gone to landfill. The success of the centre rests on both technological advances and a high performance workplace culture. Both these aspects of its success are based in the innovative capacity of a highly interdisciplinary team, fostered by deployment of BOs as a means of engaging employees in the ecological agenda. For example, as a visionary BO (Briers and Chua 2001), 'world's best practice' is translated at this Fuji Xerox plant into 'world's best practice in eco-manufacturing', widely recognised as such within the global Fuji Xerox organisation and the sector as a whole.

HR tools have been instrumental in developing the capacity upon which the perceived legitimacy of this visionary BO rests. For example, the firm has differentiated between recycling and remanufacturing with carefully specified HR management strategies defining the appropriate skills and capabilities that need to be allocated to these different technologies. The company is currently focused on challenges such as how to accommodate cultural differences in the distribution and levels of skill in other countries where manufacturing occurs and how to transfer the cultural change processes deployed in Sydney to build employee commitment, engagement and multi-skilling (Benn *et al.* 2011). Further research could explore the role that BOs in the form of HR tools could play in addressing these challenges.

Turning a strategic priority into practical initiatives saw another Australian organisation, the water utility Yarra Valley Water (YVW), engage in organisational learning around sustainability. First, supported by The Natural Step, the management team at YVW then decided they needed more practical and strategic direction setting and embarked on the widespread implementation of life-cycle analysis (LCA) (Crittenden *et al.* 2011). Acting as a structural BO, the LCA enabled the economists, accountants and engineers to each build their own disciplinary, quantitative understanding of what reducing environmental impact might mean.

We suggest that the reason the LCA has been so successful in supporting the sustainability implementation programme at YVW[1] is that it was incorporated into the organisation's HR systems. The HR manager utilised the LCA as a BO tool to motivate wider employee engagement and to foster recognition of the sustainability impacts

---

1   Yarra Valley Water has been awarded a number of sustainability-linked awards and prizes.

in social, environmental and economic dimensions. LCA was deployed in the Orientation HRM phase (Fig. 9.1), figuratively displayed as the 'YVW Sustainability Roadmap' which featured in murals and on PC screensavers across the organisation. It became an aspect of the Evaluation and Development and Training phases of HRM (Fig. 9.1), incorporated into the reward and recognition system of YVW, and operationalised into a range of job descriptions and training programmes. Effectively bringing the YVW organisation together as a community of practice, the LCA BO supported the development of a shared understanding and a strategic perspective across organisational functions of what sustainability might mean for the organisation as a whole. Hence, the LCA enabled the triple bottom-line to become individually meaningful to the range of internal and external stakeholders.

The above examples illustrate how BOs can function as change agents by creating and sharing new knowledge and practices across diverse functions in organisations. Likewise, these examples illustrate how BOs, functioning as change agents, create more sustainable organisations by integrating and/or expanding sustainability and sustainable practices in organisations.

Critical perspectives

When criticisms are levelled at BOs, they are typically levelled in three areas: power; calcification; and lack of critique/reflection. A number of writers argue that BOs have a performative power, altering the relationships of what is represented and favouring some aspects above others (e.g. Iedema 2003; Oswick and Robertson 2009), hence enhancing certain power distributions. Researchers and practitioners need to be aware of this potential when recommending or using BOs (Carlile 2004).

BOs may also 'calcify' as standards and thus become a barrier to change. Another related problem is that BOs may have a stultifying effect on change by maintaining control over tasks and limiting innovation (Oswick and Robertson 2009). With respect to HRM tools, we argue that standardised policies, criteria and programmes may be effective BOs to diffuse sustainability throughout the organisation. To guard against possible calcification or stultification as a result of using these types of structural BOs, metaphoric BOs could be introduced as a means of generating new understandings across organisations and their partners, suppliers and other stakeholders (Koskinen 2005). For example, a sustainability 'roadmap' which defines the sustainability vision and the steps needed to get there can help members of cross-functional teams with different knowledge backgrounds to develop a shared way to approach a sustainability change programme. Organic metaphors that badge the organisation as 'living cell' or 'ecosystem' can also help guide individuals towards a common, but evolving, focus on sustainability.

As is often the case with change agents, a potential problem with BOs is use without critique or reflection. However, this problem, as well as the problems with power, calcification and lack of critique/reflection, can be mitigated if BOs are used within the context of learning, collaboration and reflection.

Future directions

Sustainability is a highly diffuse concept, whose meaning can be differently interpreted by a range of interest groups and vested interests within organisations. Tradeoffs are made between and among the different elements of sustainability depending on the power and influence of various stakeholders and such interests (Angus-Leppan *et al.* 2010). Future research can explore how BOs are deployed by different sources of power, and to what ends, in terms of a holistic approach to sustainability. In addition, future research can also test whether deploying BOs within the context of change models that are rooted in collaboration, learning and reflection can result in a more holistic and collaborative approach to sustainability in organisations.

Conclusion

This chapter has demonstrated a novel approach to using HRM tools as BOs in order to translate, transfer and/or create knowledge across diverse functions for the purpose of creating and maintaining more sustainable organisations, thus addressing the boundary problems that have impeded the integration of sustainability. Practical examples specifically addressed environmental, social and economic/financial sustainability in organisations. In addition, organisational examples demonstrated how BOs in the form of HRM tools are also change agents, as they translate, transfer and/or create knowledge about sustainability throughout the organisation, and facilitate organisations' paths to sustainability. While we recognise that use of HRM tools as BOs has potential downsides, if carefully utilised as an aspect of an HRM programme that is reflective and participative, they have great potential to not only bring different aspects of the organisation to share sustainability understandings, but to bring new knowledge together into a more holistic integration of sustainability. More generally, the chapter illustrates how the HR function of the organisation can be leveraged to contribute to the change processes needed to implement sustainability.

References

Angus-Leppan, T., S. Benn and L. Young (2009) 'A Sensemaking Approach to Tradeoffs and Synergies Between Human and Ecological Elements of Corporate Sustainability', *Business Strategy and the Environment* 19.4: 30-244.

Angus-Leppan, T., L. Metcalf and S. Benn (2010) 'Leadership Styles and CSR Practice: Sensemaking, Institutional Drivers and CSR Leadership', *Journal of Business Ethics* 93: 189-213.

Basu, K., and G. Palazzo (2008) 'Corporate Social Responsibility: A Process Model of Sensemaking', *Academy of Management Review* 33.1: 122-36.

Benn, S., and E. Baker (2009) 'Advancing Sustainability Through Change and Innovation: A Co-evolutionary Perspective', *Journal of Change Management* 9.4: 383-97.

Benn, S., D. Dunphy and T. Angus-Leppan (2011) 'A Case Study in Strategic Sustainability: Fuji Xerox Australia', in S. Benn, D. Dunphy and B. Perrott (eds.), *Cases in Corporate Sustainability and Change: A Multidisciplinary Approach* (Prahhan, Australia: Tilde University Press): 28-41.

Benn, S., and A. Martin (2010) 'Learning and Change for Sustainability Reconsidered: A Role for Boundary Objects', *Academy of Management Learning and Education* 9.3: 397-412.

Boudreau, J.W., and P.M. Ramstad (2005) 'Talentship, Talent Segmentation, and Sustainability: A New HR Decision Science Paradigm for a New Strategy Definition', *Human Resource Management* 44.2: 129-36.

Briers, M., and W.F. Chua (2001) 'The Role of Actor-networks and Boundary Objects in Management Accounting Change: A Field Study of an Implementation of Activity-based Costing', *Accounting, Organizations and Society* 26.3: 237-69.

Brown, J.S., and J. Duguid (2001) 'Knowledge and Organization: A Social–Practice Perspective', *Organization Science* 12.2: 198-213.

Caldwell, R. (2001) 'Champions, Adapters, Consultants and Synergists: The New Change Agents in Human Resources Management', *Human Resources Management Journal* 11.3: 39-52.

Carlile, P.R. (2002) 'A Pragmatic View of Knowledge and Boundaries: Boundary Objects in New Product Development', *Organization Science* 13.4: 414-42.

Carlile, P.R. (2004) 'Transferring, Translating, and Transforming: An Integrative Framework for Managing Knowledge Across Boundaries', *Organization Science* 15: 514-55.

Casler, A., M.J. Gundlach, B. Pesons and S. Zivnuska (2010) 'Sierra Nevada Brewing Company's Thirty-year Journey Toward Sustainability', *People and Strategy* 33: 44-51.

Crittenden, P., S. Benn and D. Dunphy (2011) 'Learning and Change at Yarra Valley Water', in S. Benn, D. Dunphy and B. Perrott (eds.), *Cases in Corporate Sustainability and Change: A Multidisciplinary Approach* (Prahhan, Australia: Tilde University Press): 147-61.

Dunphy, D., A. Griffiths and S. Benn (2007) *Organizational Change for Corporate Sustainability: A Guide for Leaders and Change Agents of the Future* (Abingdon, UK and New York: Routledge).

Dyllick, T., and K. Hockerts (2002) 'Beyond the Business Case for Corporate Sustainability', *Business Strategy and the Environment* 11.2: 130-41.

Elkington, J. (1997) *Cannibals with Forks: The Triple Bottom Line of 21st Century Business* (Mankato, MN: Capstone Publishers).

Hart, S.L., and M.B. Milstein (2003) 'Creating Sustainable Value', *Academy of Management Executive* 17: 56-67.

Iedema, R. (2003) *Discourses of Post-bureaucratic Organization* (Amsterdam, The Netherlands: John Benjamins Publishing).

Ivancevich, J. (2009) *Human Resource Management* (New York: McGraw Hill).

Jabbour, C., and F. Santos (2008) 'The Central Role of Human Resource Management in the Search for Sustainable Organizations', *The International Journal of Human Resource Management* 19.12: 2133-54.

Jamali, D., and T. Keshishian (2009) 'Uneasy Alliances: Lessons Learned from Partnerships Between Businesses and NGOs in the context of CSR', *Journal of Business Ethics* 84: 277-95.

Koskinen, K. (2005) 'Metaphoric Boundary Objects as Co-ordinating Mechanisms in the Knowledge Sharing of Innovation Processes', *European Journal of Innovation Management* 8.3: 323-35.

Lutters, W., and M. Ackerman (2007) 'Beyond Boundary Objects: Collaborative Reuse in Aircraft Technical Support', *Computer Supported Cooperative Work* 16: 341-72.

Nidumolu, R., C.K. Prahalad and M.R. Rangaswami (2009) 'Why Sustainability is Now the Key Driver of Innovation', *Harvard Business Review* September: 57-64.

Ny, H., J. MacDonald, P. Broman, G. Yamamoto and K-H. Robert (2006) 'Sustainability Constraints as System Boundaries: An Approach to Making Life-cycle Management Strategic', *Journal of Industrial Ecology* 10: 61-78.

Oswick, C., and M. Robertson (2009) 'Boundary Objects Reconsidered: From Bridges and Anchors to Barricades and Mazes', *Journal of Change Management* 9.2: 179-94.

Pfeffer, J. (2010) 'Building Sustainable Organizations: The Human Factor', *Academy of Management Perspectives* 24: 34-45.

Porter, T. (2008) 'Managerial Applications of Corporate Social Responsibility and Systems Thinking for Achieving Sustainable Outcomes', *Systems Research and Behavioural Science* 25: 397-411.

Ramus, C.A. (2002) 'Encouraging Innovative Environmental Actions: What Companies and Managers Must Do', *Journal of World Business* 37: 151-64.

Rusinko, C.A. (2007) 'Green Manufacturing: An Evaluation of Environmentally Sustainable Manufacturing Practices and Their Impact on Competitive Outcomes', *IEEE Transactions on Engineering Management* 54: 445-54.

Sammalisto, K., and T. Brorson (2008) 'Training and Communication in the Implementation of Environmental Management Systems (ISO 14.001): A Case Study at the University of Gävle, Sweden', *Journal of Cleaner Production* 15.3: 299-309.

Sapsed, J., and A. Salter (2004) 'Postcards from the Edge: Local Communities, Global Programs and Boundary Objects', *Organization Studies* 25.9: 1515-34.

Scarbrough, H., J. Swan, S. Laurent, M. Bresnen, L. Edelman and S. Newell (2004) 'Project-based Learning and the Role of Learning Boundaries', *Organization Studies* 25.9: 1579.

Seitanidi, M.M., and A. Crane (2009) 'Implementing CSR Through Partnerships: Understanding the Selection, Design and Institutionalisation of Non-profit Business Partnerships', *Journal of Business Ethics* 85: 413-29.

Selsky, J., and B. Parker (2005) 'Cross-sector Partnerships to Address Social Issues: Challenges to Theory and Practice', *Journal of Management Education* 31.6: 849-73.

Shena, J., A. Chandaa, B. D'Nettob and M. Mongaa (2009) 'Managing Diversity Through Human Resource Management: An International Perspective and Conceptual Framework', *The International Journal of Human Resource Management* 20.2: 235-51.

Sherriton, J., and J. Stern (1997) 'HR's Role in Cultural Change', *HR Focus* 74.4: 27.

Soliman, F., and K. Spooner (2000) 'Strategies for Implementing Knowledge Management: Role of Human Resource Management', *Journal of Knowledge Management* 4.4: 337.

Star, S.L. (1989) 'The Structure of Ill-structured Solutions: Boundary Objects and Heterogeneous Distributed Problem Solving', in M. Huhns and L. Gasser (eds.), *Distributed Artificial Intelligence 2* (Menlo Park, CA: Morgan Kaufman): 37-55.

Star, S.L., and J. Griesemer (1989) 'Institutional Ecology, "Translations" and Boundary Objects: Amatuers and Professionals in Berkeley's Museum of Vertebrate Zoology, 1907–39', *Social Studies of Science* 19: 387-420.

Storey, J. (1992) *Development in the Management of HR: An Analytical Review* (Oxford, UK: Blackwell).

Thompson, M. (2005) 'Structural and Epistemic Parameters in Communities of Practice', *Organization Science* 16.2: 151-64.

Ulrich, D. (1997) 'Measuring Human Resources: An Overview of Practices and a Prescription for Results', *Human Resource Management* 36.3: 303-20.

Wee, J.S., and H.A. Quazi (2005) 'Development and Validation of Critical Factors of Environmental Management', *Industrial Management and Data Systems* 105: 96-114.

Wenger, E. (1999) *Communities of Practice: Learning, Meaning and Identity* (Cambridge, UK: Cambridge University Press).

Wirtenberg, J., J. Harmon, W.G. Russell and K.D. Fairfield (2007) 'HR's Role in Building a Sustainable Enterprise: Insights From Some of the World's Best Companies', *Human Resource Planning* 30: 10-20.

Suzanne Benn is Professor of Sustainable Enterprise at UTS Business School, University of Technology, Sydney. She has a background in the sciences and social sciences, and a PhD in environmental studies from the University of New South Wales. She has published four books and more than 90 chapters and journal articles on the topic of business and sustainability.

Cathy A. Rusinko earned a PhD in management and organisation at Pennsylvania State University, and is Professor of Management and Sustainability Co-ordinator at Philadelphia University. She researches sustainability in corporations and in higher education, and has published over 60 journal articles, chapters and professional publications. She co-edited a special issue of *Journal of Management Education* (2009) on sustainability in the management curriculum.

10

Climate change is everyone's business

Brendan Mackey

Griffith Climate Change Response Programme, Griffith University, Queensland, Australia

No escape

In discussing the climate change problem with people working in the private sector, I typically hear the following kinds of questions. How should my business respond to the climate change problem? Why all the fuss? Is it something I can ignore? What should my business be doing? How does climate change relate to other ideas I hear about such as sustainable development and, more recently, the 'green economy'? Why should my business care about climate change?

Many credit Al Gore (2006) with raising global popular concern for the climate change problem following release of his somewhat ironically titled book and video *An Inconvenient Truth*. Close on his trail was the UK government's *Stern Report* which focused on the long-term economic implications of failing to reduce emissions of carbon dioxide from burning fossil fuel to a level that prevents dangerous climate change (Stern 2007). These two 'eco-warriors' spent much of 2006 travelling the globe urging the world community to face up to the reality of the climate change problem. Both were backed by good public relations campaigns, attracting media coverage and achieving impressive popular reach. Domestically, civil society organisations piggy-backed on the positive public response and launched their own successful public advocacy campaigns which, in turn, fuelled significant political impetus for national governments to adopt progressive climate change policies. This momentum carried forward into the 2009 UN Copenhagen Climate Change Conference (UNFCCC 2009), where the nations of the world met to negotiate what many hoped would be 'the real deal'—a legally binding agreement for reducing emissions of greenhouse gases, especially fossil fuel carbon dioxide—to levels that would stabilise average global warming at no more than 2°C above the pre-industrial climate; the so-called 'guard rail' that science estimates is likely to prevent dangerous climate change.[1]

Alas, the climate change negotiations did not pan out as the advocates and optimists had hoped. Major carbon polluting countries were not ready to make the commitments to the necessary deep and rapid cuts in fossil fuel carbon dioxide emissions. To cut a long scientific story short, to restrict global warming to 2°C requires that no more than about 1,000 billion tonnes of carbon dioxide is emitted between now and around 2080.[2] I call this the 'global carbon budget pie' and it is equivalent to only about 44 years of current annual global emissions. The main game at the climate change negotiations is reaching a mitigation agreement about how the global carbon budget pie is going to be shared among 7–9 billion people, living in 193 countries, over the next 70 years.

The deep and rapid cuts in fossil fuel emissions needed to avoid dangerous climate change can only be achieved by not using fossil fuels as a source of energy for generating electricity and transportation. This is primarily because fossil fuel emissions exceed the capacity of natural sinks to absorb them (i.e. the uptake from the atmosphere of carbon dioxide by oceans and ecosystem such as forests; Le Quéré 2012). Carbon and capture technology may eventually make a modest contribution to addressing the problem, but has not been demonstrated at a commercial power station and the permanent storage of technologically captured carbon is probably not feasible (Viebahn 2009). Significant increases in energy efficiency and the rapid deployment of alternative sources of energy are therefore essential mitigation actions (OECD/IEA 2012). A lot is at stake as fossil fuel is currently the main source of energy driving economic development. Not surprisingly, there is a strong correlation between fossil fuel carbon dioxide emissions, GDP and life expectancy (Pan 2002). Developing countries, including nations with big economies but with a large proportion of the population still living in poverty (such as China, India and Brazil), do not want their use of fossil fuel energy curtailed. Unfortunately, these countries will be responsible for more and more of the carbon pollution in the coming century. China is already the number one carbon-emitting nation. Not surprisingly, rich countries, which are responsible for most of the fossil fuel carbon dioxide in the atmosphere to date, do not want to stop using fossil fuel energy. Australia, for example, generates around 77% (Commonwealth of Australia 2011) of its electricity from coal-fired power stations and is the world's largest coal exporting country.

---

1 L. Wicke, H.J. Schellnhuber and D. Klingenfeld, *The 2°max Climate Strategy—A Memorandum*, Concise English version of PIK-Report No.116—updated, www.pik-potsdam.de/research/publications/pikreports/.files/english_short_pr116, accessed 3 March 2013.

2 I have estimated this value from Anderson and Bows 2008, WBGU 2009 and Friedlingstein 2010.

Ultimately, when it comes to global climate change, there is no escape. How bad can it get? Well, actually, really bad. Scientists use various statistics to indicate the extent to which the climate is likely to change. A commonly-used metric is the average surface temperature for the planet. As any gambler knows, averages can be misleading. The annual average daily maximum temperature for Canberra (the Australian capital) is 20°C and the minimum is 7°C.[3] The record low for the South Pole is −82°C. In July 2009, Death Valley in California (USA) experienced a maximum daily temperature of 49.6°C.[4] To take the average daily surface temperature of the planet is not particularly helpful in the common sense way we think about the weather. For people living in cold climates, increasing the temperature by a couple of degrees above the current norm may sound like a good idea.

The scientific reality, however, is that this simple statistic correlates with massive changes in many aspects of Earth's climate system, including the frequency and intensity of extreme weather-related events such as heat waves, cyclones, storm surges, bush fires, floods and droughts. As the atmosphere warms, so do the oceans and their waters expand leading to rising sea levels, further exacerbated from melting ice on land (glaciers, the Greenland ice cap and, eventually, Antarctica). As hard as it is to believe, there is up to 3–6 m of sea level rise in the Greenland ice cap alone. Reduced ice cover on land and ocean results in less incoming sunlight being reflected back into space, resulting in accelerated warming (the kind of 'positive feedback' scientists worry about). As the oceans warm, the patterns of ocean circulation alter which impacts on local climatic conditions in places such as Western Europe. Rising concentrations of carbon dioxide in the atmosphere increase the acidity of the oceans, changing the fundamental chemistry of marine ecosystems (Parry *et al.* 2007).

Avoidance behaviour is certainly a very human response from children when confronted by the inconvenience of being told they must change their harmful behaviour. But as we mature and grow up, we learn the benefits of acting strategically by investing today for benefits that will be reaped in the future. Successful businesses are no different as, to survive and flourish, they must make long-term investments or risk being overwhelmed by technological innovation, ever-shifting markets and new competitors. In the real world of adults, avoidance behaviour can be lethal for individuals, families, communities, businesses and governments. When it comes to the climate change problem, there will come a point when we must face up to our individual and collective responsibilities, adopt an adult approach, stop avoiding the problem, and take decisive action.

---

3 Climate Data Online, Australian Government Bureau of Meteorology, www.bom.gov.au/climate/data/index.shtml?bookmark=200, accessed 3 March 2013.
4 NOAA National Climate Data Centre, www.ncdc.noaa.gov/sotc/national/2009/7, accessed 3 March 2013.

No more can business be usual

Mitigation

Despite the lack of 'the real deal', the world's governments are making progress on greenhouse mitigation negotiations. The agreement that came out of the Copenhagen Climate Change Conference, the Copenhagen Accord, simply asks countries to make voluntary emissions reduction commitments as they see fit. To date, countries representing some 83% of global emissions have engaged with the Copenhagen Accord (Flannery *et al.* 2012). Submitted national reduction targets, if achieved, would limit global warming to about 3.3°C.[5] While this is above what science estimates is the guard rail of 2°C, it is a step in the right direction and the accord's commitments are being used to lever national-level mitigation responses.

In 2011 the Australian parliament passed the *Clean Energy Futures Act*[6] which encompasses a package of legislation aimed at reducing emissions of carbon dioxide and other greenhouse gases from fossil fuel and land use. Put simply, the government is placing a price on carbon and creating a national carbon market. Furthermore, this price will be linked with international markets, starting with the EU emissions trading system in 2015.[7] If you are a big company with a large carbon footprint, there is now a financial incentive in many national economies to reduce your carbon dioxide emissions. If you use a lot of electricity generated from coal-fired power stations, then you have an incentive to achieve those significant energy efficiencies your sustainability office has been arguing for.

Globally, the trend is clear—even if the nations you operate in do not have a price on carbon; and, in the case of Australia, you are not one of the top 294 Australian carbon polluters that are required to track their emissions and purchase permits based on the quantity of greenhouse gases they emit. As the world community increasingly accepts what the science is saying and faces up to climate change, there will be growing political, public and economic pressure for businesses to play their part in solving the problem. We can anticipate more and more of our economy being implicated directly and indirectly in policies and mechanisms aimed at reducing emissions from all sources. Increasingly, a company's reputational value will be linked to being seen as a 'climate responsible' business operation.

Now is the time to audit your enterprise's 'carbon footprint'. Conduct an audit to quantify and audit carbon dioxide emissions from all your business activities. Undertake an energy audit to identify where your power is sourced, and identify options for moving to a green energy supplier, reducing energy use and generating your own energy on-site.

5 Climate Action Tracker, www.climateactiontracker.org, accessed 3 March 2013.
6 The Clean Energy Legislative Package, Australian Government, www.cleanenergyfuture .gov.au, accessed 10 March 2013.
7 For details see www.cleanenergyfuture.gov.au/linking-and-australian-liable-entities, accessed 1 April 2013.

Climate change means 'no more business-as-usual'; avoidance behaviour is not an option and 'greenhouse gas mitigation' must become a component of your strategic and operational business planning. Depending on the nature of your enterprise, this may involve all or some of the following responses: understanding the rapidly evolving international and national regulatory frameworks; knowing your carbon and energy footprint; having a plan for minimising your greenhouse gas emissions and energy use, and seeking green energy sources; and communicating with the community and your customers about how you are a 'climate responsible' enterprise.

Adaptation

In the lexicon of climate change, 'mitigation' refers to reducing emissions of greenhouse gases, especially carbon dioxide. The other side of the 'climate change coin' is 'adaptation'—adapting to the unavoidable impacts of a rapidly changing climate. Climate change adaptation means taking action to avoid or minimise the potential harm from climate change impacts. It can also mean responding in ways that take advantage of these changes. Therefore, from a business perspective, adapting to climate change risks can bring both associated costs and possible benefits.

Climate change adaptation can be thought of in terms of risk assessment and adaptive management. Identifying and managing risks by changing what we do to avoid or minimise harm is a standard part of business operations. Factoring in climate change-related risk is therefore readily mainstreamed into business practice. Similarly, adaptive management is a widely understood and applied approach whereby information gleaned from monitoring and evaluation can be used to improve key aspects of business operations.

When undertaking climate change adaptation assessment, a distinction is made between impacts and vulnerabilities. Impacts vary depending on the severity of the changing climate, how exposed your business is to these changes, and the sensitivity of the business to this exposure. By analogy, two men sitting on a park bench have the same exposure to the midday sun, but the bald headed one is more sensitive. The vulnerability of the two men also depends on their adaptive capacity. The bald headed man can be considered more adaptive if he anticipated a sunny day and had the foresight to bring a broad brimmed hat, thus making him less vulnerable than his more hirsute neighbour. However, the hirsute man can reduce his vulnerability by taking the adaptive response of leaving the park bench and seeking shelter from the sun. A company's exposure, sensitivity, adaptive capacity and vulnerability are, of course, context related; it all depends on the what, how, where and when of the enterprise.

A critical factor in adaptation assessment is the relevant time horizons over which your business operates, as this frames the magnitude of the climate change to which you will be exposed, the nature of the impacts and the kinds of adaptation responses called for, all of which increase in intensity the further into the future we gaze. Assuming the world community continues along the current path of fossil fuel use, global warming will cross the +2°C guard rail by around 2040–2050, continuing to +3–5°C by 2100, and beyond that in the following centuries; climate change impacts will continue for millennia. As the average global temperature increases, so do climate-related risks including the frequency and intensity of extreme weather events. For many businesses, the next five-year period is critical, but for others their return on investment is calculated over longer time periods such as 20 years when much more serious climate change impacts can be expected to occur.

Climate change can directly affect commercial operations depending on the type of business. Agriculture is an obvious example of where there are direct climate change impacts. For instance, if your business involves growing, transporting, manufacturing, or the wholesale or retail of wheat or wheat-based products, then climate change may bring risks you need to assess. The following details from an agriculture department's fact sheet (van Gool 2009) help illustrate the complex web of potentially relevant factors. Grain yields are normally limited by rainfall and temperature. For wheat, as an example, the general optimum growing temperature is about 23°C. With a moderate rise in temperatures some winter growth could increase, but this may be offset if rainfall is less. Increasingly, lower or higher temperatures will eventually slow growth, though the largest short-term impact will likely be from changing rainfall. Less rain in areas where rainfall levels are low will reduce yields. In areas where there is currently excess rainfall, a further reduction may increase yields on land that is not well drained, such as valley floors through reduced waterlogging. Extreme climatic events and greater seasonal variability, predicted to become more frequent with climate change, will also affect yield.

The further up the value chain your business operates the more indirect the potential climate change impacts and the more implicated the sector as a whole. Even more indirect effects may need to be considered such as the broader impacts of single, large-scale extreme weather events and what are being called 'event clusters and sequences', which can disrupt vital supply chains, food grains or fuel. The prospects of such event clusters are now on the intelligence community's radar as a major threat to national, regional and global security (Steinbruner *et al.* 2012). Climate change risks for business could, therefore, include an increase in the frequency and intensity of extreme weather-related events and consequently increased insurance costs, damage to property, disruption of power and water or shortages of other key resources, the inability of customers to visit or contact your business, suppliers being unable to deliver goods or services, or decreased demand for your goods and services.[8]

Undertaking a climate change vulnerability and risk assessment for your business will provide the information you need to determine adaptation options; that is, the kinds of climate change adaptation actions you should consider undertaking.

---

8 Details in this paragraph are quoted from *Environmental Risks to Your Business*, Queensland Government, Australia, www.business.qld.gov.au/business/running/environment/ environment-your-business/environmental-risks, accessed 3 March 2013.

Given that adaptation responses are part of a forward-looking business strategy, and the future remains full of uncertainty, a sensible approach is to adapt the 'scenario → policy pathway → options' framework (Low Choy *et al.* 2012). For a given scenario, a set of desirable policies can be identified and, for each policy, a set of appropriate adaptation response options. For example, one scenario might assume that climate change risks are manageable within the current business model. Therefore, the policy pathway will be to build up the resilience of the business so that it can cope with projected impacts. A set of options is then examined that reduce the exposure and sensitivity of the enterprise to these impacts. A different scenario is to anticipate that, such is the extent of projected climate change, radical changes are needed in the enterprise's business model. One policy pathway would be to have a phased move out of the sector altogether into a different line of business. Considering different scenarios and policies is important because of 'policy pathway dependency'—the longer and more deeply an organisation travels along a given route, the harder and more expensive it is to change directions. Within a given policy pathway there is rarely a single option as the world is too full of surprises to allow for such certainty. Planning in all fields is best assisted by identifying a set of appropriate options; that is, a menu of actions that can be selected from as circumstances dictate.

There is plenty to consider for businesses—big and small—when it comes to climate change. Typically, 'urgency' trumps 'importance' and, for many businesses, mitigation issues are the more immediate concern if the enterprise has a significant carbon footprint and high levels of energy use. However, risks associated with climate change, both direct and indirect, will increase over time in all sectors so adaptation assessment needs to become an integrated component of strategic planning.

Where there is change, there is opportunity

Discussion of climate change is usually negatively framed in that we consider the potential adverse impacts of climate change and how these will impose additional burdens and costs on the community and businesses. However, this is not the whole story as any change, while disruptive (and possibly even deadly and destructive), will inevitably present business opportunities for those with the capacity to exploit and to meet the social needs for repair and reconstruction. I use 'exploit' here in the positive sense of taking fair advantage of entrepreneurial opportunities, and not in the morally offensive sense of taking advantage of the harm that befalls humans and nature from climate change impacts. We must remain mindful of our duty to contribute to mitigation efforts and to help those who are vulnerable to climate change impacts and who lack adaptive capacity. Nonetheless, the fact is that meeting the challenges of mitigation and adaptation generates an urgent need and demand for innovation in all areas, including new products and services, new technologies, new approaches to management, new information systems, new apps, new materials, along with new policies, institutional arrangements and laws.

The scale of the climate change challenge can be gleaned by the fact that the international community through the United Nations Framework Convention on Climate Change (UNFCCC) has committed to establishing a Green Climate Fund with the goal of increasing climate aid to US$100 billion per year by 2020. The purpose of the Green Climate Fund is to make a significant and ambitious contribution to the global efforts towards attaining the goals set by the international community to combat climate change. The fund will contribute to the achievement of the ultimate objective of the UNFCCC. In the context of sustainable development, the fund will promote the paradigm shift towards low-emission and climate-resilient development pathways by providing support for developing countries to limit or reduce their greenhouse gas emissions and to adapt to the impacts of climate change, taking into account the needs of those developing countries particularly vulnerable to the adverse effects of climate change.[9]

Governments have a critical role to play in terms of negotiating international agreements, implementing climate change policies, establishing regulatory frameworks and incentives, along with facilitating research into knowledge gaps and helping the community understand what is at stake and needs to be done in the coming years and decades. However, much of the innovation needed to implement mitigation and adaption actions will come from the private sector.

The EU plus 13 countries are responsible for about 83% of global emissions. The 13 countries in addition to the EU are Japan, Russia, Ukraine, Australia, Canada, USA, Brazil, Indonesia, Mexico, South Africa, South Korea, China and India (Flannery *et al.* 2012). In these countries, there will be increasing demand for innovative ways of avoiding and reducing emissions of greenhouse gases and especially carbon dioxide emissions from burning fossil fuel. Achieving a 'zero-carbon economy' (or at least an economy working towards reducing emissions to zero by around 2080) will require, among other things: innovative sources of clean energy; reducing emissions from fossil fuel energy production; reducing energy use through 'greener' town planning and public transportation; and more sustainable building design and construction, manufacturing and consumer products. The imperative for a zero-carbon economy will help create the demand for a green economic revolution, and the private sector will provide the engine that drives and delivers the necessary innovation.

Adaptation has been understood as largely a problem for developing countries as they are generally seen as lacking the adaptive capacity to make the necessary adjustments given inadequate financial resources and expertise in key areas, while simultaneously struggling to address the pressing problems of poverty alleviation. However, the impact of Hurricane Sandy in the USA has made it clear that wealthy countries also face enormous challenges in adapting to future climates, especially where this involves an increase in the intensity and frequency of extreme weather events

9 Details about the fund in this paragraph are quoted from information posted on the Green Climate Fund website, gcfund.net/home.html, accessed 3 March 2013.

(Hansen *et al.* 2012). The adaptation challenge encompasses, but extends beyond, adapting to weather extremes. Much of the climate change to come, such as rising temperatures and sea levels, will be gradual and continuous over decades. Therefore, adaptation will involve integrating responses into medium and long-term strategic planning. This long-term thinking about potential future climate change impacts and adaptation responses is critical for major infrastructure investments and large-scale developments where the return on investment will be exposed to new risks.

The climate change adaptation challenge is typically seen as a cost burden that must be financed by public or donor funds. However, given the innovative solutions needed to meet adaptation problems, the private sector has a vital role to play here. For example, in the agricultural sector, innovative approaches to water use efficiency will be needed in areas suffering increased drought conditions as will new cultivars to cope with rising temperatures. In the coastal zone, rising sea levels and storm surges will create demand for new approaches to the design and construction of human settlements and associated infrastructure. While the business opportunities arising from mitigation are, perhaps, more obvious given the growing carbon economy, adaptation will increasingly present opportunities as well as risks for the business sector.

What is your business plan for climate change?

Given that climate change brings both risks and opportunities for the private sector, each enterprise needs a business plan for climate change that includes consideration of the following components:

1. A carbon and energy audit and mitigation strategy

2. A risk assessment and adaptation strategy

3. Evaluation of emerging climate change-related business opportunities

4. A review of regulatory frameworks and policy engagement

5. Public relations and communications

The fourth point warrants further comment. An increasingly important component of a business plan for climate change is to review national and international policy regimes. The international climate change policy agenda includes mitigation, adaptation, technology and finance. Understanding the implications of these rapidly evolving policy regimes can provide important intelligence to inform strategic evaluations and planning. At a national level, there may be new national regulatory reporting requirements for your business and penalties may apply for non-compliance. It may also be useful to consider if your industry representative group should be engaged in the public policy dialogue, ensuring your sector is not being unfairly treated, that governments understand your needs, and that you are aware of emerging regulatory frameworks and economic opportunities.

Promise the Earth

While I have argued here that climate change is everyone's business, the fact is that for many enterprises their carbon footprint is small and they are not commercially exposed to climate change impacts in the short-term. Many will be tempted to ask why they should bother investing now for benefits that may or may not accrue to others in the future.

In many respects, the challenge of climate change is unlike any other environmental issue. The mitigation problem demands, among many other things, globally co-ordinated action, the development and widespread application of alternative energy sources, fundamental changes in modes of production and patterns of consumption, along with new approaches to the design and construction of human settlements. The same level of engagement is needed for climate change adaptation and, together, all aspects of our economies are implicated as societies are asked to make significant changes and investments now for benefits that will accrue to others in the future. Indeed, the longer we gaze into the future, the more visible these benefits appear and the more cost-effective is early action. The fact is that we—the current generation—are being asked to make sacrifices now to avoid harm to future generations. This ethical concern for the wellbeing of those yet to be born is the foundation of sustainability. It builds upon an ethic of care, and reflects a sense of universal responsibility. It is essentially a moral position. Ethical issues are also central to the ways we collectively address the mitigation and adaptation problems of developing countries that are most at risk from climate change impacts, often have minimal adaptive capacity to respond, and are the least responsible for causing the problem.

Ultimately, solving the climate change problem requires a whole-of-society approach, the re-engineering of our economies, and the social engagement and political will that typically only arises during times of war. But the metaphor of war is inadequate and unhelpful in the face of the complex root causes of the climate change problem and the diversity of solutions it calls for. Given the long time-scales involved, the motivation to solve the climate change problem is essentially moral in character and an ethical choice about the kind of world we want our children to inherit. Good aspirations, however, can only be realised when we have the new technologies, designs and lifestyles, along with the means to deploy them across sectors and nations. Climate change is, indeed, everyone's business.

References

Anderson, K., and A. Bows (2008) 'Reframing the Climate Change Challenge in Light of Post-2000 Emission Trends', *Philosophical Transactions of the Royal Society A* 366: 3863-82.

Commonwealth of Australia (2011) *Energy in Australia 2011* (Australian Government Department of Resources Energy and Tourism; www.ret.gov.au/energy/Documents/facts-stats-pubs/Energy-in-Australia-2011.pdf).

Flannery, T., R. Beale and G. Hueston (2012) *The Critical Decade: International Action on Climate Change* (Canberra: Climate Commission Secretariat, Department of Climate Change and Energy Efficiency, Commonwealth of Australia).

Friedlingstein, P. (2010) 'Update on CO_2 Emissions', *Nature Geoscience* 3: 811-12.

Gore, A. (2006) *An Inconvenient Truth: The Planetary Emergency of Global Warming and What We Can Do About It* (Emmaus, PA: Rodale Books).

Hansen, J., M. Sato and R. Ruedy (2012) 'Perception of Climate Change', *Proceedings of the National Academy of Sciences of the USA* 109.37: E2415-23.

Le Quéré, C. (2012) 'The Global Carbon Budget 1959–2011', *Earth System Science Data Discussions* 5: 1107-57.

OECD/IEA (Organisation for Economic Co-operation and Development/International Energy Agency) (2012) *World Energy Outlook 2012* (Paris: OECD Publishing).

Pan, J. (2002) *Understanding Human Development Potentials and Demands for Greenhouse Gas Emissions: With Empirical Analysis Using Time Series and Cross-sectional Data* (Beijing: Chinese Academy of Social Sciences).

Parry, M.L., O.F. Canziani, J.P. Palutikof, P.J. van der Linden and C.E. Hanson (eds.) (2007) *Impacts, Adaptation and Vulnerability: Contribution of Working Group II to the Fourth Assessment Report of the Intergovernmental Panel on Climate Change* (Cambridge, UK and New York: Cambridge University Press).

Steinbruner, J.D., P.C. Stern and J.L. Husbands (eds.) (2012) *Climate and Social Stress: Implications for Security Analysis* (Washington, DC: National Academy of Sciences).

Stern, N. (2007) *The Economics of Climate Change: The Stern Review* (Cambridge, UK: Cambridge University Press).

UNFCCC (UN Framework Convention on Climate Change) (2009) *Copenhagen Accord*, COP 15/CMP5 (unfccc.int/meetings/copenhagen_dec_2009/meeting/6295.php, accessed 3 March 2012).

van Gool, D. (2009) *Climate Change Effects on WA Grain Production*, Western Australia Fact Sheet Note 380 (South Perth, Australia: Department of Agriculture and Food).

Viebahn, P. (2009) *Carbon Capture and Storage* (Washington, DC: Worldwatch Institute).

WBGU (German Advisory Council on Global Change) (2009) *Solving the Climate Dilemma: The Budget Approach. Special Report* (Berlin: WBGU).

Brendan Mackey is Professor and Director of the Griffith Climate Change Response Programme, Griffith University, Queensland, Australia. He serves on the governing council of the International Union for Conservation of Nature and is a member of the Australian Climate Commission's science advisory panel. He has published over 150 academic articles in the fields of climate change, biodiversity and conservation, environmental science and sustainability.

11
Industry transformation through sustainable entrepreneurship
Examples in the apparel and energy industries

Stefan Schaltegger and Erik G. Hansen
Centre for Sustainability Management, Leuphana University Lüneburg, Germany

Introduction

The key idea of a sustainable economy is the lasting, worldwide guarantee of individual opportunities to secure basic needs as well as attain a greater quality of life while, at the same time, preserving nature and promoting humane social relationships (cf. for example WCED 1987). Changed and changing market, legal, political and social conditions challenge companies to take greater account of sustainability. The rate of sustainability-oriented industry transformation varies from one country to the next; however, it is always influenced, or even shaped, by the changes in corporations. In this context corporate sustainability does not mean (superficial) 'repair' or 'corrections' of corporate activities, but instead the forging of deep changes (i.e. making sustainability principles an integral element of corporate value creation), knowing that engagement is most credible when it is comprehensive and lasting, and contributing not only to social and ecological development but also to corporate success.

Sustainable entrepreneurship as 'creative destruction'

Corporate innovativeness, triggered by sustainability-oriented business leaders and processes, has initiated a dynamic process in Germany and many other countries worldwide that has driven fundamental structural change in the economy and society. This has shaped growth and change processes in companies and industries, as well as in the economy as a whole, and in society. This in turn has influenced the kind of management increasingly needed to successfully lead a company today.

Corporate sustainability and sustainability-oriented innovation includes not only the optimisation of ongoing production processes and existing products and services, but also the core business and revenue logic (i.e. business model) and thus is the central element of a company's role in shaping society (Hansen *et al.* 2009). It is about which societal change processes are initialised or facilitated by a company's value creation and related production processes, products and services. Sustainable development requires deep changes. Unsustainable products and production processes, or even entire technological regimes, must be abandoned and new ones created in their place. In the Schumpeterian sense of the 'creative destroyer' (Schumpeter 1987), a sustainable entrepreneur is expected to see unsustainable conditions as occasions for creating new and more sustainable products, services and organisational forms, which can then replace existing structures, making them unattractive or even obsolete. This usually needs to be done in the face of resistance from most of the actors in the existing arrangements or regime (e.g. legal or political hurdles, missing finance and initial customer support). Following this line of thought has inspired an entirely new research field of 'ecopreneurship' (Blue 1990; Bennet 1991; Schaltegger 2002, 2005; Petersen 2010) and 'sustainable entrepreneurship' (Wüstenhagen 1998; Larson 2000; Cohen and Winn 2007; Hall *et al.* 2010; Hockerts and Wüstenhagen 2010; Schaltegger and Wagner 2011; Plieth *et al.* 2012).

Following Schumpeter, the 'entrepreneurial function' is not limited to the owner or founder of a business—rather it is a person or even a group of co-operating individuals successfully implementing 'new combinations' (Schumpeter 1987; Hagedoorn 1996). Thus, sustainable entrepreneurship can also take very different forms (Fig. 11.1). On one hand, motivated by their own personal values, pioneers introduce sustainable products and services or radically new business models to the market or develop markets in a correspondingly new fashion—these are entrepreneurs in a conventional sense. On the other, entrepreneurs also exist in established companies, also called 'intrapreneurs' (Schaltegger and Wagner 2011), as they enable, initiate and lead change processes towards greater sustainability. Today, this often means that sustainability managers work together with other managers in order to induce sustainability-oriented business transformation. This can only succeed in and with a company if the social and ecological issues are dealt with in a way that enhances the long-term success of the company.

Figure 11.1: **Forms of sustainable management**

Sources: Schaltegger and Wagner 2011; see also Schaltegger and Petersen 2001; Schaltegger 2002

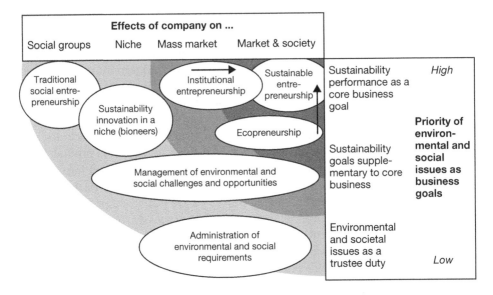

In discussions about sustainability these two idealised types of companies have so far been too often studied separately (e.g. Goldbach *et al.* 2003; Kearins *et al.* 2010; Plieth *et al.* 2012), with initiatives by both being often judged as not very effective regarding the overall transformation of an industry. Pioneer companies, for example, are accused of operating in niches and, as a result, are unable to demonstrate that they have had a real impact on economic sustainability. Similarly, conventional companies taking their first steps towards sustainability, for example by launching an eco or organic product line, have been accused of changing little in the company's essential 'unsustainability' and even of 'greenwashing'.

Although both arguments are to an extent right, considered on their own they are too limited. These two idealised types of companies have rarely been studied together and, in particular, they have not been studied dynamically over time. And yet a sustainability-oriented transformation of economic sectors and the economy itself may only be possible with contributions from both forms of sustainable entrepreneurship. This is the idea behind an evolutionary economics perspective on sustainable entrepreneurship, which unites in a common framework both the development of sustainability pioneers (so-called 'bioneers'; Schaltegger 2002) from niche to mass market and the change processes of conventional companies through sustainability management (cf. Schaltegger and Hansen 2012; Schaltegger and Petersen 2001; Schaltegger and Wagner 2011; Wüstenhagen 1998; Wüstenhagen *et al.* 1999, 2008). These two forms of sustainable entrepreneurship and their contribution to a sustainable economic change have also been characterised as 'emerging Davids' and 'greening Goliaths' (Hockerts and Wüstenhagen

2010; Wüstenhagen 1998; see also Baumol 2002a, b for his 'David-Goliath Symbiosis'). The sustainability-oriented industry transformation calls for the development of mass markets, either through the growth of sustainability pioneers or the transformation of conventional companies towards sustainability (Fig. 11.1). These two idealised types of developments do not take place independently, but instead interact in a complex fashion also referred to as a co-evolutionary process (Wüstenhagen 1998). While there are other interactions, such as spin-offs, capital investments and acquisitions, we are more interested in the interactions through market shares. Few empirical studies exist so far looking at this dynamic perspective on the transformation of industries (see, for example, Illge and Preuss 2012 for a case on the apparel industry; Wüstenhagen 1998 for illustrative cases from the energy and food sectors). Based on the results of an earlier study by the authors (Schaltegger and Hansen 2012), the goal of this paper is to illustrate these interactions with exemplary cases.

Two examples of the transformation of economic sectors

From the perspective of sustainable entrepreneurship, the sustainability-oriented transformation of industries and the entire economy occurs in the interplay of radical change by sustainability pioneers ('bioneers') in niche markets and incremental improvement strategies of conventional companies in mass markets (Wüstenhagen 1998; Hockerts and Wüstenhagen 2010). A detailed analysis of individual companies and their classification as 'sustainable' or 'unsustainable' is unable to adequately describe these interactions and change processes. It is much more instructive to analyse these transformation processes and interactions within specific industries, as will be done here for the apparel and energy (electricity) industries. For the sake of analytical clarity, the focus will be on a single important ecological issue for the sustainability-oriented transformation: organic cotton and renewable electric energy for the apparel and energy industries respectively (of course there are numerous other issues requiring simultaneous attention, such as social conditions in the supply chain or carbon dioxide emissions in production and transport).

Example 1: Change towards sustainability in the clothing industry

Clothing is a basic human need. Over the last few decades the apparel industry has faced price pressure that has exacerbated its efforts to become more sustainable. The pursuit of comparative cost advantage has led to the outsourcing of much of European and US clothing production to emerging and developing countries in

Asia. This covers most of the value chain from fibre production, spinning, fabric production, dyeing and finishing, to clothing production (cf. Goldbach *et al.* 2003). The value creation remaining in Western countries is mostly limited to value-added services and overall brand management. This change is accompanied by difficult-to-manage problems with suppliers concerning working conditions and environmental pollution. Another problem is the price pressure on raw materials. The effort to produce cotton in greater quantities at lower prices has intensified monoculture cultivation with correspondingly high levels of fertiliser, pesticide and water use (Goldbach *et al.* 2003). Furthermore, inexpensive synthetic fabrics, such as polyester, are being increasingly used, although they are non-renewable, petrochemical materials which may create various environmental and health problems.

In spite of these developments, a number of pioneer companies have entered the market with an alternative value creation model. After its foundation in 1976, the pioneer German company Hess Natur has built up a completely new and comprehensive organic apparel and textile chain (Paulitsch 2001; Schaltegger 2002; Iilge and Preuss 2012), developing a new market for organic cotton through close partnerships with its suppliers. Hess Natur probably developed the world's most stringent sustainability criteria for the apparel and textile supply chain which strongly influenced standards and certification schemes in Germany (Paulitsch 2001), for instance the Global Organic Textile Standard (GOTS; Pay 2009: 4). Based on the principles of regionality and short transportation routes, the bulk of Hess Natur's products are not just sold, but also produced in Europe. To date, organic cotton is an important trend in the apparel industry, particularly in the USA and Europe (Willer and Kilcher 2011; Memon 2012).

Some of these trends were then taken up by conventional producers in the 1990s, not only through dedicated organic product lines but also through blending strategies where organic and conventional cotton is mixed (Hustvedt and Dickson 2009) and through 'integrated production' aiming at more efficient agricultural production by reducing pesticide and chemical fertiliser use (IOBC/WPRS 2004). An 'early follower' was the Otto Group, the largest textile direct merchant in Germany (Table 11.1). By the 1980s Otto had already acknowledged the importance of environmental protection and made it a corporate goal (Goldbach *et al.* 2003; Seuring *et al.* 2004). Otto confirmed its engagement by purchasing organic cotton and developing its own label, Ecorepublic. Since the opening up of the market for organic cotton, Otto has become one of the largest buyers and has actively promoted the sustainable production of cotton. More recently it founded the initiative Cotton Made in Africa.

In the last few years other conventional textile retailers have entered the market for organic cotton clothing (Table 11.1). For example C&A has bought organic cotton since 2006 and, in 2009, founded its own brand Organic Cotton for 100% organic clothing (C&A 2012a). Today C&A, after the Otto Group the second largest textile retailer in Germany, has taken a leading role in the purchase of organic cotton, making it one of the world's largest buyers of organic cotton. In terms of quantity it has long overtaken the pioneers Hess Natur, Patagonia and Otto (Textile Exchange 2010). As strongly growing demand is faced with a very limited supply

Table 11.1: **Transformation in the German apparel industry**

Sources: TextileExchange 2010; Hess Natur-Textilen GmbH: *Consolidated Financial Statement 2010*; Mass Naturwaren GmbH: *Consolidated Financial Statement 2010*; Otto GmbH & Co KG: *Die Kraft der Verantwortung*; Adidas AG: *Annual Report 2010, Nachhaltigkeitsbericht 2010*, Handelsblatt Online: 'Adidas steigt auf nachhaltige Baumwolle um', 21 March 2011; C&A 2012a; C&A 2012b

Company name	Established	Turnover 2010/11 (€ bn)	Start of organic cotton use	Organic products in whole range (%)	Purchased organic cotton in global comparison	Goal
Hess Natur	1976	0.065	Since foundation	100%	n.a. Global #10 (2008)	Market growth; Promoting the growing of organic cotton since 1990s
Maas Naturwaren	1984	0.01	Since foundation	100%	n.a.	Market growth
Otto Group	1949	11.4	Since ~2005; Organic brand Ecorepublic since 2009	1.5% (2011)	Global #10 (2010)	To 2012/13 (Otto's own brands): 5% of products with organic cotton; Promoting the growing of Cotton Made in Africa (less pesticide and fertiliser) and sourcing goal of 10%
Adidas	1949	11.9	Since ~2009 (Integration through blending)	n.a.	Global #5 (2010)	Promoting the growing of integrated cotton labelled as Better Cotton (low levels of water and pesticides); Attaining integrated cotton sourcing goals of 40% (2015) and 100% (2018)
C&A	1841	6.59	Since 2005; Organic label Organic Cotton (since 2009 in the EU)	13% (2012)	Global #2 (2010)	Promoting the growing of certified organic cotton through Organic Exchange and increasing sourcing share; Promoting the growing of cotton from integrated production (lower levels of pesticide, fertiliser and water) through Cotton Connect; Sourcing goal of 100% in 2020

market, C&A has had problems similar to those Hess Natur had as the industry was beginning to change. Its response was to set up the initiative Cotton Connect to promote the planting of organic cotton (C&A 2012a: 106). According to a current press release, C&A is planning to increase sales of organic-certified clothing; additionally its goal is to meet its total need with cotton from integrated production (which it calls 'sustainable cotton') (C&A 2012b). The announcement by Adidas Group (2011), the second-largest sportswear manufacturer in the world, is notable in that it plans to implement a 100% conversion to cotton from the Better Cotton Initiative by 2018.

In general it can be said that innovative pioneer companies and conventional global traders, who have often borrowed their strategies from the pioneers, have initiated a notable change in the German apparel industry. This can be seen in the forecasts of most of the market studies, predicting strong growth in the area under cultivation of organic cotton and in an increasing need for retailers to rethink their strategy in terms of sustainability (cf. Pay 2009; Textile Exchange 2010; Wilcher and Kilcher 2011; Memon 2012). The currently low share of organic cotton in the global cotton market, currently less than 1% (Pay 2009: 5), is thus expected to grow considerably.

Example 2: Change towards sustainability in the energy industry

The restructuring of the energy industry towards sustainability is one of the greatest levers in the transformation to a more sustainable society. Energy is fundamentally important for both companies and for private consumers. There has been great interest in ideas about how the energy system can be reoriented towards renewable energy since the oil crises in the 1970s (Wüstenhagen and Boehnke 2006; Richter 2012) and the growth of renewable energy production has been rising steeply worldwide (e.g. US DoE 2012). Germany has been considered a pioneer and leader in the adoption of renewable energy (Wüstenhagen and Bilharz 2006; US DoE 2012). This has been possible primarily through the German feed-in tariff policy which pays a fixed price for every kilowatt hour of produced electricity from renewable energy sources, but also due to its liberated power markets which allow sales of green power (Wüstenhagen and Bilharz 2006; Bechberger and Reiche 2007). The German society has become increasingly critical of nuclear power, especially after the accidents at Chernobyl in 1986 and Fukushima in 2011, resulting in increasingly concrete energy initiatives. For example, after the Chernobyl accident, a citizens' initiative in Schönau, Germany, was founded to help restructure energy supply. At first this was done through information campaigns, energy savings competitions and the first combined heat and power projects, culminating in an electrical power station in Schönau (EWS) in 1994.[1] Shortly after

---

1 www.ews-schoenau.de/ews/geschichte, accessed 31 August 2012.

the liberalisation of the energy market in Germany in 1998, EWS was one of the first companies in Germany to provide green electricity (so-called 'rebel electricity'). Other companies such as Lichtblick, Naturstrom and Greenpeace Energy also entered the market in this phase as green electricity providers (Table 11.2). All of these pioneers attained very rapid customer acquisition growth rates at the expense of conventional energy companies. Lichtblick, for example, had over 500,000 customers in 2011. In summary, these pioneers were able to develop a market for green energy, acquire a critical mass of customers, and so demonstrate that an alternative, renewable energy supply is technically and, as growing demand showed, commercially feasible.

In 2000, when the government decided to phase-out nuclear power, a number of conventional providers began to react to these changes in the market, including large utility companies. For example, the German utility HEAG Südhessische Energie AG (HSE), made continuous and consistent progress towards its goal of becoming a 'sustainability company' (HSE 2011). Instead of being a conventional business-as-usual energy provider, a new business strategy was implemented in 2008 with the goal of 'avoiding, reducing, and compensating CO_2'. In fact this can be considered as a business model innovation (Schaltegger *et al.* 2012). Since approximately 2001 regenerative energy has been part of its electricity mix, and in 2007 it followed with a product offering of 100% green electricity. Today HSE, and its distribution company Entega, is one of the leading German green electricity providers in terms of volume sold.

For a very long time, the four major energy companies in Germany—E.ON, RWE, EnBW and Vattenfall—followed reactive strategies and were, at best, accused of greenwashing. This was especially due to their low investments in renewable energy, as well as their focus on nuclear power and 'clean coal' as climate protection solutions (Greenpeace and IÖW 2009). However, even these companies have been undergoing a noteworthy change, most recently as a result of the political decision in 2011 to completely phase-out nuclear power in Germany. Today, all four major energy companies offer, sometimes through subsidiaries, green energy. Even if these products themselves do not contribute to the energy 'turning point'—as they only bundle energy supplies from the company's own hydroelectric power capacities (often old production plants which have been available for decades) into a separate product (Greenpeace and IÖW 2009)—this is, nevertheless, a first step in their re-evaluation of the role of green electricity in their corporate strategy. That the providers still dominating the mass market are actually beginning to change is also shown by the strong growth in their investment in renewable energy, including major projects in offshore wind energy. According to current press statements, even plans for nuclear energy plants abroad have been discontinued, with the investment capital instead being redirected to renewable energy projects (Flauger 2012). While planned investment has so far been made almost exclusively in large-scale projects, E.ON's strategy is now planning to enter the area of decentralised energy supply and is offering concrete solar energy products for private homes (E.ON 2012).

Table 11.2: **Transformation of the German energy sector (descending in annual turnover)**

Sources: Stiftung Warentest (2012); 'Not every product is green', *Test 2*: 62–66; Naturstrom AG: *Annual Report 2010*; Greenpeace Energy: *Consolidated Financial Statement 2010*; EWS Vertriebs GmbH: *Consolidated Financial Statement 2010*; LichtBlick AG: *Consolidated Financial Statement 2010*; HSE: *Consolidated Financial Statement 2010, Sustainability Report 2010*, HSE Company Portrait 'Nachhaltig Wirtschaften'; Entega GmbH & Co Kg: *Consolidated Financial Statement 2010, Sustainability Report 2011*, Eprimo press release of 15 August 2011: 'Ökoangebot weiter stark nachgefragt', *RWE Factbook Renewable Energy 2011*; E.ON AG: *Annual Report 2011, CR Report 2010, Facts & Figures Report March 2012*

| Provider | Annual turnover 2010 (€ million) | Green power product | | Total renewable energy (overall) | | | Planned investment in renewable energy: |
Name (establishment)		Since approx.	Customers	Sales (million kWh) (% total sales)	Production[1] (million kWh) (% total)	Capacity[1] (MW) (% total)	
Natur-strom (1998)	53	1999	79,500	287 (100%)	*	*	Invests 1 cent per sold kWh in new plant and expansion
EWS Schönau (1994)	78	1999	115,000	450 (100%)	*	*	Extension of Sonnen-cent programme Promotion of mini CHP electricity plants
Greenpeace Energy (1999)	79	1999	96,000	448 (100%)	*	*	New electricity customers are supplied by new plants after 5 years at the latest Expansion with renewable 'wind gas'
Lichtblick (1998)	560	1999	520,000	2,600 (100%)	*	*	Expansion with 100,000 decentral mini CHP electricity plants
Entega/HSE (1999/ 2003; 1912 as HEAG)	3,743	2007	450,000	1,900 (47.5%)	477 (17.9%)	235.0 (n.a.)	Expansion of green energy plants Expansion of services for efficiency and CO_2 compensation Investment of €1.2 billion by 2015 in own renewable energy production capacity (increase to 455 MW)

EnBW (1997; merger of utility companies)	17,509	2010[2]	n.a.	n.a.	238 (0.4%)	238.0 (1.8%)	In 2011 16% of total investment in renewable energy (€217 million) 2012–2014 30% of investment in renewable energy Expand capacity to 20% (2020) and 50% (2030) and own capacity by 3,000 MW
RWE (1898)	53,320	2008[3]	150,000[5]	n.a.	6,497 (2.9%)	2,151.3 (4.4%)	Expand own production capacity in renewable energy to 4,500 MW (under construction/in operation by 2014) €4 billion investment in renewable energy by 2014 From 5.6% (2010) to 20% (2020) production of renewable energy Compensation by certificates
E.ON (2003; 1923 as Viag)	92,863	2001[4]	n.a.	n.a.	8,431 (3.1%)	4,016.0 (7.1%)	2011: €1.1 billion investment in renewable energy Double production capacity in renewable energy (2020) Expansion of decentral energy products (e.g. 'solar roofs')

Notes: * Practically no own production plants; electricity is purchased externally (mostly abroad); profits, however, are invested in new and existing plants; [1] Without old (mostly already amortised) hydroelectric power stations (own calculations based on company data); [2] e.g. EnBW Natur Max; also through subsidiaries, e.g. Natur-Energie-Plus (2010); [3] e.g. RWE Pro-Klima (2008); also through subsidiaries, e.g. eprimo Prima-Klima; [4] e.g. E.ON Aqua-Power; [5] eprimo Prima-Klima.

In general it can be seen that in Germany the development of new technologies and markets for renewable energy has largely been driven by pioneer companies for over 30 years. Their leading role was essential to show that regenerative energies are technically and economically feasible. In the next phase a number of large utility companies have promoted the change in energy supply by entering the mass market and radically modernising their business strategies. This has also given politicians a strong impetus to make successive changes in the framework conditions for markets and to persist in the face of crises. Until recently the four major energy corporations have behaved in a reactive manner, but they have now begun, after fundamental changes in markets and political regulation, to adapt their strategies and shift their investments towards renewable energies. These markets still face further steps in implementation; the transformation towards sustainability is, however, in full swing.

Discussion of the findings

These two examples illustrate the different roles sustainable entrepreneurship plays in the transformation towards sustainability in various industries. The example of the apparel industry shows how the diffusion of the certification of organic cotton and the transformation of the market was accomplished by the efforts of market actors alone. Conventional mass market retailers (e.g. C&A) have only recently entered the sustainability market but are already leading purchasers of organic cotton and have ambitious change goals for their companies and the market. This rapid transformation of a few conventional players in the market has taken place for at least three reasons:

- *Value through healthy products.* The introduction of organic textiles can, when there is a high level of health awareness and the intangible value of the product is increased, represent additional customer benefits

- *Reputational risk.* The risk of scandal accompanying conventional apparel products has a significant effect on brand value

- *Maintenance of existing production processes.* Even if the scarcity of organic cotton is a huge challenge and requires the immediate expansion of areas of cultivation, the change to organic cotton regarding the overall production process is relatively simple as it does not change requirements for production technologies (e.g. machines) and work processes (this, of course, changes once the sustainability focus is expanded from the mere cotton production to the overall supply chain including processes such as dyeing). Furthermore, no substantially new investments in production technologies (e.g. for spinning, weaving, etc) are needed, thus neither endangering existing sunk costs nor causing new ones

The transformation of the German energy sector shows a number of special features. In contrast to organic cotton in the clothing industry, green electricity is indistinguishable from conventional alternatives. When there is no direct, visible, personal added-value from a product that is often also more expensive, it is a great challenge for energy providers to acquire customers. New technologies and markets, which have been developed over the decades by pioneers, have been continuously supported in German politics since the 1990s (e.g. demonstration projects, feed-in legislation, feed-in tariffs; Wüstenhagen and Bilharz 2006; Lüthi 2010). This support may have been essential to protect niche markets and facilitate the development of mass markets. For a long time the four major energy companies persevered in their reactive attitude against green electricity, even after the first political decision was made in 2000 to phase-out nuclear energy. This energy oligopoly, protected and promoted over the decades by German politicians, demonstrated enormous inertia and attempted to resist political changes in market framework conditions. Fixed capital investments worth billions of euros—although old power plants have been amortised long ago—reinforced their limited capacity to realise strategic change. Furthermore, due to sector characteristics such as the long duration of power plant projects, the major providers have difficulties in overcoming path dependencies in the short term unless political decisions are made to provide clear framework conditions promoting transformation (Nill and Kemp 2009). This may have already been accomplished by the government decision in 2011 for a final nuclear power phase-out. It is important to point out, however, that these political decisions were encouraged and then made only after the feasibility of green energy was demonstrated in niche markets by pioneer companies.

These examples show the crucial importance of a dynamic, evolutionary view of the transformation of the economy, its industries and companies, instead of a narrow focus on the sustainability of a single company or on politics at an abstract level. Sustainable economic change is a complex process, involving both progress and setbacks, and is characterised by developments taking place over a very long time—in our two examples typically more than 25 years. The co-evolutionary lens taken by the concept sustainable entrepreneurship focuses narrowly on the interaction between different types of corporations, while other actors are set aside. The examples clearly show that both pioneer companies and incumbents are equally necessary for the sustainability-oriented transformation of industries, even if both forms of sustainable entrepreneurship react to the challenges of sustainability with different strategies and programmes. Complete sustainability may never be fully achieved. Instead, this process should be seen as a visionary orientation, in which the sustainability-oriented transformation of industries is characterised by pragmatic continuous improvement processes. The apparel industry, for example, does not become 'sustainable' through the exclusive use of organic cotton; other ecological improvements are also necessary, such as in dyeing or the cultivation and further optimisation of pesticides and water use by means of integrated production. And other dimensions of sustainability must also be addressed more strongly; for example, social conditions in the supply chain. The creative destruction of unsustainable companies can also be seen in the apparel market. New brand manufacturers are emerging—manomama in Germany (Plieth *et al.* 2012), Switcher in Switzerland or American Apparel in the USA[2]—with innovative business models based on regional value creation through vertical integration and also providing solutions to broader social and ecological problems.

The importance of sustainable management for economic change can also be seen in liberalised energy markets, which have provided the conditions in Europe, and especially in Germany, for an offensive pursuit of the turning point to renewable energy. Similarly, in the energy sector it has become clear that by setting normative goals politicians can exercise major influence on the transformation of individual economic sectors, especially when improvements in sustainability are not linked with direct customer benefits. The decisions to phase-out nuclear power in Germany have given great impetus to the transformation process, and, possibly, its decisive orientation. It also shows that it is both the combination of markets and business, together with a policy creating sustainability-oriented market framework conditions, that is especially promising in transforming sustainability-oriented niches into mass markets. These co-structuration processes illustrate that companies (seen here as political actors) have themselves possibilities to influence developments and are challenged to help shape market framework conditions that move the economy towards sustainability.

Implications for practice

These findings also have implications for corporate sustainability management in 'sleeping' markets or in those that are just setting out to become more sustainable. Sustainability managers should carefully analyse the pioneers in their sector and, through imitation, co-operation or takeover, gather experiences for new markets. Timing also plays an important role in strategy here. If conventional companies commit themselves to sustainability too quickly and radically, they may be asking too much of their customers, employees and investors. If, on the other hand, they wait too long, then market shares may be lost or even the existence of the company itself may be endangered. This was the case in the German energy sector, where conventional companies seemed surprised by the sudden changes taking place. Pioneer companies can also learn by observing developments in the market and the strategies of companies in the mass market. After all, having once achieved pioneer status does not protect a company from more intense competition from newly changing conventional companies. And mass market companies setting out to transform themselves may also be able to copy pioneer achievements and then

---

2 www.americanapparel.net/aboutus/verticalint, accessed 31 August 2012.

offer products and services on more competitive terms. Sustainability pioneers have then sufficient stimuli to develop new niche markets and become the spearhead of sustainable economic change.

References

Adidas Group (2011) *Sustainability Report 2010: In the Real World Performance Counts* (www.adidas-group.com/en/ser2010/_assets/downloads/adidasSR2010_full.pdf, accessed 31 August 2012).

Baumol, W.J. (2002a) 'Entrepreneurship, Innovation and Growth: The David–Goliath Symbiosis', *Journal of Entrepreneurial Finance and Business Ventures* 7.2: 1-10.

Baumol, W.J. (2002b) *The Free-market Innovation Machine: Analyzing the Growth Miracle of Capitalism* (Princeton, NJ: Princeton University Press, 1st edn).

Bechberger, M., and D. Reiche (2007) 'Diffusion of Renewable Feed-in Tariffs in the EU-28: An Instrumental Contribution for the Dissemination of Renewable Energies', in L. Mez (ed.), *Green Power Markets: Support Schemes, Case Studies and Perspectives* (Essex, UK: Multi-Science): 31-50.

Bennett, S.J. (1991) *Ecopreneuring: The Complete Guide to Small Business Opportunities from the Environmental Revolution* (New York: Wiley).

Blue, R.J. (1990) *Ecopreneuring: Managing for Results* (London: Longman Higher Education).

C&A (2012a) *We Care: Acting Sustainably* (www.c-and-a.com/uk/en/corporate/fileadmin/templates/master/img/fashion_updates/CR_Report/CR_Report_E.pdf, accessed 8 June 2012).

C&A (2012b) 'C&A will bis 2020 vollständig auf nachhaltig angebaute Baumwolle umstellen', press release, Düsseldorf, Germany, www.c-and-a.com/de/de/corporate/fileadmin/mediathek/de-de/Pressemitteilungen/C-und-A_will_bis_2020_vollst%C3%A4ndig_auf_nachhaltig_angebaute_Baumwolle_umstellen.pdf, accessed 29 March 2013.

Cohen, B., and M.I. Winn (2007) 'Market Imperfections, Opportunity and Sustainable Entrepreneurship', *Journal of Business Venturing* 22.1: 29-49. DOI: 10.1016/j.jbusvent.2004.12.001

E.ON (2012) *Geschäftsbericht 2011* (www.eon.com/content/dam/eon-com/de/downloads/e/E.ON_Geschaeftsbericht_2011.pdf, accessed 28 March 2012).

Flauger, J. (2012) 'Eon Investiert in Erneuerbare statt in Atomkraftwerke', *Handelsblatt Online* (29 March 2012; www.handelsblatt.com, accessed 30 March 2012).

Goldbach, M., S.A. Seuring and S. Back (2003) 'Co-ordinating Sustainable Cotton Chains for the Mass Market: The Case of the German Mail-Order Business OTTO', *Greener Management International* 43: 65-78.

Greenpeace and IÖW (Institut für Ökologische Wirtschaftsforschung) (2009) *Investitionen der Vier Großen Energiekonzerne in Erneuerbare Energien: Bestand, Ziele und Planungen von E.ON, RWE, EnBW und Vattenfall konzernweit und in Deutschland.* (Hamburg, Germany: Greenpeace e.V.).

Hagedoorn, J. (1996) 'Innovation and Entrepreneurship: Schumpeter Revisited', *Industrial and Corporate Change* 5.3: 883-96. DOI: 10.1093/icc/5.3.883

Hall, J.K., G.A. Daneke and M.J. Lenox (2010) 'Sustainable Development and Entrepreneurship: Past Contributions and Future Directions', *Journal of Business Venturing* 25.5: 439-48. DOI: 10.1016/j.jbusvent.2010.01.002

Hansen, E.G., F. Große-Dunker and R. Reichwald (2009) 'Sustainability Innovation Cube: A Framework to Evaluate Sustainability-oriented Innovations', *International Journal of Innovation Management* 13.4: 683–713. DOI: 10.1142/S1363919609002479

Hockerts, K., and R. Wüstenhagen (2010) 'Greening Goliaths Versus Emerging Davids. Theorising About the Role of Incumbents and New Entrants in Sustainable Entrepreneurship', *Journal of Business Venturing* 25.5: 481-92. DOI: 10.1016/j.jbusvent.2009.07.005

HSE (HEAG Südhessische Energie AG) (2011) *Geschäftsbericht 2010: Energie für Menschen* (www.hse.ag/fileadmin/user_upload/downloads/konzern/hse_gb2010.pdf, accessed 2 April 2012).

Hustvedt, G., and M.A. Dickson (2009) 'Consumer Likelihood of Purchasing Organic Cotton Apparel: Influence of Attitudes and Self-identity', *Journal of Fashion Marketing and Management* 13.1: 49-65. DOI: 10.1108/13612020910939879

Illge, L., and L. Preuss (2012) 'Strategies for Sustainable Cotton: Comparing Niche with Mainstream Markets', *Corporate Social Responsibility and Environmental Management* 19.2: 102-13.

IOBC/WPRS (International Organisation for Biological and Integrated Control of Noxious Animals and Plants/West Palearctic Regional Section) (2004) *Integrated Production. Principles and Technical Guidelines* (Dijon, France: IOBC/WPRS, 3rd edn; www.iobc.ch/iobc_bas.pdf, accessed 22 June 2012).

Kearins, K., E. Collins and H. Tregidga (2010) 'Beyond Corporate Environmental Management to a Consideration of Nature in Visionary Small Enterprise', *Business and Society* 49.3: 512-47. DOI: 10.1177/0007650310368988

Larson, A.L. (2000) 'Sustainable Innovation Through an Entrepreneurship Lens', *Business Strategy and the Environment* 9.5: 304-17. DOI: 10.1002/1099-0836(200009/10)9:5<304:: AID-BSE255>3.0.CO;2-O

Lüthi, S. (2010) 'Effective Deployment of Photovoltaics in the Mediterranean Countries: Balancing Policy Risk and Return', *Solar Energy* 84: 1059-71.

Memon, N.A. (2012) 'Organic Cotton: Biggest Markets are Europe and the United States', *Pakistan Textile Journal* March: 42-43.

Nill, J., and R. Kemp (2009) 'Evolutionary Approaches for Sustainable Innovation Policies: From Niche to Paradigm?', *Research Policy* 38: 668-80.

Pay, E. (2009) *The Market for Organic and Fair-trade Cotton Fibre and Cotton Fibre Products* (Rome, Italy: FAO).

Paulitsch, K. (2001) 'Hess Natur: Acting for the World of Tomorrow. Resource Management in the Textile Chain', in M. Charter and U. Tischner (eds.), *Sustainable Solutions. Developing Products and Services for the Future* (Sheffield, UK: Greenleaf Publishing): 381-92.

Petersen, H. (2010) 'The Competitive Strategies of Ecopreneurs: Striving for Market Leadership by Promoting Sustainability', in M. Schaper (ed.), *Making Ecopreneurs: Developing Sustainable Entrepreneurship* (Farnham, UK: Gower/Ashgate, 2nd edn): 223-37.

Plieth, H., A.C. Bullinger and E.G. Hansen (2012) 'Sustainable Entrepreneurship in the Apparel Industry: The Case of Manomama', *Journal of Corporate Citizenship* 45: 121-34.

Richter, M. (2012) 'Utilities' Business Models for Renewable Energy: A Review', *Renewable and Sustainable Energy Reviews* 16: 2483-93. DOI: 10.1016/j.rser.2012.01.072

Schaltegger, S. (2002) 'A Framework for Ecopreneurship: Leading Bioneers and Environmental Managers to Ecopreneurship', *Greener Management International* 38: 45-58.

Schaltegger, S. (2005) 'A Framework and Typology for Ecopreneurship: Leading Bioneers and Environmental Managers to Ecopreneurship', in M. Schaper (ed.), *Making Ecopreneurs: Developing Sustainable Entrepreneurship* (London: Ashgate Publishing): 43-60.

Schaltegger, S., and E.G. Hansen (2012) 'Wirtschaftswende Durch Nachhaltiges Unternehmertum', in G. Altner, H. Leitschuh-Fecht, G. Michelsen, U.E. Simonis, J. Sommer and E.U. von Weizsäcker (eds.), *Wende überall? Von Vorreitern, Nachzüglern und Sitzenbleibern. Jahrbuch Ökologie 2013* (Stuttgart, Germany: Hirzel): 64-75.

Schaltegger, S., F. Lüdeke-Freund and E.G. Hansen (2012) 'Business Cases for Sustainability: The Role of Business Model Innovation for Corporate Sustainability', *International Journal of Innovation and Sustainable Development* 6.2: 95-119. DOI: 10.1504/IJISD.2012.046944

Schaltegger, S., and H. Petersen (2001) *Ecopreneurship. Konzept und Typologie* (Lüneburg, Germany/Luzern, Switzerland: Centre for Sustainability Management/Rio Management Forum).

Schaltegger, S., and M. Wagner (2011) 'Sustainable Entrepreneurship and Sustainability Innovation: Categories and Interactions', *Business Strategy and the Environment* 20.4: 222-37.

Schumpeter, J. (1987 [1934]) *Theorie der wirtschaftlichen Entwicklung: Eine Untersuchung über Unternehmensgewinn, Kapital, Kredit, Zins und den Konjunkturzyklus* (Berlin, Germany: Duncker & Humblot, 7th edn reprint of 4th edn from 1934).

Seuring, S.A., M. Goldbach and J. Koplin (2004) 'Managing Time and Complexity in Supply Chains: Two Cases from the Textile Industry', *International Journal of Integrated Supply Management* 1.2: 180-98.

Textile Exchange (2010) *2010 Global Market Report on Sustainable Textiles: Executive Summary* (O'Donnell, TX: Textile Exchange).

US DoE (US Department of Energy) (2011) *2010 Renewable Energy Data Book* (Golden, CO: DoE; www.nrel.gov/analysis/pdfs/51680.pdf, accessed 23 July 2012).

WCED (World Commission on Environment and Development) (1987) *Our Common Future* (Oxford, UK: Oxford University Press).

Willer, H., and L. Kilcher (2011) *The World of Organic Agriculture: Statistics and Emerging Trends 2011* (Bonn, Germany: IFOAM, FiBL).

Wüstenhagen, R. (1998) *Greening Goliaths Versus Multiplying Davids: Pfade einer Coevolution Ökologischer Massenmärkte und Nachhaltiger Nischen* (St. Gallen, Switzerland: IWÖ).

Wüstenhagen, R., and M. Bilharz (2006) 'Green Energy Market Development in Germany: Effective Public Policy and Emerging Customer Demand', *Energy Policy* 34: 1681-96.

Wüstenhagen, R., and J. Boehnke (2006) 'Business Models for Sustainable Energy', in *Proceedings: Perspectives on Radical Changes to Sustainable Consumption and Production*, workshop of the Sustainable Consumption Research Exchange (SCORE!) Network: 253-58.

Wüstenhagen, R., A. Meyer and A. Villiger (1999) 'Die Landkarte des Ökologischen Massenmarktes', *Ökologisches Wirtschaften* 99.1: 27-29.

Wüstenhagen, R., J. Hamschmidt, S. Sharma and M. Starik (eds.) (2008) *Sustainable Innovation and Entrepreneurship* (Cheltenham, UK and Northampton, MA: Edward Elgar).

Dr **Erik Hansen** is Research Associate and 'Habilitand' at the Centre for Sustainability Management (CSM) at Leuphana University Lüneburg, Germany. His research interests are focused on innovation, entrepreneurship and transformation in the context of sustainable development. Besides research, he also teaches in graduate, post-graduate and executive programmes. Prior to his current position, he was a Visiting Researcher at Cranfield University, UK and received his PhD at Technische Universität München, Germany.

Professor **Stefan Schaltegger**, PhD, is Professor of Sustainability Management and Head of the CSM at Leuphana University Lüneburg, Germany. His research deals with corporate sustainability management including sustainable entrepreneurship, sustainability accounting and management control, performance measurement, management methods, strategic management, stakeholders and the business cases for sustainability. Stefan is Head of the MBA Sustainability Management and the Sustainability Leadership Forum, which he founded in 2003.

12

Public policy processes for transition to a sustainable enterprise society
The case of extractive industries

Ciaran O'Faircheallaigh
School of Government and International Relations, Griffith University, Queensland, Australia

Introduction

Public policy processes, or the way in which policies are conceived, developed, endorsed and implemented, have a profound impact on policy content. Yet while there is a large body of research on the substantive content of policies required to facilitate a transition to sustainability, much less attention has been paid to the sorts of policy processes that are likely to yield appropriate policy outcomes, or on how existing policy processes must change if such outcomes are to be achieved. This constitutes a significant gap in the knowledge required to support a transition to sustainability. Existing policy processes have developed incrementally over long periods of time when sustainability was not an explicit goal of government policy, and they are not simple or easy to change (Howlett 2002: 241). If the same policy processes that have led to unsustainable forms of development continue to dominate political systems, how can policies emerge that will enable and support sustainable enterprise and progress towards a sustainable society?

What aspects or components of policy processes are relevant to sustainability and what sorts of policy processes are required to facilitate its pursuit? Where governments are committed to pursuing sustainable societies, what sorts of processes should they change *to*? This chapter identifies critical components of policy processes that are likely to affect the prospects for achieving environmental, economic and social sustainability. These include: patterns and degrees of public participation in policy-making; the locus of control over policy decisions; criteria used in policy-making; and time-frames used both in taking policy decisions and in assessing the expected impacts of policy options.

The chapter illustrates the potential impact of alternative approaches to these components of the policy process in relation to public policies on exploitation of non-renewable resources, an area that raises in sharp focus the challenges of a transition to a sustainable enterprise society. Given the non-renewable and ultimately finite nature of mineral resources, it could be argued that the concept of sustainability is not even relevant to extractive industries. But while individual mineral deposits must inevitably be depleted, and so are not themselves 'sustainable', their exploitation can contribute to, detract from or even destroy, environmental, social and economic sustainability. Two examples will illustrate this point.

The first involves the Ok Tedi copper/gold mine in the Western Province of Papua New Guinea. The mine has destroyed the resource base of hundreds of villagers, as a result of the devastating environmental impacts of the release of its tailings and waste rock into the Ok Tedi and Fly rivers. This outcome emerged in large measure from the decision of the Papua New Guinea government to allow the project to proceed after the companies developing it refused to continue its construction if they were required to build a tailings dam after the original dam site was inundated by a huge land slip. There have also been serious failings in the environmental management and regulatory systems for the mine, which resulted for instance in release of cyanide into the Ok Tedi river in 1984, killing thousands of fish, crocodiles and turtles. It will take decades for the river systems to return to health, and large areas of agricultural land have been permanently lost (Kirsch 1997: 121-26; MMSD 2002: 348). In this case, an extractive activity has destroyed sustainability, a fact that has reflected corporate and government decisions, in particular decisions to proceed with mining in the absence of a tailings retention facility. Those decisions have emerged, in turn, from specific types of policy processes.

The second example relates to a bauxite mine on Cape York in northern Australia, operated by Rio Tinto Alumina (formerly Comalco Ltd) since the early 1960s. For the first four decades of its life few economic benefits accrued to the traditional Aboriginal owners of the land on which mining occurs, and at the same time they incurred significant social, cultural and environmental costs (O'Faircheallaigh 2005). In 1992 Australia's High Court recognised Indigenous ownership of land in Australia prior to European settlement ('native title') in the *Mabo* case, and in the following year the federal government provided legislative recognition of native title through the introduction of the *Native Title Act 1993*. A number of traditional owner groups subsequently lodged native title claims over sections of Comalco's mining leases. Partly in response to these changes, Rio Tinto invited traditional owners to negotiate a legally-binding agreement covering a range of issues and impacts associated with Comalco's operations. The Western Cape Communities Co-existence Agreement (WCCCA), signed in 2001, includes a system for minimising or avoiding damage to

Aboriginal cultural heritage and for enhancing environmental outcomes. In terms of economic and social sustainability, a critical part of the agreement involves payment of substantial royalties to the traditional owners by Queensland's state government and by the project operator, and investment of over half of this revenue flow in a long-term capital fund. Income is reinvested for 20 years, after which it becomes available for current expenditure, but the capital base is to be preserved in perpetuity (O'Faircheallaigh 2005).

It can be argued that, in this case, mining contributes to sustainability because future generations will enjoy a substantial and ongoing revenue flow, and the economic and social opportunities associated with it, that would not be available in the absence of mining. This example highlights again the critical impact of public policies. Indeed the contribution of mining to sustainability increased dramatically over a short period of time because of the High Court's recognition of Indigenous rights in land, the federal government's action in giving legislative expression to this recognition, and the Queensland government's decision to divert a share of its own royalty income into the WCCCA.

Policy processes and policy outcomes

The fact that public policy processes shape the content and impact of public policies is well documented across a wide variety of political systems and policy contexts. For example, Alston and colleagues (2006) found that the 'driving force' behind policies in contemporary Brazil is the specific nature of interactions between key political actors in different policy arenas, and that 'the dynamics of the policy-making game' in these arenas yield predictable outcomes in terms, for example, of the stability and adaptability of policy. The specific features of policy-making processes are, in their view, 'key determinants of the characteristics of public policies', characteristics they label as 'the dependent variable' (Alston *et al.* 2006: 6-11). Howlett (2002) found that the nature of policy-making subsystems in Canada influenced both the pace and nature of policy change, and that changes in policy-making processes were linked in a predictable manner to changes in the nature and rate of policy change (for other examples see Connick and Innes 2001; Gains 2003; Aninat *et al.* 2006; Stein *et al.* 2008). At a more specific level, Howard (2007) shows how one aspect of the policy process—the availability to participants of information on the probable impact of policy alternatives being considered—influenced the likelihood of departures from the status quo in relation to water management policy in Australia. Stratford and Jaskolski (2004: 321-32) argue that another specific aspect of the policy process—absence of appropriate leadership—acted as a barrier to the development of policies conducive to sustainability in local government in Tasmania.

To the extent that policy processes attract attention in the wider literature on sustainability or in writing on extractive industries and sustainability, this tends to focus heavily on the issue of public participation and stakeholder engagement

(Day and Affum 1995; Lyons *et al.* 2001; Cheney *et al.* 2002; MMSD 2002; Stratford and Jaskolski 2004). But public participation is just one of many variables shaping policy processes. In an earlier publication (O'Faircheallaigh 2009) I identified, based on a review of general literature on public policy-making and the literature on sustainability and extractive industries, nine variables that, individually and in combination, play a critical role in shaping the way in which policies that affect sustainability are made. The variables and some key questions in relation to each are presented in Table 12.1. The following sections analyse each variable in turn, demonstrating their impact on policy and their relevance to sustainability, and starting to explore the way in which interactions between individual variables generate particular types of policy processes.

Table 12.1: **Nine variables that shape the character of public policy processes**

Source: Adapted from O'Faircheallaigh, C. (2009) 'Public Policy Processes and Sustainability in the Minerals and Energy Industries', in J. Richards (ed.), *Mining, Society, and a Sustainable World* (New York: Springer): 445

Variable	Some key questions
1. Participation in policy-making	Who participates and who is excluded? What mechanisms foster, or militate against, inclusion? How much priority do those included/excluded attach to sustainability?
2. Authority over outcomes	What sources of power are available to participants? Who has the capacity to determine outcomes? How 'open' or 'closed' is decision-making in terms of participation and influence over outcomes?
3. Decision alternatives	What range of alternatives is considered? How do these relate to the policy status quo? How is the range of alternatives affected by the degree of openness in decision-making?
4. Criteria used in policy-making	Which impacts and issues are considered in policy-making, and which are excluded? What weight is attached to various impacts?
5. Time period over which effects of policy decisions considered	What time-frames are utilised? Who determines these time-frames?
6. 'One off' or adaptive decision-making	Do policy decisions tend to be 'one off', or can they be revisited regularly? What are the implications of this for sustainability?
7. Time allocated for decision-making	How much time is available for policy-making? How and by whom is this determined?
8. Resources available to support decision-making	What resources are available to support decision-making, and to whom are they made available? Are there major disparities in the resources available to different participants?
9. Information available to support policy-making	What sorts of information are available to inform policy-making? Are specific types of information privileged, or discounted?

Inclusion: who participates in policy-making?

The first issue involves the identity and interests of those who participate in policy-making. Sustainability will not be prioritised if those participating in decision-making do not value it and if those who do value sustainability are excluded. The importance of this issue is highlighted by the examples mentioned above. Villagers were completely excluded from decisions about the Ok Tedi development, and Aboriginal owners from decisions about the Weipa bauxite mine for the first four decade of its life. Many other similar cases can be cited; for example, phosphate mining on the Pacific island of Nauru. For over 60 years from the early 20th century no provision was made for investment of Nauru's phosphate revenues in economic, environmental or social sustainability. Policy-making involved only the colonial powers that controlled the island, and they were only concerned about securing cheap and reliable supplies of phosphate for farmers in their home countries. The ultimate result was to destroy the sustainability of Nauruan society (Weeramantry 1992; O'Faircheallaigh 2009).

Historically, policy-making in relation to extractive industries in free-market economies has been dominated by companies and a small number of government agencies, in particular treasuries and mines and energy departments. Companies play a critical role as mineral development is driven fundamentally by their investment decisions (where to explore, what to explore for, which projects to develop, which projects to close and when to close them), and because larger companies in particular have substantial capacity to lobby public policy-makers (Libby 1989). Mining companies may be very concerned about sustainability in corporate terms, but do not necessarily attach priority to the economic, social or environmental sustainability of communities, regions or countries (Trebeck 2007). While in theory democratic governments should reflect the diversity of interests that comprise their electorates, in reality they have often been driven by the need to demonstrate their ability to foster economic growth, particularly by supporting large projects that offer highly visible additions to employment and exports. As a result they have in the past prioritised rapid development of mineral resources (Harman and Head 1981).

More recently the introduction of environmental impact assessment (EIA) legislation has provided an opportunity for other interests to participate in public policy processes, for instance through public submission and objection processes that allow interested groups to argue that projects should not proceed, should be modified substantially before proceeding, or should be subject to environmental and other conditions (Cheney *et al.* 2002: 2). Growing national and international recognition of Indigenous rights has provided an avenue for Indigenous participation in decision-making, while the adoption of corporate social responsibility (CSR) policies by many of the world's leading mining companies creates another opportunity to expand the range of interests involved in policy-making. BHPBilliton (2012), for instance, 'seeks to work with relevant stakeholders, and especially those most affected by our operations, to identify and address their concerns and expectations and to maximise potential benefits from our business'. However, the trend towards participation of a broader range of interests is by no means uniform or cumulative. For example, the Canadian federal government has recently introduced new EIA legislation that 'undoes decades of progress', in part because it 'eliminates many opportunities for public participation and limits the potential range of public contributions, probably excluding the most significant public concerns' (Gibson 2012: 184).

Authority: who determines policy outcomes?

Participation in policy-making is one matter, but the capacity to determine outcomes is another (Howard 2007). Companies and governments have sources of power and influence that are unequivocal and substantive, and particularly in relation to individual resource projects each enjoys a 'yes/no' power of decision over whether or not development will proceed. Companies have an investment veto, as in a free-market economy governments cannot force companies to invest; however, governments have a regulatory veto, as projects cannot be developed without government approvals. The power to decide whether or not a project will proceed provides both parties, in turn, with substantial influence over a range of other decisions, as companies and governments can insist that they will only invest in a project, or approve a project, under the 'right' conditions. For companies, these conditions may relate to royalty rates, public funding of mine infrastructure, project scale or environmental conditions. For governments, they may relate to company funding of infrastructure that will have multiple users, domestic processing of minerals or allocation of a proportion of energy output to domestic markets.

The capacity of environmental, community or other civil society groups to shape policy outcomes is less clear cut. It can be substantial in some cases. For example, environmental groups successfully mobilised public opinion and lobbied Australia's federal government to maintain a ban on development of new uranium projects for more than a decade after 1983. Environmental groups prevented development of the proposed Windy Craggy copper mine in British Columbia in 1993. However, in relation to mining projects that do not attract widespread public attention because of the mineral being mined or their location in environmentally or culturally sensitive areas, in reality the vast majority, the power of environmental or community groups in public policy-making is still limited.

In some cases (for instance Aboriginal freehold land in Australia's Northern Territory; limited areas within comprehensive land claim settlements in Canada) Indigenous people do have a legal right to determine whether or not development can proceed, affording them a central role in decision-making. In other cases Indigenous people may be able to use political pressure to win for themselves a de facto right of veto. For example after Innu and Inuit traditional owners halted development of Inco's Voisey's Bay nickel project through direct action and litigation, the government of Newfoundland and Labrador informed Inco that it would not allow the project to proceed without the consent of the Innu and Inuit (Newfoundland and Innu Nation 2002). Voisey's Bay provides a clear example of the way in which control over decision-making affects sustainability issues. One of the conditions on which the Innu and Inuit eventually allowed the project to proceed was that annual nickel output would be less than half that originally planned. This reduced environmental impacts and provided local communities much more time to capitalise on opportunities created by Voisey's Bay (for instance skills and enterprise development), allowing them to build an economic base that could survive the end of mining.

The extent to which policy processes incorporate, and confer power upon, a wide and diverse range of interests determines the degree of openness that characterises policy-making. However, a high degree of openness in itself is no guarantee that policy processes will promote sustainability, as an open policy process can admit opponents of sustainability as easily as its supporters, a point often lost on analysts who assume that broadly-based participation is inherently conducive to sustainability. It is therefore critical to consider not only who is involved in policy-making, but also a range of variables that shape the basis on which policies are developed and decisions are taken.

Policy alternatives

One such variable involves the range of policy alternatives that are considered. In some cases an incremental approach is adopted, with only a narrow range of alternatives, representing minor adjustments to the status quo, being assessed. At the other end of the spectrum, the full range of conceivable alternatives may be evaluated (Pal 2006: 271-93). In the context of mineral development and sustainability, an incremental approach might involve a continuation of traditional approaches based essentially on economic calculations, with gradual adjustments being made to project design and operations to enhance environmental and social sustainability. These might involve, for instance, reduction of water and energy consumption (which may, of course, improve project economics in any case), or establishment of corporate foundations to channel additional social benefits to affected communities. Alternatively, a much wider and more radical range of alternatives might be considered. These could include fundamental changes to project scale and design to enhance sustainability, and a 'no project' alternative where prospects for sustainability appear poor. The latter alternative is sometimes considered in conventional EIA, but is usually immediately dismissed on the basis of the economic benefits that would be foregone (see, for instance, Chevron Australia Pty Ltd 2005: 14). The new Canadian environmental legislation actually eliminates mention of assessing alternatives to a proposed project, focusing exclusively on mitigating adverse effects the project proposed by the developer (Gibson 2012: 184). Given the magnitude of environmental and social problems associated with recent patterns of industrial development, it can be argued that an incremental approach is no longer adequate, because at least in the short- to medium-term it replicates approaches that have caused the problems in the first place.

It seems logical to assume that the range of decision alternatives considered would be linked to the openness of decision processes. A closed process dominated by interests that have benefited from the status quo is unlikely to facilitate a consideration of radical alternatives, whereas 'opening up' the decision process is likely to have the opposite outcome. This is illustrated by the example of Voisey's Bay. It is very unusual for a mining project to proceed at half the scale identified as optimum by the project proponent, and this outcome followed on from the success of the Innu and Inuit in 'opening up' the decision process and establishing themselves as powerful actors within it. However, I am not aware of any systematic research that focuses on the relationship between openness of policy processes and the range of alternatives considered.

Criteria for policy-making

Another issue involves the decision criteria that are employed by policy-makers. Which impacts of policies and decisions are considered and which are excluded? What weight is attached to different impacts, for example as between economic, social and environmental effects? What weight is attached to short-term impacts as opposed to long-term impacts? To express this last point somewhat differently, what discount rate is applied by policy-makers? Application of a high discount rate will mean that short-term effects are weighted much more heavily than long-term effects (MMSD 2002: 347), while use of a lower rate will moderate this effect.

Historically, assessment of mining projects has tended to focus almost entirely on economic criteria. Introduction of EIA and environmental protection legislation in the 1970s required a focus on the physical environment, but a great deal of latitude remained, and remains today, in determining *which* environmental impacts or issues are taken into account. For instance, in September 2007, Australia's Federal Court rejected an attempt by environmental groups to challenge the federal Minister for the Environment's decision in relation to a proposed coal mine, on the basis that the Minister had not properly assessed the adverse effects on greenhouse gas emissions that would be caused by burning coal produced by the mine. In addition, social or cultural effects often receive scant attention, and even when they are considered the analysis often lacks the rigorous, quantitative analysis applied in assessing economic impacts (Chevron Australia Pty Ltd 2005; Moolarben Coal Mines Pty Ltd 2006a). This is important, because it may be difficult for policy-makers to insist on project changes to address potential social and cultural impacts expressed in general, tentative or hypothetical terms, given anticipated economic benefits that are clearly quantified and substantial, and so appear certain to eventuate.

Another key issue involves the discount rate applied to future expected costs and benefits. In calculating economic benefits of mining projects, the conventional approach for companies is to use a discount rate which is equivalent to their average cost of capital. Using a discount rate in the region of 10% (van Rensburg and Bambrick 1978: 151-52) would obviously render negligible the current value of any benefits or costs accruing to 'future generations', in comparison to short-term benefits or costs. Public policy-makers may use discount rates somewhat lower than companies; though treasury bond rates, which are sometimes used as a basis for discount rates, are often in the range of 5–10%. If calculations are made over periods of 40 or 60 years, for instance, application of such discount rates would still have the effect of rendering negligible the current value of long-term benefits and costs. At a more fundamental level, it can be argued that affording quantitative cost–benefit techniques, such as discounting, a central role in decision-making immediately devalues the importance of factors that are not quantifiable or not easily quantifiable, such as Indigenous attachment to ancestral land, unique cultural heritage values or ways of life, or biological diversity.

Time periods over which effects of policy alternatives are considered

Central to the concept of sustainability is a consideration of the effects of current actions and choices on future generations. Thus, the time-frame over which the policy process considers the impacts of policy actions or policy alternatives is critical. If future generations are to be considered, time-frames must obviously be extended (for instance 60–100 years if the impacts on two generations is to be considered).

In reality, the time-frames over which the impacts of major mining and energy projects are analysed as part of public policy-making are generally much shorter than this. Typically, the time-frame on which attention is focused is the life of project (see, for example, Blacktip Joint Venture 2004; Moolarben Coal Mines Pty 2006b). This can be as short as ten years. The assumption generally is that economic impacts, for instance, only need to be considered during project life, and that environmental impacts will be remediated before a project is abandoned. In reality, while the direct economic impacts of a project may largely coincide with its productive life, its indirect effects may last longer, and indeed *must* last longer if the project is to make a lasting contribution to economic and social sustainability. There are many cases of 'legacy' mines whose environmental impacts persist long after mining has stopped (MMSD 2002: 407-408). Thus, a policy process that considered whether a project would generate net public benefits over an operational life of 20 years might yield a different outcome to one that assessed net benefits over 40 years.

'One off' versus adaptive policy-making

Another dimension of policy-making involves the issue of whether a process focuses on single, 'once and for all' decisions in relation to mining projects, or creates systems that allow for ongoing, adaptive changes to project design and operation. The link between adaptive management and sustainability, and the necessity for utilising adaptive management in specific areas such as climate change, are well established in the literature (Norton 2005; Otto-Zimmermann 2011). However, in extractive industries a single critical set of decisions tends to determine whether a project can proceed and, assuming it can, the environmental and other conditions under which it will operate for the remainder of project life, or at least over long periods of time (Howitt 2003: 337-38; O'Faircheallaigh 2007: 322-33). These matters are rarely revisited. I am not aware of any legislation, for example, that requires a further EIA to be undertaken after, say, ten years, to establish whether project impacts are as expected and whether the decision to allow the project to operate, or the conditions imposed on it, should be revisited.

It can be argued that such an approach is inadequate if sustainability is to be achieved. Given the rapid changes that can occur in understanding of environmental and social impacts, and in mining, mineral processing and waste treatment technologies, it may be essential to develop adaptive approaches that regularly revisit relevant issues and enhance responses to them. The requirements for adaptive management have started to attract substantial attention in the academic literature, and attempts are being made to apply them in the environmental management of some projects (Morrison-Saunders and Arts 2005; O'Faircheallaigh 2007). There are also increasing efforts to ensure that lessons learned from operating projects are applied in assessing and setting conditions for new ones (Baines *et al.* 2012). However, it can be argued that policy-making systems are still very much dominated by a 'one off' approach, as indicated by the fact that even where adaptive approaches are required by legislation, they are rarely applied in practice (O'Faircheallaigh 2007).

Time allocated for policy-making

The time period allowed for policy-making is an important variable because it influences the potential to involve a range of interests in decision-making and the ways in which they can be involved. It also shapes the type and range of information considered in making decisions (discussed below); for instance, because considerable time may be required if policy-makers are to gain access to information dealing with long-term natural cycles, or information from oral sources such as interviews with Indigenous elders. Generally speaking, the shorter the time-frame applied, the narrower the opportunities that exist in terms of involving diverse interests and a wide range and depth of information.

Two influences tend to be paramount in setting time-frames for policy-making in extractive industries. The first are statutory requirements, with mining and environmental assessment legislation usually establishing requirements on government to take decisions within specific time periods (see, for example, Government of Western Australia 2012). The second are the financial and market pressures facing mining and energy companies, which often mean that they are working to tight time-frames, especially if they are competing with other potential suppliers to meet limited market opportunities.

Mining companies tend to press hard-to-minimise decision-making time-frames, and governments tend to be responsive to what they see as commercial imperatives. The result can be that insufficient attention is paid to sustainability issues in policy-making. This is not to argue for open-ended time-frames. However, mineral industries cannot be developed in a way that contributes to sustainability if time-frames for decision-making make it impossible to incorporate groups or interests that seek sustainable outcomes, or to gather and analyse information that is critical in establishing requirements for sustainability. If mineral and energy industries are serious about pursuing sustainability, they cannot insist that time-frames be driven solely by commercial considerations. This is particularly so given that, in the event, projects rarely meet company schedules because of technical or regulatory issues, with the result that adequate time would, in fact, have been available for more rigorous information collection and analysis. For example, project proponents and the Government of Western Australia insisted that Indigenous impact assessment studies in relation to a proposed liquefied natural gas (LNG) facility in the Kimberley region be completed within six months, making it impossible to undertake adequate assessment work or fully develop strategies to enhance the contribution of the proposed project to environmental, economic and social sustainability (KLC 2010). In the event, commercial obstacles and problems in the government's own regulatory processes led to a succession of project delays, meaning that plenty of time would have been available to undertake comprehensive Indigenous impact assessment studies.

Resources available to support policy-making

Another important variable involves the availability of resources to support participation in policy-making. Resources are required both within public agencies seeking input into policy-making, and for groups and individuals seeking to participate. Not only financial resources are needed. Effective participation also requires skills, both on the part of those seeking to participate and those seeking to learn from participants, and dissemination of appropriate information is also critical. Indeed as Ogden (2006) notes, many people with a key interest in public policy decisions are not sufficiently informed to even know that they will be affected by those decisions. Ultimately, of course, other forms of resources such as information and access to appropriate forms of participation and arenas for participation have a financial cost.

Corporations fund their participation in decision-making on the assumption that they can recoup their costs from projects that proceed, and government agencies have access to public budgets. For other potential participants, in particular Indigenous and civil society groups, obtaining the resources required to participate in policy-making is often difficult. In certain jurisdictions, intervener funding is sometimes available to support participation in EIA processes. However, the resources involved are often very limited, for example a total of C$1.5 million for all non-government groups wishing to make submission to the EIA for the Mackenzie Valley Pipeline, one of Canada's largest proposed resource projects (Green 2008).

The resources available to support policy-making, and the time available for making decisions, are inter-related, but in ways that are variable and contextual and require further research. For example, provision of additional resources can allow specific activities required for policy-making (e.g. collection of information) to be undertaken more rapidly. On the other hand, resources may be used wastefully if insufficient time is available to develop a coherent and logical plan to identify, collect and analyse relevant information.

Information for policy-making

If policy-making is to attach value to and promote sustainability, then decision-makers must have access to relevant information and, in particular, to information regarding the likely impacts of proposed projects over extended periods of time, without which likely impacts on future generations cannot be assessed. Information must also be available to consider the economic, environmental and social dimensions of sustainability.

Illustrating the way in which different components of the policy process can interact, the fact that the time-frames over which project effects are considered are often short means that information regarding impacts on future generations is frequently unavailable. In relation to environmental impacts, an additional and particular problem arises from the fact that baseline data is often available only for the limited time period over which a project developer has been undertaking environmental studies in a particular area. Given uncertainty regarding the nature of the 'background' environment over longer periods of time, project proponents may argue that it is, in fact, impossible to accurately assess the implications of the impact represented by a mining project, and may use the absence of existing information as a rationale for not attempting to do so. Quite apart from the issue of whether projects should be approved if their long-term impacts cannot be evaluated, application of traditional ecological knowledge (TEK) held by Indigenous groups may assist in providing long-term baseline information, since the observations of living generations, combined with knowledge inherited from their forebears, can cover extensive periods of time. Given its overwhelmingly oral nature, access to that information requires the participation of the people who possess it. Issues relating to decision time-frames and resources to support participation in decision-making must be addressed if Indigenous people are to participate actively and make their TEK available to policy-makers, highlighting again the links that exist between different components of the policy process.

Conclusion

Public policies are critical in ensuring that the operation of extractive industries, which will continue to be indispensible to human society, are consistent with environmental, economic and social sustainability. The content and impact of public policies are shaped, in turn, by the nature of public policy processes. This fact is rarely recognised in the literature on sustainability in general, or on the relationship between extractive industries and sustainability, and there have been few if any attempts to analyse the variables that determine the nature of policy processes or their implications for sustainability. This chapter identifies nine key variables that characterise public policy processes in relation to mineral development and examines how they relate to sustainability. For example a failure to provide the resources required to allow participation by Aboriginal or environmental interests, to consider social sustainability as a decision criteria, or to consider more than a narrow range of decision alternatives, will undermine the prospects for sustainability.

There is considerable scope for further research on the implications of policy processes for sustainability. One issue is whether there are other important variables, apart from those identified here, that should be considered. There is also a need for detailed analysis of the way in which individual variables interact in actual policy-making processes. Some initial insights into this area have been offered in the discussion of the nine variables but, for instance, more systematic attention could usefully be focused on the interaction between time, information and values (i.e. the time-frames applied to the policy process, the information available to policy-makers, the criteria applied in policy-making, and the time periods over which the effects of policies are considered). Additional work is also required to consider how analysis of the nine variables might be applied in developing a normative approach to policy-making, for instance through use of a matrix that systematically relates the variables to economic, social or environmental dimensions of sustainability; or through development of a weighting system that affords greater importance to certain variables depending on the prevailing policy context and policy goals.

References

Alston, L.J., M.A. Melo, B. Mueller and C. Pereira (2006) *Political Institutions, Policymaking Processes and Policy Outcomes in Brazil* (Washington, DC: Inter-American Development Bank).

Aninat, C., J. Landregan, P. Navia and J. Vial (2006) *Political Institutions, Policymaking Processes and Policy Outcomes in Chile* (Washington, DC: Inter-American Development Bank).

Baines, J., J. Baker, L. Brophy, A. Rielly, J. Thompson and Y. Yasin (2012) 'Social Monitoring Can Contribute to Ex-ante SIAs: A Case Study of New Zealand Wind Farm Planning', *Impact Assessment and Project Appraisal* 30.3: 195-206.

BHPBilliton (2012) *Working with Integrity: Code of Business Conduct* (Melbourne, Australia: BHPBilliton; www.bhpbilliton.com/home/aboutus/ourcompany/Documents/2012/BHP BillitonCodeofBusinessConduct_2012.pdf, accessed 25 March 2013).

Blacktip Joint Venture (2004) *Social Impact Assessment Blacktip Project Wadeye, Northern Territory* (Brisbane, Australia: Impaxisa Consulting).

Cheney, H., R. Lovel and F. Solomon (2002) *People, Power and Participation: A Study of Mining–Community Relationships* (Melbourne, Australia: Mining Minerals and Sustainable Development).

Chevron Australia Pty Ltd (2005) *Draft Environmental Impact Statement/Environmental Review and Management Programme Executive Summary* (Perth, Australia: Chevron Australia Pty Ltd).

Connick, S., and J. Innes (2001) *Outcomes of Collaborative Water Policy Making: Applying Complexity Thinking to Evaluation* (Berkeley, CA: Institute of Urban and Regional Development, University of California).

Day, J.C., and J. Affum (1995) 'Windy Craggy: Institutions and Stakeholders', *Resources Policy* 21: 21-26.

Gains, F. (2003) 'Executive Agencies in Government: The Impact of Bureaucratic Networks on Policy Outcomes', *Journal of Public Policy* 23.1: 55-79.

Gibson, R. (2012) 'In Full Retreat: The Canadian Government's New Environmental Assessment Law Undoes Decades of Progress', *Impact Assessment and Project Appraisal* 30.3: 179-88.

Government of Western Australia (2012) *Environmental Protection Act 1986: Environmental Impact Assessment (Part IV Divisions 1 and 2) Administrative Procedures 2012* (Government of Western Australia; edit.epa.wa.gov.au/EPADocLib/Environmental%20 Impact%20Assessment%20Administrative%20Procedures%202012.pdf, accessed 7 March 2012).

Green, J. (2008) 'Information Underload', *Uphere Business* March: 23-27.

Harman, E.J., and B. Head (eds.) (1981) *State Capital and Resources in the North and West of Australia* (Nedlands, Australia: University of Western Australia Press).

Howard, J. (2007) 'Do Stakeholder Committees Produce Fair Policy Outcomes?', in A.L. Wilson, R.L. Dehaan, R.J. Watts, K.J. Page, K.H. Bowmer and A. Curtis (eds.), *Proceedings of the 5th Australian Stream Management Conference* (Thurgoona, Australia: Charles Sturt University): 157-62.

Howitt, R. (2003) *Rethinking Resource Management: Justice, Sustainability and Indigenous Peoples* (London and New York: Routledge).

Howlett, M. (2002) 'Do Networks Matter? Linking Policy Network Structure to Policy Outcomes', *Canadian Journal of Political Science* 35.2: 235-67.

Kirsch, S. (1997) 'Is Ok Tedi a Precedent? Implications of the Law Suit', in G. Banks and C. Ballard (eds.), *The Ok Tedi Settlement: Issues, Outcomes and Implications* (Canberra, Australia: Australian National University): 118-40.

KLC (Kimberley Land Council) (2010) *Kimberley LNG Precinct Strategic Assessment Indigenous Impacts Report Volume 3: Aboriginal Social Impact Assessment* (Broome, Australia: KLC; www.dsd.wa.gov.au/documents/Appendix_E-3.pdf, accessed 23 March 2011).

Libby, R. (1989) *Hawke's Law: The Politics of Mining and Aboriginal Land Rights in Australia* (Nedlands, Australia: University of Western Australia Press).

Lyons, M., C. Smuts and A. Stephens (2001) 'Participation, Empowerment and Sustainability: (How) Do the Links Work?', *Urban Studies* 38.8: 1233-51.

MMSD (Mining Minerals and Sustainable Development) (2002) *Breaking New Ground: Mining Minerals and Sustainable Development* (London: International Institute for Environment and Development).

Moolarben Coal Mines Pty Ltd (2006a) *Moolarben Coal Project: Socio-economic Impact Assessment* (Hamilton, Australia: Hunter Valley Research Foundation).

Moolarben Coal Mines Pty Ltd (2006b) *Moolarben Coal Project: Environmental Assessment Report Vol. 1* (East Maitland, Australia: Wells Environmental Services).

Morrison-Saunders, A., and J. Arts (2005) *Assessing Impact: Handbook of EIA and SIA Follow-up* (London: Earthscan).

Newfoundland and Innu Nation (2002) *Memorandum of Agreement Concerning the Voisey's Bay Project* (St John's, Canada: Newfoundland and Innu Nation).

Norton, B.G. (2005) *Sustainability: A Philosophy of Adaptive Ecosystem Management* (Chicago, IL: University of Chicago Press).

O'Faircheallaigh, C. (2005) 'Creating Opportunities for Positive Engagement: Aboriginal People, Government and Resource Development in Australia', paper presented at the *International Conference on Engaging Communities*, Brisbane, Australia, 12–17 August 2005.

O'Faircheallaigh, C. (2007) 'Environmental Agreements, EIA Follow-up and Aboriginal Participation in Environmental Management: The Canadian Experience', *Environmental Impact Assessment Review* 27.4: 319-42.

O'Faircheallaigh, C. (2009) 'Public Policy Processes and Sustainability in the Minerals and Energy Industries', in J. Richards (ed.), *Mining, Society, and a Sustainable World* (New York: Springer): 437-67.

Ogden, L. (2006) 'Public Participation in Environmental Decision-making: A Case Study of Ecosystem Restoration in South Florida', *Cahiers d'Economie et Sociologie Rurales* 80 (clusters.fiu.edu/Meet-FIU-Researchers/10-20-09/Ogden-Cahiers.pdf, accessed 7 March 2013).

Otto-Zimmermann, K. (ed.) (2011) *Resilient Cities: Cities and Adaptation to Climate Change. Proceedings of the Global Forum 2010* (Dordrecht, The Netherlands: Springer).

Pal, L.A. (2006) *Beyond Policy Analysis* (Toronto, Canada: Thomson Nelson).

Stein, E., M. Tommasi, C. Scartascini and P. Spiller (2008) *Policymaking in Latin America* (Boston, MA: Harvard University Press).

Stratford, E., and M. Jaskolski (2004) 'In Pursuit of Sustainability? Challenges for Deliberative Democracy in Tasmanian Local Government', *Environment and Planning B* 31: 311-24.

Trebeck, K. (2007) 'Tools for the Disempowered? Indigenous Leverage Over Mining Companies', *Australian Journal of Political Science* 42.4: 541-62.

van Rensburg, W.C.J., and S. Bambrick (1978) *The Economics of the World's Mineral Industries* (Johannesburg, South Africa: McGraw-Hill).

Weeramantry, C. (1992) *Nauru: Environmental Damage Under International Trusteeship* (Melbourne, Australia: Oxford University Press).

Ciaran O'Faircheallaigh is Professor of Politics and Public Policy at Griffith University, Brisbane. His research and professional practice focus on the inter-relationship between large-scale resource development and Indigenous peoples, and on the effects of mining on social and economic sustainability. He works with Indigenous organisations in Australia and Canada on social impact assessments, and on negotiation of agreements with resource development companies.

13

Sustainable development
Continuing to re-earn our license to operate

Fiona Nicholls
Rio Tinto Energy, Brisbane, Australia

> For Rio Tinto, leadership in sustainable development performance is a key success factor in achieving our vision. Alongside our core values (accountability, respect, teamwork and integrity) and a framework to ensure effective corporate governance, sustainable development drives the manner in which we conduct ourselves as a business: the way we work.

Introduction

The mining industry is rarely out of the news in Queensland. The media reminds us every day that society's expectations of our industry are high. But is this attention new? Has our industry really been ignoring the rest of the world with the arrogance that the headlines suggest? Or, conversely, are the complaints all wrong? Is the attention unjustified? The answer to all of this is: 'No'.

But it is true that we are operating in a changing world, and that a long-term commitment to sustainable development helps us navigate through it. What has happened, both internally and externally, since the concept of sustainable development came to prominence in the late 1980s? Between then and now has anything changed? Or have the goal posts moved? And how do we bridge the ever-widening expectations gap and maintain our social license to operate? An ongoing commitment to sustainable development, and to continuing to evolve our work in this area, is one way we can try to close the gap and ensure sustainable development remains relevant in a fast-paced and changing world.

What does sustainable development mean for the mining sector?

In the years following Brundtland, mining companies and industry spent a lot of time debating and defining what sustainable development meant for us. How were we going to interpret and practically implement this concept that meant different things to different people? In most places sustainable development was about integrating environment, social and economic considerations—the triple bottom-line—and then a fourth dimension of governance was added.

Several initiatives then happened in parallel that developed the thinking in the mining industry further:

- In 1996 the Mining Council of Australia developed the Code for Environmental Management which required all who signed up to publicly report their environmental performance

- The Global Reporting Initiative, formed in 1997, looked at what types of non-financial numbers should be reported

- In 1999, the mining industry, led by the then Rio Tinto Chairman Sir Robert Wilson, began the Global Mining Initiative. This independent analysis included the Mining and Metals in Sustainable Development (MMSD) study and extensive global stakeholder interviews from all levels of society. The findings recognised the industry's potential contribution and identified core challenges. One of the main outcomes of the study was the establishment of the International Council on Mining and Metals in 2001, which aims to improve sustainable development performance in the mining and metals industry.

Adopting sustainable development

Industry's adoption of the sustainable development concept has been characterised by three phases:

- Definition
- Tools development
- Integration

All of the work on the definition of sustainable development led to what could be characterised as the second stage—tools development. Tools were developed to help companies unpack the sustainable development concept into practical implementation. Many companies came up with complicated diagrams and methods that tried to summarise the process. For Rio Tinto, adopting the concept was essentially characterised by:

- Enhancing human potential and well-being
- Maximising resource efficiency and minimising environmental damage
- Optimising economic contribution

Then came the third stage—integration. At Rio Tinto we understand our sustainable development contribution will be maximised if it is integrated or embedded into everything we do—from high level business planning through to everyday tasks.

In practice, to Rio Tinto, sustainable development means:

- Understanding stakeholder expectations, balancing conflicting expectations and changing behaviours appropriately
- Working with customers and suppliers to maximise the use of our products and minimise adverse effects
- Engaging with people inside and outside the business
- Managing operations responsibly, to maximise resource use and minimise social or environmental effects
- Having open and accountable governance frameworks
- Delivering year-on-year improvement

We also recognise that sustainable development is not something a single organisation can achieve on its own, nor is it a single project that can be completed and ticked off as it is finished. It is about the way we continuously work, within our business and in our interactions with others, to meet the multiple objectives of social wellbeing, environmental stewardship and economic prosperity, throughout the life of a mine and beyond. For our Australian coal business, our business strategic map also forms our sustainable development framework; further highlighting that the concept needs to be part of the way we do business.

Sustainable development in decision-making

Rio Tinto's sustainable development decision-making criteria ensures the concept's principles can be incorporated into any business-related initiative, project or activity. For example, within Rio Tinto Coal Australia, the sustainable development decision-making criteria are considered in our capital expenditure application process for amounts over AU$100,000. We also consider the full range of sustainable development threats and opportunities in our risk assessment processes.

It was this type of thinking that led to the development of an ongoing programme of work called Clermont Preferred Futures. Rio Tinto operates the Clermont and Blair Athol coal mines in the Clermont area. The programme is managed and implemented by Isaac Regional Council and the Clermont community in regional Queensland to plan for their future beyond mining. We participate as a member of the community and are working in collaboration on shaping their region's future.

The first step in this was the development of a vision for the future and a plan for ongoing engagement and implementation. Now that the vision and plan have been developed, Rio Tinto Coal Australia supports ongoing implementation through:

- The appointment of a new position in council—the Preferred Futures Implementation Officer—to help implement the strategy. This position is jointly funded by Rio Tinto and the council

- An increase in funding to the company's community development fund—to enable community projects to have access to funding. The community have used this fund to develop a fully-scoped town development plan and to develop a business plan for the establishment of a Clermont Community Business Group

The process of engagement enables constructive discussion around mine/town issues such as fly-in-fly-out (FIFO) and long-term accommodation strategies, including low-cost housing for those not in the mine workforce.

Today, it is the community leaders who are responsible for managing and developing the town and its businesses for the future. Nominated by the Isaac Regional Council, the programme was recognised at the 2011 Australian National Awards for Economic Development Excellence, winning the highly commended award for the community economic development category. This type of recognition helps bring us greater acceptance in the communities in which we operate. And when we are recognised for this sustainable approach, it helps us to maintain our license to operate.

Embedding sustainable development in our culture

A consequence of embedding the sustainable development concept into our businesses has been a change in behaviours so that sustainability is part of our culture. Today, we do much of what we ten years ago characterised as 'a sustainable development approach' without thinking about it too much.

While we still have work to do, sustainability has increasingly become part of our everyday culture—the way we do business. However, public perception often does not adequately reflect our internal sustainable development emphasis, and this has contributed to a disconnect between the programmes and reporting. For example, Rio Tinto Coal Australia publicly publishes a complete sustainable development report each year. Some see this as PR spin when, in reality, it is just the tip of the iceberg when it comes to sustainability and the emphasis our businesses place on it.

Many researchers and commentators now talk about how there has been an over-emphasis on the shorter-term reputational benefits achieved through sustainable development initiatives which, paradoxically, undermines our efforts to deliver on sustainability objectives because it is not seen by our stakeholders as having built long-term value. There is a clear and increasing expectation from local communities that our operations will bring benefits in terms of economic development. This goes to the heart of our social license to operate. Through our operations, we make a significant direct and indirect contribution to the local, regional and national economy, through:

- Export revenue

- Purchasing goods and services from suppliers

- Paying salaries and benefits

- Paying rates, royalties and other taxes to governments, which are used for the provision of services and infrastructure

- Community investments

Many of the contributions outlined have a component that is spent within the local areas and states where we operate. For example:

- Creating jobs, as well as job and career opportunities through training, apprenticeships and traineeships

- The majority of our employees (73%) are residential, which means that they are likely to spend at least some of their salaries and wages locally (RTCA 2011). The remainder are FIFO or bus-in/ bus-out, and tend to live within the state or regions where we operate

- Buying goods and services from suppliers. During 2011, 29% of what we spent on goods and services was done so in the local areas of our operations

For years we have said local procurement is important and developed local procurement plans and set targets. But for years reality worked against it and the rhetoric didn't match the practice. In reality, there are many things that work against local procurement, for example buying competitive, bulk items such as tyres, which are typically sourced from overseas. Of course we will always be looking for competitive suppliers, but is there opportunity to do more of that locally? How do we challenge our thinking so that we start to see ourselves as part of the economic web of our host region? How do we assist local suppliers to develop?

Maybe the value will be the same or better for our business, and for local suppliers. That is why we have sought to better understand our 'spend' on goods and services and to examine challenges and opportunities in local procurement development plans—but plans that align our business needs with those of the local economy. It will not help to create local subsidies. That is not sustainable for any business in the long term and only increases dependency and creates non-competitive businesses; which is in no one's interests. Furthermore, business and the local economy must recognise that local suppliers will never be able to supply everything—but that does not mean we have no role to play in where these interfaces can occur. It is just as important to us that we have increased supplier competitiveness that will drive cost and performance improvements for our business, and a sustainable and secure supply chain which contributes to our operational stability.

Investing in the future

Another way in which we work to help meet the needs of the present and, in doing so, increase the capacity of future generations to meet their own needs, is by investing in areas which are a priority for both the community and our business, such as education and business development.

Rio Tinto Coal Australia (RTCA) currently operates eight community development funds. Funding decisions are made by committees representing RTCA and local communities. The funds are an integral part of our approach to community relations, a key objective of which is to effectively contribute to communities' long-term sustainability. The funds also contribute to our objective of building robust relationships with our communities of interest, through the relationships developed with committee members as well as individuals and organisations applying for funding. Effective operation of the funds also requires us to have a sound understanding of the needs and aspirations of each community.

Since their inception, our community development funds in Queensland and New South Wales have contributed more than AU$21 million to the communities in which we operate. Wherever possible, we seek community investment opportunities where we are not the only funding source, but are one of a number of community and/or government bodies contributing to a programme that benefits the community. In this way, the long-term sustainability of a programme is increased and community dependence on mining activities decreases over time. Some examples of the work our funds support include:

- The Hail Creek Mine Community Development Fund which supports the Building Better Business super series, a programme aimed at improving knowledge on employee attraction and retention strategies, marketing in a regional centre, online retailing and planning for growth

- Kestrel Mine Aboriginal Community Development Fund, the Wiri Yuwiburra Trust and the Coal & Allied Aboriginal Development Consultative Committee's support for the establishment and development of local businesses owned and operated by local Indigenous groups and individuals

During 2011, Rio Tinto spent more than AU$9 million in Queensland and New South Wales to support almost 500 programmes in the areas in which we operate. In 2012, more than 40% of our investment was in the area of health and disaster management, reflecting the unprecedented number of natural disasters during the year, particularly in Queensland where over three-quarters of the state was impacted by the worst flooding in its history (RTCA 2011).

Reducing our impacts

The minerals and metals we produce contribute to society's needs and wellbeing. However, we recognise the real impacts they have on the environment. That is why a focus of our sustainable development performance is to reduce the environmental impacts of our operations.

Rio Tinto recognises the value of action on climate change. The scale of the necessary emissions reductions and the need for adaptation, coupled with the world's increasing requirements for secure, affordable energy, create large challenges that require worldwide attention. We support a co-ordinated global approach to reduce emissions. Until that is in place, as well as after, we recognise that it will be necessary for individual jurisdictions to take action.

We factor into our planning and decision-making, including our choice of investments, the costs and associated risks of emissions and business disruption, as well as the costs and benefits of mitigation and adaptation, and the opportunities created for our business by the move to a low-carbon economy. We include carbon prices in our investment decision-making and have done so for the past ten years. We work with others in this space, engaging with:

- Our customers and suppliers to reduce supply chain emissions, and make best use of our products to build a low-carbon economy

- Our host communities by listening to and working with them on energy, emissions and climate issues that are important to them

- Governments and other stakeholders to advocate constructively for policies that are environmentally effective, economically efficient and equitable

- Investors and the broader community by reporting publicly our emissions and performance, and integrating our climate related activities into our broader sustainable development programme

We also engage in policy debates, seeking policies that:

- Avoid damage to the competitiveness of trade exposed industries and displacement of emissions with no reduction in the global total

- Make use of market mechanisms, both within and across jurisdictions, to promote innovation and cost-effective outcomes

- Use revenue raised from any carbon pricing to facilitate the transition to a low-carbon economy, including through the development of new technology

- Are broadly based and predictable

Given the continued demand for our products, our challenge is to improve the contribution they make by increasing their value and reducing impacts from their supply and use. It is important that our business contributes to climate change solutions and invests in research and development initiatives to find ways to reduce our greenhouse gas emissions throughout the coal chain.

We have actively managed our energy footprint and greenhouse gas emissions profile since 1996. Our current climate change programme, launched in 2007, has objectives in four key areas:

- Active research and promotion of technologies that reduce carbon dioxide emissions from the use of coal

- Improved use of energy in our operations, projects and supply chain

- Designing future projects with energy efficiency and climate change risks considered

- Raising awareness among stakeholders that climate change is an issue that requires us all to change how we currently operate

Work on our Mine of the Future Programme is also helping to reduce our footprint through improved capability for underground operations by relying more on technologies such as remote-controlled equipment.

The use of coal contributes about 25% of global greenhouse gas emissions; therefore, climate change and greenhouse gas emissions are a key area of focus for us. In addition to the emissions produced from the energy we use, our total greenhouse gas emissions include fugitive emissions. Fugitive emissions of carbon dioxide and methane naturally occur in coal seams and are released to the atmosphere during the mining process. Capturing coal seam methane has potential value both as a saleable product and as a means to meet the challenge of climate change. In order to test the viability of capturing and flaring methane from its open-cut coal seams prior to mining, in 2011 RTCA funded a AU$7 million pilot programme at its Mount Thorley Warkworth mine in the New South Wales Hunter Valley region. As far as we are aware, this trial was a first for attempting to pre-drain methane from shallow coal seams which will be mined using open-cut methods.

Another initiative that we are supporting is a AU$6 million, three-year sponsorship into a unique carbon capture and storage facility and research project.

In keeping with our intent to help minimise emissions, we are supporting this Australian first demonstration of geological carbon dioxide storage at a field site in Victoria, along with research at the newly established Peter Cook Centre for CCS Research at the University of Melbourne. We are doing this because we believe carbon capture and storage will be a significant technology globally, and one particularly important in Australia given the role of coal as our major source of electric power, and our position as a major international supplier of fossil fuels. The project has been running since 2008 and 60,000 tonnes of carbon dioxide has already been stored and monitored.

Poverty alleviation

Access to energy can transform lives and the electricity generated by the products we produce is playing a role in alleviating poverty in developing countries. Over the past 20 years in China alone, almost 500 million people have risen out of poverty—in large part because they got access to electricity.

Demand for energy is not slowing. Even under the most ambitious climate change scenarios, the International Energy Agency (IEA) forecasts global energy demand will increase by a third from 2010 to 2035 (IEA 2011). Growth will be dominated by Asia, where urbanisation and industrialisation are driving the demand for our products. And coal as a cheap source of energy will continue to remain an important part of the global energy mix.

So with this clear demand for fossil fuels, and the mining industry's role to help meet that demand, it could be thought that sustainable development is, perhaps, incongruous. After all, mining takes things out of the ground and depletes non-renewable resources. However, the materials we mine and supply are essential to life and a quality standard of living.

Conclusion

While on our sustainable development journey, we have made many changes and seen the expectations of society and our stakeholders grow exponentially. Global volatility is impacting our businesses at a local level. This volatility will continue, and is an outcome of broader social and economic global trends which need to be understood to develop integrated strategies and programmes to better enable our business to grow.

An example is the rise of social media networks and what this means for the way we communicate, for our business, and for how we deliver and receive information. We operate in a world that demands immediacy, transparency and which is short-term focused. Our stakeholders and communities are far more socially aware. So how do we bridge this expectations gap and maintain our social license to operate? In a speech given at the Dehli Sustainable Development Summit on 7 February 2009, Björn Stigson, President of the World Business Council for Sustainable Development, makes the observation that 'business cannot succeed in societies that fail'. Conceivably, the expectations gap has another side—that we cannot have successful societies without successful businesses. And both need an inclusive government. We need all three and too much of the debate is about only one of these rather than their inter-dependency. The most value comes at the intersection of what business wants and what society wants; that is, where there is alignment of goals. This value is maximised if governments at all levels are working effectively with each other and with society and business.

When reflecting on our sustainable development journey from the late 1980s to today it is clear that sustainable development contains two implicit concepts. First, that it is long-term and, therefore, is about the journey rather than the destination and, second, that no one stakeholder is solely responsible—rather all have a contribution to make. Twenty-five years ago we talked about three intersections of sustainability—social, environment and economy. We have also been on a journey where we have adopted new terms from triple bottom-line to corporate social responsibility (CSR) to creation of shared value (CSV)—each trying to address any shortcomings or gaps in the previous approach.

It would be unfair to say that we—both Rio Tinto and the wider industry—got it 'wrong' when it comes to sustainable development. Instead of characterising this as having got it 'wrong'—and by implication now 'my new version is right'—developments are essential steps along a journey of continuous improvement. We need to consider a three-sided model as the junction between the concepts that:

- Business cannot succeed in failing societies
- Societies need successful businesses to prosper
- We all need inclusive governments to enable individuals to invest and innovate

If sustainable development is to remain relevant we do need to continue to evolve our thinking. Not because we haven't been listening—but because we need to continue the journey in a world that is changing.

References

IEA (International Energy Agency) (2011) *World Energy Outlook 2011* (Paris: IEA; www.world energyoutlook.org/publications/weo-2011).

RTCA (Rio Tinto Coal Australia) (2011) *Sustainable Development Report 2011* (Brisbane, Australia: RTCA; www.riotintocoalaustralia.com.au/sustainabledevelopment/index_sustainabledevelopment.asp).

Fiona Nicholls joined Rio Tinto in 1994 and has held a number of management positions in various Rio Tinto businesses, including General Manager Sustainable Development for Rio Tinto's Energy Product Group. Fiona holds a Bachelor of Natural Resources with Honours, a Masters of Business Administration and is a graduate of the Australian Institute of Company Directors. In 2012 Fiona received the QRC Resources Award for Women recognising her 25 years in the resource industry. Fiona served as Vice President of External Relations for Rio Tinto Energy before leaving the company in 2013.

14

Currencies of transition
Transforming money to unleash sustainability

Jem Bendell
Institute for Leadership and Sustainability, University of Cumbria, UK and Griffith Business School, Queensland, Australia

Thomas H. Greco
BeyondMoney.net

Introduction

The idea that money needs to be more 'local' to enable more environmentally sustainable and socially beneficial economies is a theme in a variety of conferences and initiatives that ally with the concept of 'transition' to low-carbon societies. The first ever Transition Town initiative sprang up in the rural British town of Totnes in 2006. One of its activities was to pioneer a local currency that one could purchase with British pounds. Subsequently, the Transition Network, which promotes the concept of Transition worldwide from its base in Totnes, has promoted similar schemes across the UK.[1] In 2012 the launch of the Bristol pound in the UK generated significant media attention, as Bristol became the first city in the UK to launch its own currency and gain the support of the local council, with the Lord Mayor spending the very first Bristol pound. People must purchase Bristol pounds by using national

---

1 www.transitionnetwork.org/blogs/josh-ryan-collins/2010-11/transition-currency-20-online-banking-system-local-money, accessed 20 February 2013.

currency, and businesses can redeem them for national currency.[2] Almost entirely ignored by mainstream media in the past, local currencies and alternative exchange systems are becoming familiar themes in mainstream newspapers such as *The Financial Times, Wall Street Journal, Guardian* and *Der Spiegel*, as well as on both local and network TV. The reports focus mainly on attempts to keep money circulating locally instead of 'leaking out', as a way of enhancing the vitality of local economies and improving the prospects of local businesses in their struggle to compete with large corporate chains. This has been the key aim expressed by the originators of the pound-backed local currencies issued in Brixton, Bristol and elsewhere.

All of that is well and good, but could miss the main point of what ails our communities—and our world. The problems facing our communities, and civilisation as a whole, stem from the mechanisms by which money is created and allocated by the members of the most powerful cartel the world has ever known. Our current monetary system is the main underlying cause for multiple crises with sovereign debt, environmental destruction, spiralling inequality and mass unemployment. Unless we transform the way money is issued, rather than repackaging it after the fact, then we are not addressing the underlying problem. This insight is not widely understood by people working on social or environmental issues, even those who work on economic dimensions. As one of the authors of the original *The Limits to Growth* (Meadows *et al.* 1972) report, Dennis Meadows explains: 'I did not think about the money system at all. I took it for granted as a neutral aspect of human society. ... I now understand ... that the prevailing financial system is incompatible with sustainability' (in Lietaer *et al.* 2012a: 1). On average, modern humans are monetarily illiterate, not understanding the essence of money, how it is created and how this influences their experience of life. This illiteracy restricts our ability to work towards transition. In this chapter, our aim is to help relevant professionals understand the monetary origins of our current malaise, the practical steps being taken by communities to manage their own economies and exchange systems, and to map out some emerging issues for research, practice and policy. In conclusion, we explain how a focus on monetary systems can re-frame how we understand the sustainability challenge, away from being a matter of exhorting each-other to behave 'better' and/ or impose more restrictions on our behaviours, towards a step-by-step liberation of communities' innate ability to thrive in the ways that they themselves determine.

The essence of money

In every developed economy, labour is highly specialised. Very little of what we need do we make ourselves. This fact makes the exchange of goods and services necessary for subsistence. But primitive barter is inefficient and dependent upon

---

a coincidence of wants or needs—'I have something you want and you have something I want'. If one of us has nothing the other wants, no barter is possible. Money was invented to enable exchanges that fall outside the local tight-knit communities in which less formalised modes of give and take are possible. It makes possible trade that is occasional and impersonal. Money is first and foremost a medium of exchange, a kind of place-holder that enables a seller to deliver real value to a buyer, then use the money received to claim from the market something that s/he needs from someone else. Archaeological research finds that the earliest records of money, engraved on stones in ancient Egypt, existed as lists of debts and credits of goods (Graeber 2011). Indeed, some of the earliest records of money were promises to deliver beer—up to two gallons a day for work on building the pyramids (Tucker 2011). This suggests that beer was useful at that time as the basis for an 'exchange medium': it would be readily accepted by many people, so could be accepted as payment even by those who did not want beer for themselves. I might, for example, have no personal use for tobacco, but knowing that many others desire it, I might accept it, or a promise to deliver it in future, in payment for my apples. The same goes for gold and silver, which eventually became the preferred commodities for use as exchange media.

Money has continued to evolve; today it is neither a 'thing' nor a promise to deliver a thing. It is *credit* in a system of accounts, which manifests mainly as 'deposits' in banks, and only secondarily, in small amounts, as paper currency notes. Every national currency is supported by the collective credit of everyone who is obliged by law to accept it.

In most countries today, it is estimated that about 3% of our money originates from government-owned mints that make notes and coins (Ryan-Collins *et al.* 2011). The rest is digital and is created by banks, out of nothing, when they issue loans. When you or your government goes to a bank to take out a loan, the bank does not lend its own money or that of its depositors. Instead it creates that money by an electronic accounting entry, in return for a contract that the borrower will pay back that amount, plus interest. Nothing is being loaned; banks simply create the money on the basis of the 'borrower's' promise to pay (Ryan-Collins *et al.* 2011).

This fact sounds unbelievable to those of us who have not thought about how modern money is issued, rather than earned. Consequently, it is often helpful to quote the central banks themselves: 'When banks make loans they create additional deposits for those that have borrowed the money', explains the Bank of England. As Paul Tucker, the Deputy Governor for Financial Stability of the Bank of England further explains: 'Banks extend credit by simply increasing the borrowing customer's current account … That is, banks extend credit by creating money' (Ryan-Collins *et al.* 2011).

Unfortunately, even the best educational institutions are teaching their students a fictional account of how this system works today. In his best-selling *The Ascent of Money*, Professor Niall Ferguson explains how students are instructed at his university:

... first-year MBA students at Harvard Business School play a simplified money game. It begins with a notional central bank paying the professor $100 on behalf of the government, for which he has done some not very lucrative consulting. The professor takes the banknotes to a bank notionally operated by one of his students and deposits them there, receiving a deposit slip. Assuming, for the sake of simplicity, that this bank operates a 10 per cent reserve ratio ... it deposits $10 with the central bank and lends the other $90 to one of its clients. While the client decides what to do with his loan, he deposits the money in another bank. This bank also has a 10 per cent reserve rule, so it deposits $9 at the central bank and lends out the remaining $8 to another of its clients ... By the time money has been deposited at three different student banks, [the monetary base, 'M0'] ... is equal to $100 but [the combined cash and demand deposits, 'M1'] ... is equal to $271 ($100 + $90 + $81), neatly illustrating, albeit in a highly simplified way, how modern fractional reserve banking allows the creation of credit and hence of money (Ferguson 2008: 49-50).

It might be neat, but it is fiction. That form of fractional reserve banking has not existed for many decades. Instead, 'changes in [a private bank's] reserves [with a Central Bank] are unrelated to changes in lending ... the textbook treatment of money ... can be rejected', explained Seth B. Carpenter of the US Federal Reserve. Vitor Constâncio, Vice President of the European Central Bank, further explains that: 'Banks [are] taking first their credit decisions and then looking for the necessary funding and reserves of central bank money'. Simply put, this means that private banks create as much money as they determine is possible to be paid back, or that they can sell on to other institutions, given their assessment of prevailing market conditions (Ryan-Collins *et al.* 2011).

The key insight from a study of the history of money is that we have allowed the 'credit commons' to be privatised so that it can be accessed only by appealing to some bank to grant a 'loan' (Riegel 1944; Greco 2009). By 'credit commons' we mean our ability, as free individuals and organisations, to issue credit to whoever we choose, in a form and volume that we decide, without paying interest to a bank in that process. Today's monopoly on credit creation by private banks now drives a range of economic, social and environmental problems. One key problem is that as banks create the amount borrowed, but not the interest to be paid on that loan, there is more debt owed to banks in the world than there is money to repay it.[3] Although individually we might pay off our debts, collectively we are in debt forever, and paying interest to the banks. That makes increasing inequality a mathematical certainty. Inequality is rising worldwide, with 2% of the world's population controlling about half the world's wealth (BBC 2006). Extreme inequality is correlated with

---

3 Hypothetically, if banks spent all their interest payments and also the velocity of monetary exchanges increased sufficiently, then the debts could be serviced without increasing amounts of lending. However, banks do not spend all their interest earnings, they add most of them to their capital and enable additional loans at interest.

major social problems, including crime and ill health of all sorts—physical, mental and emotional (Wilkinson and Pickett 2009).

The interest that must be paid to 'borrow' our own credit from a bank is not the only parasitic element in this system. Another is the inflation of the money supply that accompanies government's deficit spending. Most national governments consistently spend beyond their incomes, sucking real value out of the economy in return for counterfeit money that the banks create for them under colour of law. This debasement of the currency inevitably results in higher prices of basic necessities in the marketplace (Riegel 1978). To these drains you can add the obscene salaries and bonuses that insiders pay themselves to run the system, and the periodic bailouts that they extract from governments.

A further problem arising from our money supply being bank-issued debt is that the availability of our money depends on the sentiments and intentions of bankers. If bankers lose confidence in our ability to pay, or our government's ability to pay, or simply choose to lend in a less co-ordinated way, then the whole economy has less money. That means less money for investment, wages and jobs. Which means we stop working for each other. That is one reason why there is mass unemployment while there remains so much that needs doing to enhance human existence. While professionals working on 'sustainability' continue to focus on initiatives and debates arising from their preoccupations with environmental protection or international development assistance, the Western financial crisis has been fundamentally restructuring the societies they exist within. Greece has suffered the greatest contraction in money supply during the recent crisis, with an annual contraction of about 20% (IMF 2012). Less money in circulation has meant cuts in wages and more unemployment, which has social consequences. The suicide rate in Greece increased by 40% in 2011 (*Guardian* 2011).

The role of banks in deciding where the newly issued money goes presents another problem, as it shapes the economy and society in line with their interests, while undermining the free market, civil society and governments. Banks choose whom to issue money to in line with their aims of seeking the largest return with the lowest transaction cost and risk. So they lend to things such as consumption and property speculation, rather than to small businesses. For instance, about 80% of bank lending in the UK of late has been for property purchases. This has made house prices rise 8000% since 1950, far above the inflation in prices of other goods or assets.[4] The result of this inflation is that, if you are not fortunate enough to own a property, then the costs of rental or a mortgage means that many people are forced to work in jobs that are destructive or demeaning and to live lives they are not happy with (Bolchover 2005).

The most destructive problem from this monetary system is that it requires continual economic growth to justify the necessary growth in the money supply. This stems from the fact that money is created on the basis of interest-bearing debt,

4 www.positivemoney.org.uk/2012/09/house-prices-why-are-they-so-high-new-video, accessed 20 October 2012.

so that the amount owed increases with the passage of time. Compound interest is an exponential growth function, which means that debt grows, not at a constant steady pace, but at an accelerating rate. The global money system therefore requires the further continual expansion of debt in order to avoid financial collapse, as there is not enough money to service the ever expanding debts. New loans require further economic activity which, despite a small amount of decoupling economic growth from resource consumption, means an ever greater consumption of natural resources, and pollution of our biosphere (Lietaer *et al.* 2012a). Although in some countries increasing economic growth—the amount of money changing hands—may be what people desire to improve their lives, this monetary system imposes a growth imperative whatever the local context, and does not allow a 'steady state' economy to emerge. Some Nobel laureates and politicians have noted the inappropriateness of growth in gross domestic product (GDP) as a goal for societies, and various initiatives are working on new metrics, such as the European Union.[5] Yet with an interest-charging system of money creation we have no choice but to grow the economy, otherwise there will less new debt issued to service existing debts, and there will be defaults, foreclosures, bankruptcies, unemployment, depression and, as history shows us, crime, extremism and even war (Greco 2009).

The competition among borrowers for an insufficient supply of money also results in pressure for externalising costs onto society and environment—pollution, for instance. The interest rates charged on loans also lead to greater discounting of natural assets, as money in the bank today can be worth more than trees in a forest (Lietaer *et al.* 2012a).

The dominant system of money and banking, based as it is upon usury and the centralisation of power and wealth, has visited untold misery and injustice upon the human race and the entire web of life on planet Earth. So what is to be done? There are growing campaigns for monetary reform, such as the Positive Money campaign in the UK. These call for government to pass legislation to end fractional reserve banking and give government the role of spending and lending new money into circulation. As the ability to give credit is something we all have, this government-centric solution would not be adequate in itself. Yet the Western 'financial crisis' has revealed to us that even this small step forward is not likely, and may even be impossible. Over five years ago the 'credit crunch' occurred due to toxic loans pervading the whole financial system. The bailouts of the banks involved money that had to be 'borrowed' by governments from the banks, which then compromised future public spending by governments, threatening the future of social systems built up over many decades. Since the outbreak of the 'crisis' there have been no significant monetary reforms and few prosecutions. Instead, the corporate media turned their ire on governments and their inability to manage the fallout of the crisis. Sadly, it appears the majority of bankers, economists and politicians

---

5 www.beyond-gdp.eu, accessed 20 February 2013.

either do not know what to do in the public interest or are not sufficiently focused on serving that interest.

During 2012, one of the authors of this chapter, Jem Bendell, attended four high-level gatherings with politicians, senior bureaucrats, academics and business people, from around the world. He spoke with around 100 people and in nearly every conversation brought up the issues addressed in this chapter. His previous work had led him to believe that professionals from various sectors of society can collaborate for systemic change (Bendell 2009), and so he was hopeful of engagement on these issues. However, he discovered that, apart from two individuals, no one knew about the monetary causes of our multiple crises, and most did not want to put in the intellectual effort to understand, preferring agendas that they considered would be more politically and commercially acceptable. These were not 'bad' people, but people who were busy with other issues and, with one exception, they were not prepared to give themselves the time or take the risk to explore what an understanding of monetary systems might lead them towards. The implication is that, at present, it appears that the current monetary system will not be reformed; it can only be transcended.

Transcending the money system

The good news is that we need not be victims of a monetary system that is so obviously failing us. We have in our hands the power to reclaim the credit commons. We can reclaim that right both peacefully and without attacking the entrenched regime. It only requires that we each take control of our own credit and give it to those individuals and businesses that merit it—and withhold it from those that do not—and for us to apply our talents and energies to those enterprises that enhance community resilience (Hopkins 2008), sustainability, self-reliance and the common good.

It is possible to organise an entirely new structure of money, banking and finance, one that is interest-free, decentralised, and controlled, not by banks or central governments, but by individuals and businesses that associate and organise themselves into moneyless trading networks. In brief, any group of people can organise to allocate their own collective credit among themselves, interest-free. This is merely an extension of the common business practice of selling on open account—'I'll ship you the goods now and you can pay me later', except it is organised, not on a bilateral basis, but within a community of many buyers and sellers. Done on a large enough scale that includes a sufficiently broad range of goods and services, such systems can avoid the dysfunctions inherent in conventional money and banking. They can open the way to more harmonious and mutually beneficial relationships that enable the emergence of true economic democracy.

Mutual credit clearing: moneyless trading

This approach is no pie-in-the-sky pipe dream. It is proven and well established. Known as mutual credit clearing, it is a process used by hundreds of thousands of businesses around the world that are members of scores of commercial 'barter' exchanges which provide the necessary accounting and other services for money-less trading. In this process, the things you sell pay for the things you buy without using money as an intermediate exchange medium. Instead of chasing dollars, you use what you have to pay for what you need.

Unlike traditional barter, which depends upon a coincidence of wants and needs between two traders who each have something the other wants, mutual credit clearing provides an accounting for trade credits, a sort of internal currency, that allows traders to sell to some members and buy from others. There are reportedly more than 400,000 companies worldwide who, in this way, trade more than US$12 billion dollars worth of goods and services annually without the use of any national currency (Z/Yen 2011).

Perhaps the best example of a credit clearing exchange that has operated success-fully over a long period of time is the WIR[6] Economic Circle Co-operative. Founded in Switzerland in the midst of the Great Depression as a self-help organisation, WIR pro-vides a means for its member businesses to continue to buy and sell with one another despite a shortage of Swiss francs in circulation. Over the past three quarters of a century, in good times and bad, WIR (now known as the WIR Bank) has continued to thrive. Its more than 60,000 members throughout Switzerland trade about US$2 bil-lion worth of goods and services each year, paying each other, not in official money, but in their own accounting units called WIR credits (Greco and Magalli 2005).

Some systems are created with a more specific focus on community develop-ment, and involve individuals rather than businesses. One of the most significant of these is the Community Exchange System (CES), which was founded in Cape Town, South Africa in 2003 as a non-profit company by the community organiser Tim Jenkin. Since then it has grown to around 400 systems in over 40 countries, with over 20,000 users. The core of the system is a Web-based closed-source soft-ware that allows members to trade with each other using the clearing of positive and negative balances between members when they trade. The currencies on the system are therefore backed by a promise to supply local goods and services. The websites acts as an online marketplace with all transactions being recorded. There is also help with brokering trades. There are no printed circulating currencies associated with the CES systems. People on the different systems can now trade with people on another system in another part of the world, and CES publishes exchange rates between participating currencies based on the recommended minimum wage in each country. The costs of running the system, which include a

---

6 WIR, an abbreviation for Wirtschaftsring-Genossenschaft, is the German word for 'we'.

manager and software engineers, are funded by national currency donations and a fee charged to users that is denominated in their local currency. Jenkin's efforts led to his receiving a fellowship by the Ashoka Foundation in 2007 (Lietaer *et al.* 2012b).

Back in Switzerland, Matthew Slater and Tim Anderson believed that community exchange systems, such as the SEL, would best be supported by free and open-source software. They founded CommunityForge in 2008, which now hosts 130, largely francophone, local exchange systems, with many more using its software tools and hosting their systems themselves. As a matter of principle, they chose to base their software on Drupal, a widely understood open-source platform, so that communities which use the software need not become dependent on Community-Forge, and would also benefit from a worldwide base of programmers and support. The volume of trade of three exchanges around Geneva that use CommunityForge is greater (if calculated according to minimum wage) than the renowned Berkshares alternative currency in the USA, which reports US$22,000 circulation per year. As with CES, inter-trading between the local exchange systems is now possible, as well as payment by sending an SMS. In search of greater scale, CommunityForge has begun working with local chambers of commerce, to provide opportunities for socially-concerned businesses and organisations to trade together without money.

In times of economic recession, as bank-issued currencies become more scarce, alternative means of exchange through mutual credit clearing can become more attractive. In 2009, an alternative exchange system based on mutual credit clearing was introduced in the Greek port city of Volos. From jewellery to food, electrical parts to clothes, many goods and services are on sale through a local alternative currency called TEM. If someone sells a good or service, they gain credit, with one TEM notionally equivalent in value to one euro. They can then use their TEM earnings to buy whatever else is being offered through the network. The whole system is organised online, with members holding TEM accounts. Everyone can issue or earn credit, without the need for a loan from a bank. Everyone can exchange as much as they wish, without it being restricted by availability of euros, and everyone ends up returning to zero, so no one makes money out of issuing the currency or charging interest. The mayor of Volos supports the project and thinks it can co-exist with the euro (BBC 2012). A co-founder and co-ordinator of the Volos TEM, Yannis Grigoriou, says that there are now many similar initiatives in towns across Greece.[7] Some use CommunityForge software, some use Cyclos software, and others have developed their own.

The alternative exchange systems we mention here, and the systems that support them, are just some of thousands that have sprung up worldwide. The list of initiatives at www.complementarycurrency.org keeps growing. The low cost of computing power and the penetration of the Internet makes it far easier to establish and operate mutual credit clearing systems. People are developing them because they present a number of benefits to individuals, enterprise and whole communities. Mutual credit systems mean that underused assets can be matched with unmet

---

7 Personal communication, 10 October 2012.

needs, to the degree that people want, not to the degree that there is money around to complete a transaction. For businesses, these systems offer new sources of credit that are interest-free, reducing need for scarce bank-issued currency, as well as fostering a loyal customer base. As all credits and debits ultimately cancel each other out, there are not increasing amounts of money chasing the same amount of stuff or services, so the currency does not inflate. There is no interest charged upon the issuing of credit, so wealth is not extracted from those with lower incomes. As most mutual credit currencies are locally-focused, they encourage us to trade locally, so reducing our carbon footprint and promoting regeneration. At a time of increasing scarcity of natural resources, the more efficient exchange and use of existing resources is needed more than ever (Greco 2009).

Although many participants in mutual credit clearing systems are focused on their local communities, they increasingly understand themselves as participating in a common movement for change. In the village of Drapanos in Greece in October 2012, a two-day conference, co-facilitated by the authors of this chapter, brought together community exchange practitioners and experts from Greece and worldwide, at the European Sustainability Academy. To clarify and communicate the intention for their many initiatives, a declaration was agreed on 11 October 2012 (Box 1).

Box 14.1 **Drapanos Declaration on community exchange**

- Individuals, communities and environments are the true source of our wealth and well-being.

- Therefore we develop alternative means of exchange between individuals and organisations to foster more co-operative and equitable relations.

- Although we may focus on our own communities, we share this principle with other communities.

- Therefore we commit to work together in Greece and worldwide, to improve our practices, so that more communities connect to their own abundance.

- Our efforts are part of a greater movement to make economic activity more accountable, socially beneficial and environmentally sustainable.

- Our work must develop ever expanding circles of co-operation, exchange and learning.

- We invite others who share these aims to join us in a growing movement and emerging profession on community exchange.

Scaling up mutual credit

The challenge for any network is to achieve sufficient scale to make it useful. The bigger the network, the more opportunities it provides for moneyless trades to be made: that is, more opportunities for capacity to meet needs. In the early stages, it may require some help to find those opportunities, but as the members discover each other and become aware of what each has to offer, the benefits of participation become ever more evident and attractive. Like Facebook, QQ, Twitter, LinkedIn and other networks that are purely social, moneyless trading networks will eventually grow exponentially. The growth of mobile Internet will enable payment at point of sale, making these moneyless systems suitable for everyday transactions. These factors could mark a revolutionary shift in political as well as economic empowerment. It would be a quiet and peaceful revolution brought on, not by street demonstrations or by petitioning politicians who serve different masters, but by working together to use the power that is already ours—to apply the resources we have to support each others' productivity and to give credit where credit is due.

What will it take to make mutual credit clearing networks go viral the way social networks have? That is the key question, the answer to which has heretofore remained elusive. One reason is that many such systems have been developed for a small subset of individuals who are socially or environmentally motivated to participate in alternative lifestyles (Lietaer *et al.* 2012a). They soon become clubs of friends who gain personal benefit, but have limited incentive to expand, and little knowledge of how to bring businesses into their network. Therefore, the mutual credit clearing systems that are designed for businesses to participate are likely to achieve more scale. While the WIR has been an obvious success, it has not spread beyond Swiss borders. While commercial 'barter' has been significant and growing steadily for over 40 years, its volume is still tiny in relation to the totality of economic activity. What then is limiting such systems?

Our analysis of the commercial trade exchanges is that they appear to be self-limiting, and typically impose significant burdens upon their members. These include onerous fees for participation, exclusive memberships, limited scale and range of available goods and services within each exchange, the use of proprietary software, and insufficient standardisation of operations which limits the ability of members of one trade exchange to trade with members of other exchanges. Most of these commercial trade exchanges are small, local and operated as for-profit businesses. Although small-scale, local control and independent enterprise are desirable characteristics, when it comes to building a new exchange system, something more is required. What the world needs now is a means of payment that is controlled by its users, while being globally useful. That means giving members of a local trade exchange the ability to trade with members of other exchanges easily and inexpensively, with little risk, without any new dependencies on exchange system service providers.

From our analysis of these limitations, we propose the following characteristics for alternative exchange systems to enable them to go viral:

1. Involve businesses that produce value for the local community in the design and governance of the mutual credit clearing system, and extend them preferential credit lines if they agree to offer their full range of goods and services at their usual everyday prices.

2. Make trade exchanges open to all with little qualification, but determine lines of credit (the overdraft privilege) according to each member's ability and willingness to reciprocate (measured, for example, by his/her record of sales into the network), or through an insurance provided by other members, or the offering of collateral in case of default.

3. Manage trade exchanges in transparent, open and responsive ways, without the organiser running large negative balances unless agreed by the majority of users for defined purposes.

4. Provide members a free and unrestricted option to export all their own data, including contact information of those they have traded with, in useable formats, according to emerging protocols.

5. Seek interoperability with other trade exchanges, according to emerging protocols, so that members can trade with others on compatible exchanges. Also, seek interoperability with the growing number of companies and organisations that enable the sharing of goods and services (systems called 'collaborative consumption' (Botsman and Rogers 2010).

6. Develop revenue streams that rely on value-added services, such as advertising, brokering trades or more sophisticated payment systems, so that membership fees and transaction fees can be charged only in the mutual credit currency.

7. Exchange experiences and ideas with others working in this field, as participants in a new movement and new profession, rather than seeing others as competition.

As trade exchanges master these dimensions of design and operation, they could become models for other exchanges to follow. Then the rapid growth phase could begin, leading eventually to an Internet-like global trading network that will make money obsolete and enable a freer, more harmonious society to emerge.

Implications for movements and professions in sustainability and transition

For those of us who recognise the monetary driver of many of our social and environmental ills, the mutual credit clearing systems we have described above are a crucial part of the solution. Some people working on the sustainable monetary system agenda are currently focusing on other initiatives and campaigns. Increasing numbers focus on national and international monetary reform, to end non-reserve banking and give government the power to issue new money. The difficulty in obtaining support for such a reform is significant, perhaps impossible before a collapse, as we discussed above. Developing independent means of exchange, through mutual credit clearing, is one way to become less dependent on the bank-money system, and thus engage in national monetary reform debates from a position of greater strength. In addition, even if such a reform were possible, it would not in itself empower individuals and communities to control their own levels and direction of credit, which is key for a well-functioning society.

Others call for a return to the gold standard, arguing that this would curb inflation and promote economic stability. However, there were numerous monetary crises during periods on a gold standard. As the banks control gold and could still issue many more promises of gold than they store, so a gold standard would not, in itself, do anything to reduce the power of the banks in our economy, and the negative effects of their dominant role in issuing credit at interest. In addition, introductions of gold standards in the past have led to contractions in money supply and therefore widespread hardship (Boyle 2002).Those advocating for the role of gold in monetary systems may need to better understand the functions of money, rather than relying on misplaced assumptions about 'real' money (see Box 2, adapted from Greco 1990).

Box 14.2 **The role of gold**

In discussions of the role of gold, and a possible return to a gold standard, commentators typically fail to understand that 'measure of value' and 'means of payment' are two distinct functions of money that require two distinct approaches. We need not be restricted by the availability of gold or any particular commodity to achieve the facilitation of exchange of value. Neither should we be subject to credit instruments (currencies) issued by governments or central banks, which are almost always badly abused.

Much confusion has arisen from the fact that 'legal tender' laws have obliterated the distinction between a measure of value and a means of payment. A vendor who accepts a particular currency in payment, wants to know that s/he can receive equivalent value for it when s/he decides to spend it. What gives strength to political monies, such as the dollar, the euro, the pound, etc, is the fact that governments have enacted legal tender laws that obligate everyone in their jurisdiction to accept their currencies in payment at face value. Thus, governments and central banks are free to exploit their people and to squander the fruits of their labour by injecting into the economy money that they themselves create through loans yet which must be accepted by everyone in that jurisdiction.

It is this universal abuse of the money power by countries around the world that has caused the majority of reformers to advocate a return to hard monies such as gold and silver, and has prejudiced their minds against credit money in general. It is undeniable that political monies have been politicised, monopolised and badly abused by governments and central banks, which has led to a variety of economic and political ills, including inflation, depressions, unemployment, maldistribution of income and wealth, and, not least of all, war.

It is true that gold can be an inflation hedge by serving as a store of value, and thus provide some measure of security when political currencies are abused by improper and over issuance (causing inflation), but a return to gold as a means of payment would not provide an exchange mechanism that is sufficiently flexible to enable the economy to function optimally.

The answer lies, not in reverting to more primitive forms of exchange, but in perfecting the more evolved forms, which utilise the credit of private producers who put actual value into the economy. Credit money has the great advantage of being flexible enough to accommodate the exchange needs of an economy. Unlike gold, or any other physical commodity, it can be entirely sufficient to enable the transactions that people may wish to make. Further, its availability does not require the application of enormous amounts of labour and resources to mine and refine it, nor does its creation result in the environmental damage that attends mining operations.

If gold has a monetary role to play, it is in providing an objective measure of value that is independent of any political currency unit. However, why not define a value unit that is more stable and much harder to corner, hoard or manipulate? A composite value standard composed of a 'market basket' of basic commodities that are freely and actively traded could provide a much better benchmark for measuring the relative value of all goods, services and financial instruments, although would require better regulation of international commodities markets than currently occurs.

Another response is the issuing of local fiat currencies, where the issuer asks the users to believe the currency has value in itself. Such systems can stimulate local trade, and there are some success stories such as with Banco Palmas in Brazil (Lietaer *et al.* 2012b). However, many of these currencies eventually suffer from a lack of confidence, due to over issuance and counterfeiting, as happened in Argentina after the financial collapse. Therefore, some local fiats back their currency with bank-issued currency, which means the currencies must be bought with bank-issued currency. The local currencies in Brixton and Bristol in the UK, for instance, use British pound-backed systems. Such systems may encourage money to circulate more in the local economy, and can provide a pool of bank-money savings that can be loaned at low rates to local businesses. However, they do not provide a local autonomous source of credit, or liquidity. As such, people need to be persuaded that, due to their ethics, a sense of local pride or their liking of the designs of notes, they want to buy the local currency with their national currency. Consequently, such systems are not appealing to communities and businesses with cash flow problems, and their potential for scaling up is limited. In essence, these local currencies are not local at all, as the source of credit is the international banking system that issues the national money that is required to buy the local notes. They are, in essence, the same as the gift cards that are issued by many retail establishments. To transition to more fair and sustainable societies requires a transition away from dependence on bank-issued credit as our money supply, not a repackaging of that supply with local imagery. Many communities, both in the UK and North America, have come to realise, after many years of experience, the limited potential of currencies that are sold and redeemable for national currency. **Mutual credit clearing is the true currency of transition, because it offers means of exchange that does not rely on exploitative bank-issued interest-bearing debt as its original source.** The bank-money backed local currencies can be a step in the right direction if they do not dominate the policy space and professional standards for alternative currencies, and use their notoriety to then launch local mutual credit clearing systems. That is a difficult challenge. One option is to make the digital versions of the local currencies no longer redeemable for national currencies, and to be issued through a mutual credit system. The legal and communications issues around such a change will need careful handling. The options will depend on the contracts of initial sale of the currencies backed by national monies. Given these difficulties, our advice to communities and business networks that seek a monetary dimension to their transition effort, is to adopt mutual credit clearing in the first instance.

The organisation of mutual credit clearing exchanges is an essential first step in the transition to sustainability. It provides a locally controlled means of exchange (i.e. local liquidity based on local productive capacity). But, it will also be necessary to address a community's needs for a store of value and the financing of capital projects with long time-frames, the funding of government delivery of public services or the addressing of existing government debt levels. New innovations will be required to enable people to have better choices for storing value in a semi-liquid form rather than fixed assets. Systems for financing long-term projects with mutual credit will also need to be developed, along with ways for the organisers of mutual credit clearing systems to fund public works according to the will of their system members. In addition, relations with local and national governments will need to evolve, with governments accepting payment of taxes on mutual credit clearing transactions in the unit of the clearing system, rather than requiring payment in the national currency.

As mutual credit clearing grows, governments and foundations will begin to engage with them more, and seek to influence practices. How this relationship evolves will be key to the ultimate social usefulness of practitioners in the field of alternative currencies and exchange systems. Relations with the European Commission (EC) is a case in point. It has begun to recognise this as an area deserving greater attention. The EC funded a project called SPREAD Sustainable Lifestyles 2050,[8]

---

8 www.sustainable-lifestyles.eu, accessed 21 February 2013.

which issued conclusions on future research and policy for scaling up sustainable lifestyles. One of the five pivotal issues in SPREAD's First Policy Brief was: 'The emergence of non-monetary systems: reward schemes, alternative currencies and the principle of reciprocity to incentivise people to rethink the value of services and goods in terms of their actual costs and benefits' (SPREAD 2012b: 15). It recommends 'a toolbox for change makers' to 'enable the transition' that should include 'alternative currencies and reward schemes ...' (SPREAD 2012a: 5). In its Memorandum on Directions for Future Social Scientific Research on Sustainable Lifestyles SPREAD states that: 'The impacts of alternative money systems, complementary currencies, micro-credit, micro-finance etc. on consumption patterns, well-being, health and lifestyles' (SPREAD 2012b: 10) needs to be researched, as well as 'how credit systems can be designed to support sustainable lifestyles' (SPREAD 2012b: 10). This builds on the findings of one of its workshops, that 'innovation is needed to make communities more cost-effective and capable to interact conveniently ... [for this] they also require new forms of non-monetary exchange, such as reward and credit systems, with local rules (alternative currencies)' (SPREAD 2011: 8). That is a positive development, but the involvement of large donors might begin to influence strategies in unhelpful ways. For instance, in 2012, EU funds have been provided for development, promotion and evaluation of local currency systems that are backed by bank-issued debt-money, rather than mutual credit clearing systems. Practitioners who engage in this field to help the transition to greater sustainability will need to devote more attention to the truly transitional approaches.

In this chapter we have described how a new movement and a new profession is emerging in the area of alternative currencies and exchange systems, and the key role of mutual credit clearing (as recognised in the Drapanos Declaration). As such, it will require more analysis, knowledge sharing and capacity building. Here, then, is a role for institutions involved in research and education. Our literature review of journals of international development, human geography, business and management, sociology, environmental policy, as well as specialist journals on business ethics and corporate responsibility, has concluded that the implications of mutual credit systems for either business or sustainable development have not been well-researched or recognised (as has been stated in previous reviews; Schroeder *et al.* 2011). There are books on the topic (for instance Greco 1990, 1994, 2001, 2009; Lietaer, *et al.* 2012b) and a specialist journal (*International Journal of Community Currency Research*) but mainstream academic analysis has not focused on them. There is much to learn about good exchange system design and management. For instance, as we mentioned above, in Argentina the community currencies helped people during the financial collapse, but they subsequently collapsed due to poor (and sometimes fraudulent) management and counterfeiting, which eroded confidence. Avoiding the repetition of these mistakes will require professional approaches informed by good research, education, and oversight. With this in mind, practitioners present at the October 2012 workshop in Greece identified the issues they believe to be important to advancing the field (Box 3).

Box 14.3 **Emerging issues for practitioners in community exchange and mutual credit clearing**

The following questions were identified by participants during a workshop on community exchange at the European Sustainability Academy, Greece, on 11 October 2012. They are listed in order of priority, according to participants' expressed preferences:

- How can community exchanges be well governed in ways that encourage initiative to be taken by more and more participants?
- How can we work together on common values and identity, and then communicate that attractively?
- How can businesses be better engaged for mutual benefit?
- How should community exchange systems and their members relate to the tax authorities? What principles and practical issues are there to consider?
- What issues are there to consider, and options, for software systems and potential payment systems?
- How can political support for community exchange systems be increased, both nationally and internationally?
- How to grow the networks and increase diversity of offers, such as food, to increase convenience.
- Can credits be issued by co-ordinators to contract community work, to provide public goods and, if so, how, and with what relationship to local governments?
- How can community exchanges relate to each other within a country and worldwide?
- How can capital intensive projects be supported by community exchange systems, or in relation to them?
- What are the limitations, or even potential negative effects, of community exchange systems on positive social change?

In addition to working with the issues that emerge from practitioner dialogues over time, research will also need to mobilise relevant theories and provide greater context to help inform the policy and practice for positive social outcomes. Some of these broader questions include:

- What kind of finance (grant-funding, private investment, community financing or self-sufficient) and co-operation strategies do mutual credit clearing systems embrace in order to increase impact? How do they finance themselves sustainably in ways that do not restrict their catalytic function, and what is the role for non-profit, for-profit, small- and large-scale enterprise in community exchange systems?

- What are the technological issues, including software, software standards, skills, resources, intellectual property and digital privacy issues that are key to scaling these exchange systems?

- What institutional, political, cultural and economic environments favour the development and survival of mutual credit systems, their potential for growth and positive outcomes (in terms of local economic development, jobs, well-being and the environment)? How can mutual credit systems be encouraged and fostered in policy-making processes at local, national or international level?

- How do mutual credit systems impact on consumer-producer relations, behavioural change and community cohesion?

- What is best practice in the design, management, evaluation and funding of mutual credit systems?

- What metrics are appropriate to measure the health and impact of mutual credit systems?

- How do executives in businesses, local government, national government and civil society best learn about mutual credit systems and explore relevant roles, risks and opportunities?

- What kind of skills are helpful for developing and scaling-up mutual credit systems?

We map out these initial lines of inquiry not only to inform future research, but also to indicate the breadth and depth of this field of mutual credit, and therefore the need for large-scale engagement by non-governmental organisations, chambers of commerce, local governments, aid agencies and foundations. If you are new to this topic, then the complexity of the field may seem daunting, just as the invitation to understand mainstream banking and its effects on economy, society and environment can be daunting at first. That is why you are needed. Too many people turn away from monetary critiques and solutions because it takes them beyond their comfort zone. **Yet lasting solutions to most economic, social and environmental ills will not be found without fundamental transformation in the way money is issued and credit allocated.** It is also worth pursuing because engagement with this topic can be personally rewarding, as it encourages a shift of awareness that can deeply influence one's outlook on life. It is something that must be experienced to be understood, but we can try to explain.

Many of us also assume that such ideals as ending hunger are not affordable. Yet there seems to be ample money for spending on weapons, lavish buildings or luxuries. We assume that this indicates something essential about human nature or the way we function in large groups, such as nations. Many people assume that human nature is naturally competitive and selfish and thus needs to be moderated or controlled by force for the common good (Crompton 2010). By analysing the monetary system, and seeing the energising effect of creating alternatives, we gain insight on a different perspective. We see evidence that some of the selfishness arises from a fear of scarcity that is based on the current monetary system. We see evidence that the reason why there is money for skyscrapers but not free schools is partly an outcome of how the issuing of credit is in the hands of bankers seeking high returns, low transaction costs and secure collateral. We begin to see people, in general, to be more like the people we know the best, our closest friends; that is, as people who care.

We have found that many people working towards 'sustainability' assume that it requires new checks and balances on personal behaviour, and calling on each other to be more responsible; pay more for this, don't travel on that, switch off this, don't buy that. Yet by working on monetary issues, we begin to see that people and communities are being hampered in their ability to organise for mutual benefit. We begin to see that through mutual credit clearing, communities can connect to their own abundance. We begin to see that people can lose the delusion that 'money' is wealth and recognise, as Cumbria's John Ruskin wrote more than 150 years ago 'THERE IS NO WEALTH BUT LIFE' (Ruskin 1860, author's capitalisation). Although the past decade has seen a shift towards sustainability professionals couching their message in a positive way, about increasing personal well-being, in general the discourse is one of progress through limitation, rather than through reclaiming freedoms. Instead, by working on monetary issues a liberational environmentalism is possible, where we seek to unleash human nature, not curb it. Our goal is to liberate the wealth of communities, to unleash sustainable ways of living.

The past 20 years of environmentalism, and indeed other areas of social concern such as human rights and poverty alleviation, have seen a focus on incorporating these concerns into existing institutions, whether business, government, media, civil society, and into existing cultural assumptions, norms and values (Crompton 2010). This may have seemed like a good tactic to some, and is one where individuals pursuing it in their own work can pursue well-paid careers in relevant institutions. However, this attempt at incorporation reflects a fundamental insecurity about one's views and roles. It can be fundamentally debilitating, because it closes one's mind to analyses which sound too challenging to the project of incorporation. We described earlier our sense that senior people in big business, banks and governments are unlikely to lead the necessary changes. What, then, is the role for those of us who work on social or environmental issues, who now understand the necessary transformation of monetary systems? If not us, who? If not now, when?

Conclusion

There can be no intentional transition to a fairer and more sustainable world while the current monetary system remains dominant. A system where commercial banks issue our money supply as interest-bearing debt creates an unstable, unsustainable, unfair and unintelligent economy. Despite the financial crisis, and the way it has accentuated the injustices and ill effects of the current system, we know of no mainstream politicians organising effectively to deliver substantial monetary reform. People seeking transition cannot wait, but can transcend the existing system by developing mutual credit clearing systems. Promisingly, there are now thousands of such initiatives worldwide. With tools such as the Internet, cheap computing power and mobile telephony we now have the means available to massively scale up the direct clearing of credits among buyers and sellers. For such scaling to occur, mutual credit systems need to engage businesses as well as individuals, and learn from the successes and limitations of existing systems. A whole field of practice, inquiry, education and, eventually, policy is emerging that requires more active and informed participation by professionals working in the sustainability field.

Community currencies and exchange systems provide an essential toolkit for community and self empowerment, but they need to be designed in such a way as to make us less dependent upon political money and banks. Private exchange media should be issued on the basis of the value created and exchanged by local producers, especially the small- and medium-sized businesses that form the backbone of any economy. This means that a currency must be *spent* into circulation *not sold* for money. Some of the new currencies that have been gaining the most media attention are sold and fully-backed by national currencies and are therefore not necessarily part of a transition effort. For them to become steps towards transition, their initial success in gaining local support will need to be followed by adopting mutual credit clearing as their model. How they achieve this will determine their longer-term contribution to transition.

Communities around the world are showing that we can design currencies and credit systems that are always in sufficient supply to help match underused assets with unmet needs. Currencies and exchange systems can be designed to connect communities to their own abundance. This realisation presents deep implications for the concept and pursuit of sustainability or transition—to move to a message of freedom, where we might be freed to live according to our loving natures in harmonious thriving communities.

So long as people depend upon the money that bankers create for their material 'salvation' and admission to the 'good life', so the systematic destruction we have described above will continue, as well as the capture of politics and culture by banking interests. Therefore, the challenge for sustainability professionals is also a personal one—to find ways to move themselves and their own organisations away from dependence on the current money and banking system. In doing this, we may discover new truths about ourselves, our neighbours, our communities, our nations and our world.

References

BBC (2006) 'Richest 2% own "half the wealth"', Andrew Walker (5 December 2006; news.bbc.co.uk/1/hi/6211250.stm, accessed 26 March 2013).

BBC (2012) 'Greece bartering system popular in Volos', Mark Lowen (12 April 2012; www.bbc.co.uk/news/world-europe-17680904, accessed 26 March 2013).

Bendell, J. (2009) *The Corporate Responsibility Movement* (Sheffield, UK: Greenleaf Publishing).

Bolchover, D. (2005) *The Living Dead: Switched Off, Zoned Out—The Shocking Truth About Office Life* (Chichester, UK: Wiley).

Botsman, R., and R. Rogers (2010) *What's Mine Is Yours: The Rise of Collaborative Consumption* (New York: HarperCollins).

Boyle, D. (2002) *The Money Changers: Currency Reform from Aristotle to E-cash* (London: Earthscan).

Crompton, T. (2010) *Common Cause: The Case for Working With Our Cultural Values* (Godalming, UK: WWF).

Ferguson, N. (2008) *The Ascent of Money: A Financial History of the World* (London: Allen Lane).

Graeber, D. (2011) *Debt: The First 5,000 Years* (New York: Melville House).

Greco, Jr., T.H. (1990) *Money and Debt: A Solution to the Global Crisis* (Tucson, AZ: Greco Publishing).

Greco, Jr., T.H (1994) *New Money for Healthy Communities* (Tucson, AZ: Greco Publishing).

Greco, Jr., T.H. (2001) *Money: Understanding and Creating Alternatives to Legal Tender* (White River Junction, VT: Chelsea Green).

Greco, Jr., T.H. (2009) *The End of Money and the Future of Civilization* (White River Junction, VT: Chelsea Green).

Greco, Jr., T.H., and T. Megalli (2005) 'An Annotated Précis, Review, and Critique of Prof. Tobias Studer's *WIR and the Swiss National Economy*', Reinventing Money (reinventing money.com/documents/StuderbookCritique.pdf, accessed 26 March 2013).

Guardian (2011) 'Greek woes drive up suicide rate', Helena Smith (18 December 2011; www.guardian.co.uk/world/2011/dec/18/greek-woes-suicide-rate-highest, accessed 26 March 2013).

Hopkins, R. (2008) *The Transition Handbook: From Oil Dependency to Local Resilience, Transition Guides* (Totnes, UK: Transition Network).

IMF (International Monetary Fund) (2012) *World Economic Outlook: Growth Resuming, Dangers Remain* (Washington, DC: IMF, www.imf.org/external/pubs/ft/weo/2012/01/pdf/text.pdf).

Lietaer, B., C. Arnsberger, S. Goerner and S. Brunnhuber (2012a) *Money and Sustainability: The Missing Link* (Winterthur, Switzerland: Club of Rome).

Lietaer, B., M. Kennedy and J. Rogers (2012b) *People Money: The Promise of Regional Currencies* (Axminster, UK: Triarchy Press).

Meadows, D.H., D. Meadows, J. Randers and W. Behrens III (1972) *The Limits to Growth* (New York: Universe Books).

Riegel, E.C. (1944) *Private Enterprise Money* (New York: Harbinger House).

Riegel, E.C. (1978) *Flight From Inflation: The Monetary Alternative* (Tonopah, NV: The Heather Foundation).

Ruskin, J. (1860) 'Essay IV: Ad Valorem, section 77', *Unto This Last* (muff.uffs.net/skola/dejum/ruskin/texts/unto-this-last/unto_this_last.pdf, accessed 21 February 2013).

Ryan-Collins, J., T. Greenham, R. Werner and A. Jackson (2011) *Where Does Money Come From? A Guide to the UK Monetary and Banking System* (London: New Economics Foundation).

Schroeder, R.F.H., Y. Miyazaki1 and M. Fare (2011) 'Community Currency Research: An Analysis of the Literature', *International Journal of Community Currency Research* 15.A: 31-41.

SPREAD (2011) 'Emerging Visions. A Work in Progress from the SPREAD Vision Workshop', SPREAD Vision for Sustainable Lifestyles in 2050, Milan, 21–23 September 2011, Politecnico di Milano—Indaco Dept.

SPREAD (2012a) 'Emerging Visions for Future Sustainable Lifestyles. Preliminary Policy Considerations from the SPREAD Sustainable Lifestyles 2050 European Social Platform Project. Developing Pathways to More Sustainable Living', First Policy Brief, *SPREAD Sustainable Lifestyles 2050*.

SPREAD (2012b) 'Memorandum on Directions for Future Social Scientific Research on Sustainable Lifestyles', *SPREAD Sustainable Lifestyles 2050*.

Tucker, A. (2011) 'The Beer Archaeologist: By Analyzing Ancient Pottery, Patrick McGovern is Resurrecting the Libations that Fueled Civilization', *The Smithsonian Magazine* (www.smithsonianmag.com/history-archaeology/The-Beer-Archaeologist.html#ixzz2AX7yutqa, accessed 26 March 2013).

Wilkinson, R., and K. Pickett (2009) *The Spirit Level: Why Equality is Better for Everyone* (London: Penguin).

Z/Yen (2011) *Capacity Trade and Credit: Emerging Architectures for Commerce and Money* (London: Z/Yen).

Professor **Jem Bendell** is a strategist and educator on social and organisational change, with 18 years specialising in responsible business development, alliances for sustainable development, transformative philanthropy and sustainable currencies. With over 100 publications, including United Nations' reports, he is an award winning authority on business and sustainable development, and has helped create a number of leading multi-stakeholder alliances.

Thomas H. Greco Jr. is a community economist who writes and speaks on the subject of free market alternative currency and monetary systems. A former Assistant Professor at a business school, he has authored four books on monetary theory and how monetary alternatives can empower communities. These include his 2009 best-seller *The End of Money and the Future of Civilization*.

Index

For Product Safety Concerns and Information please contact our EU
representative GPSR@taylorandfrancis.com Taylor & Francis Verlag GmbH,
Kaufingerstraße 24, 80331 München, Germany

Printed and bound by CPI Group (UK) Ltd, Croydon, CR0 4YY

01/05/2025

01858343-0001